The Florentine Enlightenment

1400–1450

The Florentine Enlightenment 1400–1450

George Holmes

Clarendon Press

Oxford University Press, Walton Street, Oxford OX2 6DP

Oxford New York Toronto
Delhi Bombay Calcutta Madras Karachi
Kuala Lumpur Singapore Hong Kong Tokyo
Nairobi Dar es Salaam Cape Town
Melbourne Auckland Madrid
and associated companies in
Berlin Ibadan

Oxford is a trade mark of Oxford University Press

Published in the United States
by Oxford University Press Inc., New York

British Library Cataloguing in Publication Data
Data available

Library of Congress Cataloging in Publication Data
Data available
ISBN 0–19–820292–X

3 5 7 9 10 8 6 4

Printed in Great Britain
on acid-free paper by
Biddles Ltd.,
Guildford and King's Lynn

For Anne

Contents

Abbreviations

Alberti, *Opere*	L.B.Alberti, *Opere Volgari*, ed. C.Grayson (Bari, 1960–).
ASI	*Archivio Storico Italiano.*
Bruni, *Epistolae*	Leonardo Bruni, *Epistolarum Libri VIII*, ed. L.Mehus (Florence, 1741).
Bruni, *Schriften*	Leonardo Bruni Aretino, *Humanistisch-Philosophische Schriften*, ed. H.Baron (Leipzig-Berlin, 1928).
Poggio, *Epistolae*	*Poggii Epistolae*, ed. T. de Tonellis (reprint, Poggio Bracciolini, *Opera Omnia*, ed. R.Fubini, III, Turin 1963).
Poggio, *Opera*	*Opera* (Basle, 1538); (reprint, *Opera Omnia*, I, Turin, 1964).
	(Most of Poggio's other works are reprinted in *Opera Omnia*, II, 1966).
Traversari/Mehus	*Ambrosii Traversari Latinae Epistolae*, ed. L. Mehus (Florence, 1759).

List of Plates

List of Figures

Acknowledgement

I would like to express my gratitude
to the Rockefeller Foundation of New
York and the Institute for Advanced
Study at Princeton for making it
possible for me to undertake research on
subjects connected with this book.

G.H.

Introduction

This book contains an account of the history of ideas at Florence
and the papal court roughly in the years 1400–50. It assumes
that there is a distinguishable movement among literary men
in that milieu which can be described as one might describe,
for example, the philosophers of Paris and Oxford in the late
thirteenth century or the theorists of the Communist Revolution:
the individuals respond and react in very different ways in the
details of their thought but they are loosely connected by a
common inspiration. The assumption is that this is a movement
with a history and not a collection of individuals best considered
separately.

The primary inspiration which bound the thinkers together was
an intense enthusiasm for the study of antiquity and a belief in the
superiority of the classical world, not as an irretrievable, mythical
golden age but as a civilisation with a discoverable history which
could be studied rationally and ought to be imitated. The implications which were drawn from this overriding historical roman-
ticism were various, and the exposition of them will provide much
of the subject matter of succeeding chapters. The movement had
a literary origin. Several of its main figures were professional
rhetoricians, men who earned their living by skill in Latin composition, and they inherited the increased dignity which had been
given to that profession by the genius of their great master
Petrarch: they believed that the cultivation of an excellent Latin
style was of the highest cultural importance. Like Petrarch they

also believed that the Latin classics contained keys to wisdom which had been shamefully neglected by their barbarian ancestors and contemporaries. They devoted a great deal of time and energy to the improvement and enlargement of the stock of classical texts by searching out and copying manuscripts. They also believed, more actively than Petrarch, that if they were to be regenerators of the Roman world they must also know Greek as Cicero and some of their other heroes had done. They set great store by proficiency in that rather exotic language and regarded the translation of the Greek authors into Latin as a particularly laudable activity.

Here the common inspiration ends and the different lines of interest begin. Every reader of the classics is differently inspired by them and even within this circle there was a range of aspirations and responses. Most of the men who will be discussed were more or less affected, as Petrarch had been, by the account of moral philosophy given by Cicero. It confirmed their distaste for metaphysics and logic and encouraged them to adopt a common-sense view of philosophy and human conduct which pervades their writings and faintly foreshadows the attitudes of Montaigne and Hume. One of the main writers of the school, Leonardo Bruni, was the originator of a very influential attitude to politics which is clearly connected with this philosophy. He was the first to write philosophically about the politics of a secular city state without the apparatus of metaphysical justification with which political theory had been invested in scholastic writings, and the first to describe the contemporary history of a city as a continuous process of the application of raison d'état in the manner of some of the ancient historians. He is the forerunner of Machiavelli. Bruni was also the founder of a new tradition in the study of world history. He wrote about the ancient world for the first time in terms of cultural rise and decline instead of the providential destinies of empire and papacy. A quite different manifestation of classicism is to be seen in some of the writings of Leon Battista Alberti, the polymath who was amongst other things the theoretician of a new school of artistic realism. Alberti both reflected and encouraged the achievement of the artists who at this period suddenly introduced a new realism into the depiction of space, the human form and the emotions. His view of the artist's function was affected by Pliny and Vitruvius in the same way as Bruni's view of politics and history was affected by Cicero and Livy. The intellectual movement will be regarded here, in short, as a movement of rather extreme and sudden secularisation of ideas, under the auspices of the classics, over a broad spectrum of interests. When, for instance, the rhetorician Poggio described a great evangelist, Jerome of Prague, in terms of Roman stoicism and Donatello contemporaneously carved the Old Testament prophets in oratorical poses they were working under the same classical spell, and in both cases the imitation of antiquity facilitated and directed rapid changes of outlook.

The new ideas such men introduced were in part permanent additions to the stock of European experience. Art, history and political thought were obviously and profoundly affected in the long run. It is equally clear, however, that the movement and its tendencies existed in their fullness for only a few decades. They have inevitably been regarded as a phase in the general history of the Italian 'Renaissance'. This has been a hindrance rather than a help in historical understanding, for the intellectual and aesthetic trends of the later fifteenth century at Florence were in many ways opposed to those of the age of Bruni and Donatello. The problem of historical explanation is therefore to find circumstances which encouraged, or at least permitted, a sudden blossoming of highly original attitudes in a transitory movement. Intellectual movements involving small numbers of people with unusual opinions cannot of course be 'explained' by large environmental factors, and their causes must be sought in individual biographies; but the spectacle of a momentous intellectual change, affecting important aspects of thought in a great cultural centre, even if it emanates from a small group, challenges the historian to identify the atmosphere which made it possible. Some of the succeeding chapters suggest an approach to this problem in which the crucial factor is not the commercial society of Florence or the Florentine political experience – though these are both important – but the ecclesiastical background and in particular the relationship between Florence and the papal court which provided the backcloth for the main actors in the story. This was the age of the Schism and the councils, when ecclesiastical and papal influence in Italy were weaker than they were to be again for many generations. The circumstances of this immense institutional crisis are the essential background to the early and transient enlightenment at Florence.

Introduction to the Paperback Edition

A distinguished Italian historian described the subject-matter of this book as 'an intellectual avant-garde movement . . . destined to run its course within the span of a few decades, against the historical background, not so much of the political and social conditions of Florence, but essentially of the "immense institutional crisis" of the Schism and the Councils'.[1] Since the book was published I have become inclined to take the city background even more seriously. The Florentine Enlightenment was the product of one of the most remarkable cities in Europe at a time when cities, across Europe from Florence to Bruges, were both exceptionally free of disturbance from the monarchies of France and Germany and exceptionally rich in comparison with kingdoms dependent on small populations in the century after the Black Death.[2] The fifteenth century was the age of the independent city; the early fifteenth century was the heyday of Florence, Milan, and Venice, and the careers of Bruni and Brunelleschi and their associates should be seen against this background.

Nevertheless, it remains true that the complex interaction between the contrasting worlds of commercial Florence and papal

---

[1] Riccardo Fubini, 'il "teatro del mondo" nelle prospettive morali e storico-politiche di Poggio Bracciolini', *Poggio Bracciolini 1380-1980 Nel VI centenario della nascita* (Florence, 1982).

[2] A perspective similar in some ways was suggested by Fernand Braudel, *Civilization and Capitalism 15th-18th Century*, III, *The Perspective of the World* (London, 1984), pp. 116–38.

The Florentine Enlightenment

Rome was essential to the forms adopted by literature and art at this period. The aim of the book was, first, to present a phase of the Italian Renaissance for the sake of its aesthetic and intellectual creations, emphasizing the connections between letters and visual arts, in a manner intelligible to the general reader. It had as its second object to offer an interpretation of that movement which stressed the interdependence of Florence and Rome as a relationship without which the Enlightenment would have been unlikely to take the form it did. My view was that the dependence of Rome on Florence in this period gave the Florentines freedom and that the papal court itself provided a refuge in which they enjoyed esteem and comfort.

An interpretation of this kind might have been attacked by a historian who argued that I had misunderstood the connection between the Florentines and the papal court. As far as I know no one has taken up the cudgels in this manner. There has been an interesting study of ecclesiastical organization in Tuscany and relations with Rome by Roberto Bizzocchi[1] but not much interest in the intellectual or aesthetic developments connected with that relationship.

The Florentine mind and Florentine politics have, however, continued to excite active attention, symbolized perhaps by the very grand restoration in recent years of two major objects of Florentine art. The Masaccio frescos in Santa Maria del Carmine, which play a part in this book, were of course the most important enterprise in painting.[2] The other great restoration has been of Donatello's *Judith and Holofernes*, which presented an exceptionally intricate problem of conserving a very complex bronze sculpture. *Judith and Holofernes* may have accompanied Donatello's bronze *David* in the Palazzo Medici. Because it was probably a late work of the 1450s it was not mentioned in this book but it is an essential part of the œuvre of one of the greatest masters of the early fifteenth century.

[1] Roberto Bizzocchi, *Chiesa e potere nella Toscana del Quattrocento* (Bologna, 1987).

[2] A valuable attempt to explain the background to them was made by Anthony Molho in 'The Brancacci Chapel: Studies in its Iconography and History', *Journal of the Warburg and Courtauld Institutes*, XL, 1977.

Introduction to the Paperback edition

The Papacy of this period has not recently been an object of intense study. Much attention has been paid, however, to defining the progress of Florentine politics. Gene Brucker has written a detailed narrative from 1378 to 1430.[1] Dale Kent contributes a masterly account of the Florentine background to Cosimo de' Medici's attainment of power in 1434,[2] which, as a matter of fact, pays little attention to the Papacy. Anthony Molho has begun the elucidation of the city's finances.[3] Richard Trexler has published a fascinating anthropological approach to city politics.[4] These books are products of the American and Australian tendency to focus on Florence alone, not Florence *and* another place. But they have greatly increased our knowledge and understanding of the way the Florentines behave. The opportunities for study offered by Florence's rich archives and particularly by the *catasto*, the new taxation system introduced in 1427, which required financial statements from heads of families, have inspired the demographic studies of Christiane Klapisch-Zuber and David Herlihy,[5] which have given a more thorough account of population than is available for any other part of Europe in the fifteenth century. There are many aspects of Florentine life which remain obscure, notably the relations of the city with its subject contado[6] and the economic history, still largely in darkness. Some interesting suggestions about the relations between economics and the artistic patronage have been offered by Richard Goldthwaite in his important book about the building trades.[7] But the many volumes of merchants' accounts in the archives have not yet been organ-

[1] Gene Brucker, *The Civic World of Early Renaissance Florence* (Princeton, 1977).

[2] Dale Kent, *The Rise of the Medici. Faction in Florence 1426-1434* (Oxford, 1978).

[3] Anthony Molho, *Florentine Public Finances in the Early Renaissance* (Cambridge, Mass., 1971).

[4] Richard C. Trexler, *Public Life in Renaissance Florence* (New York, 1980).

[5] David Herlihy and Christiane Klapisch-Zuber, *Les Toscans et leurs familles* (Paris, 1978), trans. as *Tuscans and their Families A study of the Florentine Catasto of 1427* (New Haven and London, 1985). See also Christiane Klapisch-Zuber, *Women, Family and Ritual in Renaissance Italy* (Chicago, 1985).

[6] Interesting insights into this by Robert Black in *Benedetto Accolti and the Florentine Renaissance* (Cambridge, 1985).

[7] Richard A. Goldthwaite, *The Building of Renaissance Florence An Economic and Social History* (Baltimore and London, 1980).

ized to produce a picture of the city's commerce. There have been many valuable studies of the humanists and their ideas during the creative period stretching over the years from Coluccio Salutati, who was presiding over the Renaissance in 1400, to Lorenzo Valla, its most original offspring fifty years later, who was connected with Rome rather than Florence. Ronald Witt has written a comprehensive account of Salutati's intellectual biography.[1] Salvatore Camporeale has carried out a remarkable investigation of the manuscripts of Valla's works which has revealed the complicated movements of his thought and the humanist anti-clericalism which was so much more prominent in his writings than in those of other humanists.[2] Classical learning in mid-century Florence, touched on in the last chapter of this book, has been much more thoroughly explored by Arthur Field.[3] In between Salutati and Valla we can now read L. B. Alberti's *Della Pittura* in a good English translation.[4]

Connections between humanism and the visual arts are fundamental for the interpretation of the Renaissance in this period. One of the most fascinating developments in this area has been Samuel Edgerton's investigation of the invention of perspective drawing, which has linked it with the wider world of optics and the whole conception of the physical environment.[5] A different line of thought has been followed by Michael Baxandall. He has studied humanists' observations about painting from Petrarch to Valla and has also given us a subtle and original analysis of the connections between art and the visual assumptions connected with preaching, dancing and other activities, which flourished in

[1] Ronald G. Witt, *Hercules at the Crossroads The Life, Works and Thought of Coluccio Salutati* (Durham, N. Carolina, 1983).

[2] Salvatore I. Camporeale, *Lorenzo Valla Umanesimo e Teologia* (Florence, 1972). A number of Valla's works have also been newly edited: *Collatio Novi Testamenti* by Alessandro Perosa (Florence, 1970), *Gesta Ferdinandi Regis Aragonum* by Ottavio Besoni (Padua, 1973), *Antidotum Primum* by Ari Wesseling (Assen/Amsterdam, 1978), *Autidotum in Facium* by Mariangela Regoliosi (Padua, 1981), the *Epistole* by Ottavio Besoni and Mariangela Regoliosi (Padua, 1984).

[3] Arthur Field, *The Origins of the Platonic Academy of Florence* (Princeton, 1988).

[4] *On Painting and Sculpture*, ed. and trans. Cecil Grayson (London, 1972).

[5] Samuel Y. Edgerton, Jr., *The Renaissance Rediscovery of Linear Perspective* (New York, 1975).

Introduction to the Paperback Edition

the society around the artists.[1] For the age of Donatello and Ghiberti nothing was more important than imitation of the art of antiquity. As far as sculpture is concerned this has now received a full analysis which makes clear the works available to artists in the fifteenth century.[2]

Among specific studies of the work of particular artists perhaps the most interesting relate to the earlier years of Brunelleschi and Donatello, where documentary sources still left room for discoveries. R. W. Lightbown has looked again at the work of Donatello and Michelozzi in the tombs of Pope John XXIII, Cardinal Rainaldo Brancacci, and Bartolommeo Aragazzi.[3] Diane Zervas has very interestingly studied the connection between the Parte Guelfa, an august Florentine club, and the building of its new palace and the niche for Donatello's *St Louis of Toulouse* in the wall of San Michele.[4] These studies have added to our understanding of the origins of the new classical fashion. Diane Zervas makes the point that the first piece of Renaissance architecture was the St Louis niche, not the Ospedale degli Innocenti. Pursuing a different aspect of Brunelleschi's activity, perhaps less significant for Renaissance ideas but enormously important for the Florentines and very influential on later Renaissance architecture, Howard Saalman has explained in complex detail how Brunelleschi managed the feat of building the cupola of the cathedral.[5]

The wealth of new scholarship released in the past twenty years is bound, of course, to have changed our conception of Florentine thought and art in this period. The changes are not, I hope,

[1] Michael Baxandall, *Giotto and the Orators Humanist observers of painting in Italy and the discovery of pictorial composition 1350-1450* (Oxford, 1971); id. *Painting and Experience in Fifteenth Century Italy* (Oxford, 1972).

[2] Phyllis Pray Bober and Ruth Rubinstein, *Renaissance Artists and Antique Sculpture* (Oxford, 1986).

[3] R. W. Lightbown, *Donatello & Michelozzo An Artistic Partnership and its Patrons in the Early Renaissance* (London, 1980).

[4] Diane Finiello Zervas, *The Parte Guelfa, Brunelleschi & Donatello* (Villa I Tatti The Harvard University Center for Italian Renaissance Studies, 8), Locust Valley, NY, 1987.

[5] Howard Saalman, *Filippo Brunelleschi The Cupola of Santa Maria del Fiore* (London, 1980).

substantial enough to invalidate the approach which was adopted in this book. Its aim was, first, to point out the great landmarks and, secondly, to relate their story within an intelligible framework which allowed them to be regarded as a section of intellectual history. The great landmarks have not changed, though anyone interested in Masaccio or Donatello will of course derive pleasure from the latest books and articles about them and will find his appreciation made keener.

Interpretation is a slightly different matter. My view of Renaissance Italy includes the conviction that the relation between Florence and Rome has a peculiar and special importance. Florence was a commercial city with an exceptionally lively intellectual and aesthetic life. Rome was the spiritual capital of Christianity with great financial and temporal powers. The two were closely connected because Florence was one of Rome's closest neighbours and also the Papacy's chief financial partner. The connection had constant intellectual implications from the day when Dante was driven out of Florence by Pope Boniface VIII to the days when Michelangelo and Raphael, a pupil of the Florentines, went to Rome to paint for Pope Julius II. *The Florentine Enlightenment* charts a phase in that long connection, a period when the Papacy was particularly weak because of the schism and the fall in population, while Florence was in the ascendant.

The connection of both humanists and artists with Rome and the papal court was so strong that, in my opinion, the story of their work is much more intelligible if it is seen against this background. It gave the humanists an exceptional freedom of thought and it helped to give the artists the strong sense of connection with the ancient world of Rome which infused classicism into their creations. The historical background to art is always too complex to be easily definable but this particular aspect of their environment was, I suggest, so marked that it can be given a central place in the story without distortion. Early fifteenth-century 'Florence' is one of the most delightful and original episodes in the aesthetic history of Europe. It fits comfortably, and can be seen more intelligibly, when placed against the background of 'Florence and Rome'.

I

The Humanist Avant-garde

In the early years of the fifteenth century a group of enthusiastic readers of classical literature in the city of Florence shocked some of their contemporaries by parading irreverent and eccentric opinions. One of the more vivid portrayals of this new wave is contained in a piece called an *Invective against certain calumniators of Dante, Petrarch and Boccaccio*, written by a Florentine patrician with literary tastes called Cino Rinuccini.[1] It was composed at the latest in 1417 when he died, and perhaps some years earlier. Rinuccini, who was the head of one of the richer Florentine families, saw his subject from close by, with enough education to understand it and enough ironical detachment to characterise it. He described first the linguistic obsessions of

a chattering flock who, in order to appear highly literate to the crowd, proclaim in the square how many dipthongs the ancients had and why only two are known today; which grammar is better, that of the time of the comedian Terence or that of the heroic Virgil corrected; how many feet the ancients used in versifying and why nowadays we use only the anapaest of four unaccented syllables.

This sounds harmless enough, but the fastidiousness about classical Latin was only the beginning of a series of affectations extending far beyond literature, some of which had disturbing implications. 'The chattering flock' disapproved of some parts of conventional philosophy.

[1]Printed in *Il Paradiso degli Alberti*, ed. A.Wesselofsky (Bologna, 1867), I, ii, p. 303 seq. On the author see L.Martines, 'Nuovi documenti su Cino Rinuccini e una nota sulle finanze della famiglia Rinuccini', *ASI*, CXIX, 1961.

They say that logic is a sophistical science which is very long and not very useful and therefore they do not care to know whether the term is understood by its signification or by its species or by its name: the term 'man' may signify Peter, an animated sensible substance, or the human species, or a noun. Nor do they care what a Contradiction is or a Demonstrative Syllogism, or about the other parts of logic which are most valuable in disputations and philosophical demonstrations.

They were not interested in rhetoric, arithmetic, music or astrology, but they had an absurd interest in the minutiae of classical history. 'When it comes to history they discuss with great anxiety whether there were histories at the time of Ninus, how many books Livy composed, since they are not all to be found, and what errors there are in the writings of historians, affirming that Valerius Maximus is too brief and Livy interrupted and the chronicles too prolix.' Though they lived in a city which was proud to claim Dante, Petrarch and Boccaccio among its illustrious men, they took a snobbish view of the value of modern literature in comparison with the ancients.

They say poetic stories are fairy tales for women and children and that the sweet recounter of these, Giovanni Boccaccio, did not know grammar – which I do not think is true. They make fun of the works of the poet laureate Petrarch, saying that his *De Viris Illustribus* is just a Lenten scrapbook. . . . They make great debates in front of the populace in the square about whether Homer or Virgil was the great poet. And then to show the mob how very well educated they are they say that the most famous and honoured Dante was only a shoemaker's poet.

They admired Aristotle less than was customary in the medieval world and tended to put other philosophers on a higher footing.

They say that Plato is a greater philosopher than Aristotle, quoting St Augustine's statement that Aristotle was the prince of philosophers save for Plato. They do not say that St Augustine put him first because his view of the soul was more in conformity with the Catholic faith, while in natural things which require demonstration and proofs Aristotle is the master of those who know. . . . They say what a splendid account of moral philosophy Cicero gave in the *De Officiis*, but they do not know what human felicity is, that it consists not in riches or honours or bodily pleasures but in the operations of perfect virtue.

They were insufferably detached from the normal Florentine's involvement in the affairs of his commune. 'In politics they do not know which form of government is the best, the rule of one or of more, or of many, or of an elected few. They evade the responsibility, affirming that he who serves people in common serves no one, and they neither give counsel to the republic in their robes nor defend it with arms.' Finally it was even doubtful whether they accepted the basic tenets of the Christian faith. 'As for divine philosophy, they say that Varro wrote many books of the observation of the gods of the pagans in the most elegant style and they praise him excessively, secretly preferring him to the doctors of our catholic faith; and they dare to say that those gods were truer than this one, forgetting the miracles of our saints.'

Rinuccini was writing partly as a patriotic Florentine offended by the supercilious indifference to the politics of their city which some of the humanists apparently affected and by their contempt for the greatest writers of the Tuscan language. To understand why his 'chattering flock' seemed outrageous, however, one must also recall something of the intellectual conventions of Europe in 1400, particularly that it was the tail end of the great creative period of the medieval universities. William of Ockham had been dead for half a century but the world of thought which the medieval scholars had created still enjoyed enormous prestige. His successors and their hordes of pupils at Paris, Oxford, Prague and Padua studied the textbooks and debated the tenets of scholastic philosophy in the faculties of arts before they went on to fill the best benefices in the church. Canon law and theology were important avenues to success, but scholasticism in its various forms was the philosophy of the ecclesiastical establishment. Even rebels within that system, like Wycliffe or Hus, now in the middle of his university career at Prague, lectured on scholastic topics and argued in the terminology of the schools. Scholasticism was based on the classics; but like all classicisms it took what it wanted from the ancient books and ignored the rest. The scholastics concentrated on a structure of logic and metaphysics based originally on translations of Aristotle. They were not much interested in classical history or poetry. They rarely knew Greek. Their Latin was a utilitarian language, well adapted for conveying philosophical propositions, innocent of literary grace and far removed from the styles of classical Latin. This philosophical movement was less dominant in Italy than in Northern Europe, partly because most of the great masters of scholasticism had worked at Paris or Oxford, partly because the Italians had superior schools of rhetoric and a superior acquaintance with the language and literature of Cicero and Virgil. Nevertheless the prestige of scholasticism was accepted in Italy, including Florence, almost as it was elsewhere.[1]

The people whom Rinuccini described were shocking because they were propagating an alternative set of values based on a different approach to the classical world. There would be nothing unconventional in admiring Cicero and Virgil. To deny that Aristotle was the 'master of those who know' and to prefer Cicero's approach to philosophy, or to regard the niceties of Latin style as all-important while denying value to the intricacies of logic, was an intellectual rebellion more complete and bizarre – in purely intellectual terms – than the rebellion of Wycliffe or Hus. The lunatic fringe of the new humanists, as they were characterised by Rinuccini, were an avant-garde, ostentatiously observing a set of values outside the normal intellectual framework. Like other avant-gardists they were to become the masters of a new orthodoxy. The purpose of this book is to examine the precarious and brilliant history of their orthodoxy in the first half of the fifteenth century.

The attitudes lampooned in Rinuccini's invective would have been unthinkable without the influence of the poet Petrarch, who had been dead since 1374 but whose shadow loomed large over the literary landscape of Italy and especially Florence. To us, and perhaps to Rinuccini, Petrarch is the Italian poet. In 1400, how-

---

[1] In the *Paradiso degli Alberti*, which is a famous portrayal, probably written in the 1420s, of an imaginary humanist discussion in 1389, the circle of eminent men includes some important scholastic philosophers, notably Biagio da Parma and Marsilio di S. Sofia.

ever, this was not his sole, and in the eyes of many of the intelligentsia not his chief, claim to fame. Petrarch was to them primarily the author of the Latin books which we have forgotten. In these books he had made several momentous innovations. First, he had raised the study of classical literature onto a new level of understanding and historical perspective. He knew more about the Latin classics than any medieval man before him. He had himself recovered from forgotten manuscripts some works of Cicero, notably the letters to Atticus, and produced a superior edition of Livy, and he had encouraged others to continue with the task of recovering the corpus of Latin literature. Secondly he had restored Latin to the status of a living language for original composition in the style of the ancients. He had attempted to revive the manner of Cicero in his letters and to imitate Virgil in a long epic poem. Thirdly, and most important, he suggested a world of ideas in which concepts directly drawn from Latin literature were important. He was scornful of the scholastic thought built on a metaphysical amalgam of Aristotle and Christianity and of the elaborate logic and natural science connected with it. His masters were Cicero, the student of moral problems in the terms of the Stoics, especially the problem of living a virtuous life in the face of the buffets of fortune, and Augustine, the recorder of men's inner torments. He portrayed himself as an individual grappling with his moral destiny and analysing the conflict in a language learnt from the classics.

The interest in the niceties of Latin grammar and history, the horror of logic and the preference for Augustine and Plato were attitudes which the Florentines of 1400 had probably originally derived from Petrarch. But Rinuccini was defending Petrarch against them and accusing them of dispraising not only his Italian works but even *De Viris Illustribus*, which was a notable demonstration of his classical learning. In retrospect Petrarch seems an innovator of greater genius and originality than any of the fifteenth-century humanists; but Rinuccini's avant-garde, although they owed half their intellectual stock to the old master, had already left him behind. They had taken over one side of his work, the passionate acceptance of classicism and Ciceronian ideals, and developed this in isolation and with greater refinement. There was another difference. Petrarch had been a lonely genius, a man of acknowledged eminence who enjoyed the wealth which accompanied the friendship of popes and kings; he was too determined a cultivator of his own isolated genius to be a member or even the founder of a school and his life had been rootless and solitary. The Florentine classicists were a select band but they were a group, closely connected with each other and securely rooted in one society.

Rinuccini was writing at a critical point when a new generation in Florentine humanism was coming to the fore. The older generation in the last quarter of the fourteenth century had been dominated by two commanding figures, Coluccio Salutati and Luigi Marsigli, both of whom had fostered and strengthened ideals of classical humanism derived principally from Petrarch. Salutati, born in 1331, was, like many other humanists, trained to the profession of a notary.[1] After practising in various central Italian towns in the mid-century and failing to obtain a position at the papal court during the period when Urban v brought it back temporarily from Avignon to Rome, he became chancellor of Florence in 1375. Salutati was a passionate student of classical literature and, though he never met the master, a disciple of Petrarch and an enthusiastic admirer of Petrarch's revival of the Latin language. One of his most cherished ambitions was to publish Petrarch's unfinished Latin epic *Africa*. His establishment at Florence meant that Petrarchan ideals acquired a stable home. The chancellor of Florence was an important person, the head of the commune's writing office and the composer of diplomatic correspondence with other sovereign powers. Salutati was enormously successful in this position throughout the troubled years of Florentine history from 1375 until his death in 1406. It was of his letters that Florence's greatest enemy, Giangaleazzo Visconti of Milan, was reported to have said that they were worth more than a thousand horsemen.[2] His mastery of diplomatic eloquence made him a great figure in the city.

[1] B.L.Ullman, *The Humanism of Coluccio Salutati* (Padua, 1963).

[2] Aeneas Sylvius, *Opera Omnia* (Basel, 1521), p. 454, in a passage praising the Florentines for choosing humanists rather than mere lawyers as their chancellors.

His first love was classical literature. He collected a great library. He wrote many elaborate letters on literary and philosophical subjects in a heavy neo-classical style and he composed several extended works in this humanist Latin: *De Seculo et Religione* (1381), a discussion of arguments for and against the monastic life; *De Fato et Fortuna* (*c.* 1396), about free will; *De Nobilitate Legum et Medicinae* (1399), a characteristic humanist expression of preference for the more humane study of law over that of medicine; *De Tyranno* (1400), a discussion of monarchy; and, most important of all in his eyes though it was rather quickly forgotten, *De Laboribus Herculis* (*c.* 1391), a long exposition of the allegorical meanings which might be attributed to certain legends in classical poetry. Above all he fostered the study of the classics by his example and by his direct encouragement of younger men. To the modern student his figure looms a little larger than life because his prolific output happens to have survived rather well; one would gladly exchange some of his repetitive writings for a few words of other more obscure figures. But he also had a real importance. A large proportion of the abler humanists of the early fifteenth century, even men like Antonio Loschi of Vicenza and Pier Paolo Vergerio of Capodistria who were only temporarily members of his immediate circle at Florence, acknowledged his influence.[1] For the leading Florentines he was the indispensable defender of the prestige of the Petrarchan tradition.

His contemporary Luigi Marsigli wrote very little and is therefore a much more shadowy figure.[2] He was born in 1342 of a good Florentine family and became an Augustinian friar in the convent of S. Spirito. The greater part of his earlier life seems to have been spent in the long university courses leading to the doctorate of theology. He studied at Padua, met and corresponded with Petrarch, and then went on to the University of Paris probably about 1374. Sometime between 1378 and 1382 he returned to Florence to settle finally at S. Spirito until he died in

[1] See the letters of Loschi and Vergerio after Salutati's death in *Epistolario di Coluccio Salutati*, ed. F. Novati (Rome, 1891-1911), IV, pp. 478-80.

[2] Biographical records collected by C. Casari, *Notizie intorno a Luigi Marsili* (Lovere, 1900); U. Mariani, *Il Petrarca e gli Agostiniani* (Rome, 1946).

1394. Like Salutati he became an important figure in the city. He was employed as an ambassador and several times recommended unsuccessfully by the commune as a candidate for the episcopal see. But like Salutati, also, he was remembered chiefly because he preached the ideals of Petrarch. Practically no record has survived of his own thoughts. His place in history depends largely on references to him after his death which portray him as the master of a circle. When Poggio Bracciolini described Niccolò Niccoli's early humanist training, in a funeral oration written half a century later, he recalled Marsigli's cell at S.Spirito, 'always full of distinguished young men who took his life and manners as their model and visited by the best people drawn from every part as to some divine oracle.'[1] When Giovanni Gherardi da Prato, in the 1420s, reconstructed the intellectual society of Florence as it had been in 1389, in an imaginary discussion in the *Paradiso degli Alberti*, the villa of the banker Antonio degli Alberti in the suburbs of the city, he depicted Marsigli as the presiding intellectual authority to whom the other characters deferred. He placed in his mouth the crucial exposition of the evidence from Sallust for the foundation of Florence by Sulla.[2]

Marsigli had been dead for nearly two years when Salutati made his most imaginative contribution to humanism by bringing to Florence the Greek scholar Manuel Chrysoloras to remedy the ignorance of Greek which had limited the classicism of Salutati's own generation.[3] Chrysoloras first came to the West in 1394-5 as an envoy seeking aid for Byzantium against the Turks. Two young Florentine enthusiasts, Roberto Rossi and Jacopo d'Angelo da Scarperia, went to Venice to sit at his feet and Jacopo followed him back to Constantinople. The result of these early contacts was an official invitation to Chrysoloras to teach at the university of Florence at the expense of the commune. The

[1] Poggio, *Opera*, p. 271.

[2] *Paradiso degli Alberti*, III. An admiring reference to his memory is attributed to Salutati in Leonardo Bruni's *Dialogi ad Petrum Paulum Histrum* about 1401 (*Prosatori Latini del Quattrocento*, ed. E.Garin (Milan-Naples, 1952), p. 50).

[3] G.Cammelli, *I Dotti Bizantini e le Origini dell' Umanesimo*, I, *Manuele Crisolora* (Florence, 1941); R.Sabbadini, 'L'Ultimo Ventennio della Vita di Manuele Crisolora (1396-1415)', *Giornale Ligustico*, XVII, 1890.

invitation, dated 28 March 1396, was in all probability both procured and composed by Salutati and it demonstrated the strength of his influence. It pointed out that the Roman ancestors of the Florentines, as Cicero testified, had taken their learning from the Greeks; Greek and Latin were indispensable to each other. 'Moved by this opinion, wishing that our youth may drink from both founts, mixing Greek things with Latin to obtain a richer teaching, we have decided to enlist someone expert in both tongues who can teach Greek to our people and to adorn the university of the flourishing city of Florence with these advantages and splendours.'[1] Chrysoloras eventually came to Florence in February 1397 under an arrangement by which he received an official salary with only the obligation to teach Greek to those who visited him in his own home. He remained in Florence for three years, during which time his pupils included a number of people who were to be important in one way or another in the evolution of humanism, either by their social or by their intellectual influence: Palla Strozzi who was to be an outstandingly wealthy and influential citizen until his exile in 1434; Roberto Rossi translator of Aristotle's *Posterior Analytics* and teacher of Strozzi's political rival Cosimo de' Medici; Leonardo Bruni, the most brilliant luminary of Florentine humanism and a prolific translator from Greek in the years after Salutati's death; Niccolò Niccoli and Pier Paulo Vergerio. Chrysoloras left Florence in March 1400 but the rest of his life, although he was very much involved in diplomatic relations between Byzantium and the western powers and between the Eastern and Western Churches, was not without influence on the humanists. In 1410 he joined the court of Pope John XXIII, which was to become a crucial centre for humanists, and remained with it, on its movements from Bologna to Rome and then to the Council of Constance, until his death in 1415.

Again there is not much direct evidence of Chrysoloras's ideas. His historical position depends on the testimony of others to his influence; but this is so striking as to make it clear that he did more than simply teach his pupils the elements of Greek. The

[1] *Statuti della Università et Studio Fiorentino*, ed. A.Gherardi (Florence, 1881), p. 365.

tradition of his teaching was carried on by his most successful pupil Bruni, who recorded in a famous passage how he and his contemporaries were swept into the study of Greek when they were offered the opportunity of direct acquaintance with the giants, Homer, Plato, Demosthenes, after seven centuries in which Greek letters had been dead in Italy.[1] Bruni, probably because of his own preoccupation with the translation of Greek, created a legend about the sudden recovery of the language. There had in fact been other, perhaps better, opportunities of learning Greek in fourteenth-century Italy,[2] and genuine knowledge of it now grew slowly within a small circle. The inspiration of the great teacher in the fertile circumstances of Salutati's Florence mattered more than the actual linguistic knowledge which he imparted. A funeral oration composed by the Venetian Andrea Giuliano invoked the philosophers of antiquity whose traditions it had fallen to Chrysoloras to preserve – 'O wisdom of Socrates, divine intelligence of Plato, omniscience of Aristotle, schools of all the Athenian philosophers' – and recalled his 'knowledge of divine things which the Greeks call metaphysics.' For Giuliano it was the many-sidedness of Chrysoloras that was impressive; there was no aspect of life which he had not illuminated.[3] Chrysoloras was a polymath with the power to inspire others with his enthusiasm not merely for the language but for the whole of classical civilisation, and in Florence in 1397 there was a group ready to be inspired with this message of classicism.

Rinuccini's diatribe was probably not, as we shall see, directed against Salutati or Marsigli. In the early years of the fifteenth century the generation of their pupils and, perhaps more important, Chrysoloras's pupils was coming into prominence and flaunting its new enthusiasms. The oldest of the new men is the most elusive and yet perhaps the most important figure of the

[1] Leonardo Bruni Aretino, *Rerum Suo Tempore Gestarum Commentarius*, ed. C. di Pierro (Rerum Italicarum Scriptores, xix, iii), p. 431-2.

[2] K.M.Setton, 'Byzantium and the Italian Renaissance', *Proceedings of the American Philosophical Society*, c, 1956, pp. 40-57.

[3] H.Hody, *De Graecis Illustribus Linguae Graecae . . . Instauratoribus* (London, 1742), pp. 32-44.

The Humanist Avant-garde

early Renaissance, Niccolò Niccoli.[1] Niccoli, born in 1364, was a gentleman, a scion of a once wealthy family of cloth manufacturers. He scorned his inherited business interests and allowed his financial position to collapse while he devoted himself unswervingly to the study of antiquity. Practically nothing written by him has survived and he probably wrote little apart from letters, but in spite of this his character emerges powerfully from indirect evidence. He first appears as the central figure of Leonardo Bruni's *Dialogi ad Petrum Paulum Histrum*, an imaginary dialogue between humanists, written in about 1401, in which Niccoli was made to adopt an extreme position of enthusiasm for classical culture and contempt for contemporary intellectual standards.[2] Much of Bruni's correspondence in the decade after 1405, the main source of information about the humanism of the years immediately following Salutati's death, was with Niccoli and makes it clear that he was then regarded, in some sense, as the arbiter of classicism. He seems to have been a snobbish, eccentric and difficult man and much of the evidence about him comes from the complaints, fortunately lengthy complaints, of those who quarrelled with him. The earliest and on the whole the most informative account of him is a diatribe written in 1413 by Guarino Guarini, the Veronese humanist, who was invited to Florence as lecturer in Greek in 1410 after spending a considerable time in Constantinople, which had presumably given him a better command of the language than any possessed by native Florentines. Guarino's life in Florence was apparently made impossible by Niccoli, and he left in 1414. The picture which he paints fits in well with the portrait of the argumentative classicist in Bruni's *Dialogi* a decade earlier, with the humanist group in Rinuccini's *Invective*, probably written *circa* 1400-17, and also with the picture of Niccoli later in life which can be built up from various sources.[3] Guarino described with scorn his interest in the trivial minutiae of classical scholarship – parchment, orthography,

[1] G.Zippel, *Niccolò Niccoli* (Florence, 1890); L.Martines, *The Social World of the Florentine Humanists 1390-1460* (London, 1963), pp. 112-16.

[2] *Prosatori Latini del Quattrocento*, pp. 44-99.

[3] *Epistolario di Guarino Veronese*, ed. R.Sabbadini (Venice, 1915-19), pp. 35-46. See also below, pp. 89-93.

coins – his abuse of the Florentine politicians (a confirmation of one of Rinuccini's accusations), his passion for acquiring manuscripts, and the dubious extent of his knowledge of Latin and Greek. The paradoxes of Niccoli's character will have to be mentioned again. Although his enemies were not out to praise him and were out to impugn his scholarship they leave no doubt of his fanatical devotion to classical antiquity at the expense of every other conventional concern. When he died Poggio, who was not a sentimentalist, wrote of him as his father in scholarship, a man to whom he owed more than to his natural parents. Some, he said, asserted that Niccoli did not write because he could not; it would be as absurd to say this of Pythagoras, of Socrates or of Christ.[1] The natural conclusion to be drawn from a comparison of Guarino's diatribe with Rinuccini's *Invective* is that Niccoli was the leader of the most advanced humanist group.

His closest friends after the death of Salutati were probably Leonardo Bruni and Poggio Bracciolini. Bruni was in some ways the most impressive of the humanists of this generation. He managed to combine a large output, both of translations from Greek and of original compositions in Latin, with a practical competence which earned him high office at the papal court and at Florence.[2] He was born about 1370 at Arezzo and came to Florence as a law student in the last decade of the century, by which time Arezzo was a subject city. He was patronised by Salutati and instructed in Greek by Chrysoloras, and became a passionate classicist. Unlike Niccoli he was a poor man who had to earn a living. Largely through the good offices of Salutati he obtained in 1405 the eminent position of a secretary at the papal court. He stayed with the popes, serving Innocent VII, Gregory XII and Alexander V, until 1410, returned briefly to Florence as chancellor but was lured back by John XXIII with whom he

[1] Poggio, *Epistolae*, VI, xii.

[2] There is no modern biography. See G.Voigt, *Die Wiederbelebung des Classischen Altertums* (reprint, Berlin, 1960), I, pp. 306-12; Martines, *Social World of the Florentine Humanists*, pp. 117-23, 165-75; H.Baron, *The Crisis of the Early Italian Renaissance* (two editions, Princeton, 1955, 1966), *passim*; H.Baron, 'Leonardo Bruni', *Past and Present*, XXXVI, 1967.

stayed until his deposition at the Council of Constance in 1415. During his decade of papal service he kept in touch with Niccoli and others in Florence and translated several things from the Greek. In 1415 he was prosperous enough to return to Florence as a private citizen. He was granted Florentine citizenship and devoted himself to the composition of his *History of the Florentine People*, his most monumental work, which was to occupy him intermittently until his death in 1444. In 1427 he became chancellor. In spite of official commitments he was the most prolific of the early Greek scholars and poured out over the years a stream of translations from Xenophon, Plato, Plutarch, Demosthenes and Aristotle.

Although their careers were in some respects parallel, Poggio was a very different kind of man.[1] He was born a Florentine in 1380. He was educated in Florence as a notary but evidently before the end of his training had become acquainted with Salutati and Niccoli, impressed them by his command of Latin and acted as a copyist for them. He seems not to have entered the magic circle of the pupils of Chrysoloras, perhaps because he was too young, and he remained until late in life an inferior Greek scholar. In 1403 he went to Rome as a *scriptor*, a position below that held shortly afterwards by Bruni. Before the end of John XXIII's pontificate he too had become a secretary and he spent most of the rest of his life in the papal service. In his years at the Curia he kept up the same kind of relationship as Bruni with Niccoli's circle at Florence. He translated nothing and wrote little at this period and few of his letters have survived, but he was mentioned frequently by contemporaries as an active worker in the search for Latin manuscripts. It was Poggio who made the famous expeditions from the Council of Constance to uncover the treasures hidden in the dusty libraries of the abbeys and cathedrals of transalpine Europe. His manner and interests were closer to those of Niccoli than Bruni. He had none of Bruni's *gravitas*. He shared with Niccoli, and had perhaps learnt from him, a passion for the recovery of antiquity and a contemptuous detachment from the normal concerns of his contemporaries.

[1] E. Walser, *Poggius Florentinus* (Berlin, 1914).

Salutati and Chrysoloras had had other pupils but Niccoli, Bruni and Poggio appear to us now as the leading figures in Florentine humanism in the years following Salutati's death. Humanists, experts in the study of the classics, were to be found also in many other parts of Italy and some of them entered into a more or less close relationship with the Florentine school. For instance Guarino, born in 1374, probably owed nothing to Florence for his early training and developed an advanced humanism, including expertise in Greek, quite independently.[1] He went to Constantinople in 1403 to study in the household of Chrysoloras. Before he came back, about 1408, he was translating Plutarch. When he was called to Florence to lecture on Greek in 1410 he mixed with the local humanists – he dedicated Plutarch translations to two prominent patrician amateurs, Angelo Corbinelli and Roberto Rossi in 1411 – until his quarrel with Niccoli made his position too uncomfortable. Another visitor of a different kind was the Venetian nobleman Francesco Barbaro.[2] He was born in 1390 and rapidly acquired a humanistic education under masters who were independent of Florence, including Guarino. In 1415, a precocious young man, he paid a visit to Florence and, as we learn from the letters written when he returned home, fitted easily into the humanist group which included, apart from the professionals, men of his own social class. He wrote to Lorenzo de' Medici, Cosimo's brother, recalling their pleasant conversations and sending greetings to Roberto Rossi and to *literatissimus* Niccoli; and to Niccoli himself enclosing a list of Greek manuscripts which had arrived in Venice from Cyprus and sending greetings to Rossi, Bruni, the Corbinelli family and to Lorenzo. He sent a copy of Giuliano's funeral oration on Chrysoloras to the Florentine monk Ambrogio Traversari with a letter giving news of Guarino and sending greetings to Niccoli, 'the most learned and outstanding authority on antiquity', and Bruni, 'our age's light of eloquence'.[3] He then composed, no doubt with the help of Guarino and others, an

[1] R. Sabbadini, *La Scuola e gli Studi di Guarino Guarini Veronese* (Catania, 1896).

[2] P. Gothein, *Francesco Barbaro* (Berlin, 1932).

[3] R. Sabbadini, *Storia e Critica dei Testi Latini* (Catania, 1914), pp. 34-41.

elegant literary wedding present for Lorenzo de' Medici, who was to be married early in 1416, in the shape of a Latin treatise on marriage, *De Re Uxoria*, which is really a string of quotations from and allusions to classical authors designed to show off his learning and give pleasure to a refined humanist palate.[1]

One visitor who had closer and more important ties was Pier Paolo Vergerio from Capodistria.[2] Vergerio went to Florence and met Salutati when he was 16, in 1386, but he spent most of his formative years in study at Padua where, besides following university courses of logic, law and medicine, he wrote various pieces about Latin literature and busied himself, like Salutati, with the publication of Petrarch's *Africa*. In 1398 he was drawn to Florence by the prospect of studying Greek with Chrysoloras and apparently became one of the inner circle. On Chrysoloras's departure in 1400 he returned to Padua but the links with Florence and its influence remained. It was to Vergerio, as a former participant in Florentine gatherings similar to the one imagined in this work, that Bruni dedicated his *Dialogi*:

'Scarcely a day passes but the memory of you comes into our minds, but although we always desire your presence we do so especially when something is happening of the kind in which you used to take particular pleasure. For instance when there was recently a disputation with Coluccio (Salutati) I cannot say how much we wished you were there. . . . You know that no one is more serious than Coluccio; and Niccolò (Niccoli) who was on the other side is prompt in speaking and drives home the attack sharply.'[3]

Vergerio probably composed his educational treatise, *De Ingenuis Moribus*, about 1402 under the strong and recent impression of his stay in Florence. *De Ingenuis Moribus* is one of the small group of writings which, like Bruni's *Dialogi*, convey the radicalism of the movement, the sense of starting afresh on a new path. Although Vergerio is vague about the details of the course of education which he has in mind, the spirit in which he proposes it

[1] *Francisci Barbari De Re Uxoria Liber*, ed. A.Gnesotto (Padua, 1915).

[2] L.Smith, 'Note cronologiche vergeriane', *Archivio Veneto-Tridentino*, 1926, 1928; *Epistolario di Pier Paolo Vergerio*, ed. L.Smith (Rome, 1934).

[3] *Prosatori Latini del Quattrocento*, p. 44.

is clear enough and new. For him the love of praise and glory on account of virtuous activity is to be the basis of educational effort. His aim is character-building, to develop the potentialities of the *vita liberalis*, the life of a free man in the world, whether he is to devote himself to speculation or to political affairs. The most valuable studies are history and moral philosophy; one provides the precepts, the other the examples for action; and eloquence should be added to them. Grammar and logic and perhaps rhetoric are necessary but these are preparatory subjects. Poetry and music are for leisure, and mathematics and the natural sciences have their uses; medicine and law are trades rather than liberal studies.[1] This is to prepare the enlightened active layman, Quintilian's ideal of the cultivated orator adapted for a modern nobleman. It is the beginning of a new approach to education. In 1405 Vergerio was reunited with Bruni when he moved to a similar position at the papal court. Their paths diverged again after the Council of Pisa in 1409, when Vergerio remained true to Gregory XII while Bruni followed the Florentine line in defecting to the new Pisan obedience, but they were together again for a while at Constance in the court of John XXIII.

Guarino, Barbaro and Vergerio remind us that Florence was only one of a number of humanist centres in the cities of northern Italy which to some extent shared the same interests and aspirations and were linked and cross-fertilised by active correspondence and the movement of humanists in search of a living. The ideas which interest us here, however, are the ideas of Florentines, expressed mostly in Florence itself or in the other centre which became home to them, the papal court. How accurate was Rinuccini in charging them not only with an excessive devotion to the classics but also with a sweeping rejection of conventional values?

We must begin with their literary interests. Half the humanists were professional literary men, drawn to the study of the classics because there was a good living to be made by writing and

[1] Ed. A.Gnesotto, *Atti e Memorie della R. Accademia di Scienze Lettere ed Arti in Padova*, XXXIV, 1918; English translation in W.H.Woodward, *Vittorino da Feltre and other Humanist Educators* (Cambridge, 1897).

teaching Latin as rhetoricians, attracted to classical ideals because in Cicero and Quintilian these ideals were inseparably connected with the rhetorician's art.[1] Salutati, Bruni, Poggio, Vergerio and many lesser colleagues were men who actually earned their living by the pen. The conventions of Italian government and diplomacy decreed that rulers should employ the best letter-writers at the highest salaries, so that the lure of professional advancement positively encouraged the ancillary study of classical authors. Salutati would not have been such a valued diplomatist had he not been a deep student of Petrarch and Cicero. 'They have a chancellor,' said a fifteenth-century description of the Florentine constitution, 'who stays in the palace during the day and writes all the letters which are sent to the princes of the world and to any person on behalf of the commune. The chancellors are always poets and men of great scholarship.'[2] When Bruni was seeking a place in the papal court in 1405 he came into competition with another Florentine disciple of Salutati, Jacopo d'Angelo da Scarperia. To decide between them Innocent VII gave them both the task of answering a letter from the Duc de Berry. Bruni wrote the better letter and got the job.[3] There were of course also the idle rich, the Rossi and the Barbaros, who could afford to be interested in the classics for their own sake, but it was the professional usefulness of the classics which made it possible for the movement to attract a number of active and original minds. The background to their ideas about everything else was their admiration for the poets and prose writers of antiquity.

Their knowledge of the classics was by modern standards limited and one-sided. At this stage their literary culture was still

---

[1] The point is well made by J.E.Seigel, ' "Civic Humanism" or Ciceronian Rhetoric', *Past and Present*, XXXIV, 1966.

[2] Gregorio Dati, *Istoria di Firenze dal 1380 al 1405*, ed. G.Manni (Florence, 1735), p. 137. 'Poeti' may be a later interpolation as suggested by H.Baron, *Humanistic and Political Literature in Florence and Venice* (Cambridge, Mass., 1955), p. 65; but the alternative version in the edition by L.Pratesi (Norcia, 1902), p. 148 ('Il quale è sempre *pronto*') does not make very good sense, so I have let it stand.

[3] R.Weiss, 'Jacopo Angeli da Scarperia (*c.* 1360-1410)', *Mediovo e Rinascimento Studi in onore di Bruno Nardi* (Florence, 1955), II. pp. 816-17.

overwhelmingly Latin. Apart from the medieval translations of Plato and Aristotle, which the humanists despised, the best known of the Greek authors was probably Plutarch, with Xenophon coming next and most others far behind or totally unknown in the original. They had a far wider range of Latin authors at their disposal, but little knowledge of some who have since become important, such as Tacitus and Lucretius, and a strong preference for the writers of rhetorical interest, Cicero, Seneca and Quintilian. Within these limits, however, their admiration and their desire to absorb and imitate were boundless. The impulse was unquestioningly imitative. Classical Latin was superior to medieval, therefore the natural aim was to approach it as closely as possible. They did this chiefly in letter-writing after the style of Cicero and Seneca which was carefully cultivated and provides the bulk of humanist literature surviving from the period 1390-1420. They occasionally wrote poems or plays in Latin. The few lengthy original works – such as Vergerio's *De Ingenuis Moribus*, Barbaro's *De Re Uxoria* and Bruni's *Dialogi* – were also to a large extent imitative exercises to display a mastery of Latin style or to quote and refer to a large number of passages from classical authors.

A more positive concern which was widely shared was the effort to make Greek authors generally available by translation into Latin. The ideal which we may suppose Chrysoloras set before his pupils at Florence and the papal court is suggested in a letter which he wrote to Salutati, flatteringly in Greek, a year before he actually came to the city. The ancient Romans, he said, had known how to make use of Greek and to prize Greek authors without despising their own Latin. Cicero and St Ambrose were striking examples. They used Greek in their education and sent their young men to study in Athens. It might even be said that no Roman writer achieved excellence without a knowledge of Greek. In fostering the study of Greek, therefore, Salutati would be reviving an excellent Roman tradition and there could be no better author to start with than Plutarch, who bridged the gap between the two peoples.[1] The ideal was again partly

[1] Salutati, *Epistolario*, IV, p. 333.

imitative, to embrace Greek because it would help to recover the standards of Rome. Before the first decade of the fifteenth century was over a respectable start had been made. The translations were all into Latin, but translation was practised as a serious art. Translation from the Greek philosophers had of course been an important activity in the twelfth and thirteenth centuries. The new wave of translations had different characteristics. It aimed at a new literary standard of faithfulness to the originals combined with graceful Latin, and it had interests outside the authors of merely philosophical or theological appeal. Bruni stated his attitude to the old translations in the preface to a new translation of Aristotle's *Ethics* (*c.* 1419):

I undertook to translate the *Ethics* into Latin not because they had not been translated but because they had been so translated that they seemed to have been made barbarian rather than Latin. It is clear that the author of that translation – whoever he may have been, though it is evident that he was of the Order of Preachers – knew neither Greek nor Latin properly. ... Since he was frequently ignorant of excellent and tried words in existence in Latin, begging in the midst of our riches, he sometimes did not know how to render a Greek word into Latin and so in desperation and failure of understanding surrendered and left the Greek standing. Thus he was half Greek and half Latin, deficient in both languages and complete in neither.[1]

Poggio was the most spectacular worker in the other main field of positive endeavour, the search for better manuscripts of the Latin classics. In 1407 when the papal court was at Rome Bruni reported him to be visiting Monte Cassino in search of manuscripts.[2] His stay at Constance for the council opened to him a rich field in the libraries of northern Europe which he explored in three journeys between 1415 and 1417 taking in, among others, the abbeys of Cluny to the west and St Gallen to the east and the cathedral of Cologne to the north, altogether a fairly wide sweep. His investigations produced a rich haul – several unknown speeches of Cicero, the most admired of Latin prose authors, and the complete text of Quintilian's *Institutio Oratoria*, the venerated

[1] Bruni, *Schriften*, pp. 76-7.
[2] Bruni, *Schriften*, p. 107.

fountainhead of humanist educational ideas hitherto known only in a mutilated version. Poggio assumed and others confirmed that these discoveries were vital contributions to civilisation. The powers of composition and discussion, Poggio wrote to Guarino from Constance in January 1417 soon after his discovery of Quintilian, without which reason itself would be impossible, distinguished men from beasts. Hence the value of discoveries of the memorials of the liberal arts, especially those which contained rules for formal speech. Even if Cicero were lacking we could get all the guidance we need from Quintilian; and now we have Quintilian complete.[1] A few months later in July 1417 Barbaro wrote from Venice to congratulate him in the most extravagant terms, comparing Poggio's deserts with the rewards of the heroes of antiquity. His services were superior to those of victorious generals as Cicero's were to Caesar's. It was the interval between the deposition of the three popes of the Schism and the election of a new one and Barbaro hoped that he who would soon have power in the 'universal commonwealth' (*universa respublica*) would reward Poggio properly for his services to it.[2] One must make allowances for the rhetorical style; nevertheless the idea that Poggio deserved the highest honours from the pope for his services in the recovery of pagan antiquity shows how far the veneration of the classics could go.

Perhaps the most extravagant early expression of this attitude occurs in a letter written by another papal secretary, Cencio da Rusticci – not a Florentine, though he was a pupil of Chrysoloras – written in 1416 after he had accompanied Poggio to St Gallen. His anger about the barbarous illiteracy of the monks who had neglected the treasures of that monastery prompted him to air his opinion of the yet more criminal destroyers of the libraries of ancient Rome. If death was the punishment for murderers what tortures should be devised for wretches who deprived the whole human species of its nourishment? Rome had been robbed of its libraries and was still being robbed of its monuments. Those who destroyed classical sculptures of pagan gods were perpetrators of

[1] Poggio, *Epistolae*, I, pp. 25-9.
[2] *Francisci Barbarae et aliorum ad ipsum Epistolae* (Brixen, 1743), pp. 1-8.

a vulgar error. Popes had been amongst the worst culprits and their inhuman and savage folly deserved to be condemned.[1]

Slavish imitation of a dead language is a poor basis for litera-ture. Without the care for the vernacular of Petrarch before them or Alberti after, the humanists of this period were aesthetically the most sterile of their breed. Intellectually, however, it was possible for their imitative passion to have significant results. One of the implications of their interests, perhaps the most immediate, was a considerable sharpening of the historical sense. The more accurate understanding of classical texts was inevitably an historical undertaking. It encouraged a better sense of perspect-ive about the dating and circumstances of classical authors. It also led to other antiquarian interests, as Cencio's letter indicates. Poggio was the inventor in the first decade of the century of the Latin script which became popular among humanists.[2] In fact it was probably based on a mixture of the hands of Carolingian manuscripts and the style of ancient inscriptions, and reveals the common humanist failure at this period to distinguish between Roman and Romanesque remains which also influenced early Renaissance architecture. But whatever its actual failings it was an attempt to write as the ancients had written. The same im-pulse attracted them to all other aspects of the ancient world, its material remains as well as its literature. Here again Chrysoloras may have been to some extent the immediate inspirer. A long letter which he wrote to the Emperor John Paleologus from the papal court at Rome (c. 1411-13), comparing the cities of Rome and Constantinople, shows a considerable interest in, and appre-ciation of, the things to be seen at Rome, the triumphal arches with their vivid presentation of historical events and their evoca-tive inscriptions, the sculpture to be seen on every hand repre-senting Greek legends, 'works of some Phidias or Lysippus or Praxiteles or the like'.[3] Bruni on his travels with the papal court entertained Niccoli in Florence with accounts of classical

---

[1] L.Bertalot, 'Cincius Romanus und seine Briefe', *Quellen und Forschungen aus Italienischen Archiven*, XXI, 1929-30, pp. 224-5.

[2] B.L.Ullman, *The Origin and Development of Humanistic Script* (Rome, 1960), pp. 54-7.

[3] J.P.Migne, *Patrologia Graeca*, CLVI, cols. 27-30.

antiquities he had seen. When he reached Constance with John XXIII's court at the end of 1414, knowing that Niccoli would not be interested in the council, he sent back a vivid description of the route through the Alps from Verona. He ended by mentioning a marble slab which he had seen at Constance, venerated by the local inhabitants as an early Christian monument but ironically perceived by Bruni to be a Roman work inscribed 'not with the names of Christ's saints but those of the persecutors of the Christian faith'.[1] Poggio was collecting inscriptions soon after his arrival in Rome,[2] but Niccoli seems to have been the most passionate and all-embracing antiquarian. In his diatribe against him in 1413 Guarino pokes fun at his interest in Roman coins and buildings.

Between archeology and literary classicism, stimulated by both, was history proper. In this field falls the most considerable original work of humanism in the early years of the fifteenth century. When Bruni retired to Florence in 1415 he took up the writing of a comprehensive history of the Florentine people. By the middle of 1416 he had completed the first part, an account of the city from its origins to 1250, set in a general sketch of Roman and medieval history. He began with the foundation of Florence by Sulla in the first century BC and the growth of the city into a flourishing community under the Roman Republic. He then turned back in time to an account of the Etruscans and their cities, which had been the first settlements in Tuscany, and the struggles between them and the Romans. Reverting to his previous point in the first century, he dealt in his next section with the decline of Roman civilisation under the emperors, the barbarian invasions of the fifth century AD, the temporary recovery of Italy by Belisarius and its conquest by the Lombards. He then paused to comment on the decline of the Empire under the emperors and its cessation in the West for three centuries between Romulus Augustulus and Charlemagne and the passing of the empire to the Germans. Then he went back again to the survival of Florence and other Tuscan cities through the barbarian

---

[1] Bruni, *Epistolae*, III, iii; *Corpus Inscriptionum Latinarum*, XIII, no. 5249.
[2] Walser, *Poggius Florentinus*, p. 28.

invasions and Dark Ages, continued with their relations in the early medieval period and the rise of the Guelf and Ghibelline factions, and ended with the destructive consequences of the reign of the thirteenth-century Emperor Frederick II.[1]

Bruni's *History* is for several reasons a work of extraordinary originality. The first is that much of it was based on genuine historical research in the modern sense, which overturned established but erroneous traditions about distant events. The first paragraphs, for instance, contain a new account of the foundation of Florence. Medieval traditions of Florentine historiography attributed the foundation for sentimental reasons to Caesar. Bruni, as we shall see, had sentimental reasons as a modern Florentine republican for rejecting Caesar, and his history has a partly polemical purpose; but it was also based firmly on Cicero, Sallust and Pliny and therefore presented a good account from the literary materials available at that time. Another deep-rooted medieval tradition was that ancient Florence had been destroyed by the Ostrogoth Totila in the sixth century and refounded by Charlemagne. Bruni, using the authority of Procopius, correctly believed that Totila had not destroyed Florence and also deduced that the idea of Charlemagne refounding the city with a colony from Rome was an absurdity.[2] Bruni got the story right partly because he was a devoted reader of the classics and really valued the truth about the ancient world. The fascinated interest in the details of Roman history which fills many tedious letters of Salutati had born fruit in a surer grasp of the actual succession of events. The novelty of the approach is striking if Bruni's work is compared with the standard history of Florence composed in the early fourteenth century by Giovanni Villani, the early parts of which are largely built around the errors which Bruni exposed. Bruni was still capable of stupendous historical howlers. He appears for instance to have thought that one of the institutions

[1] Leonardo Bruni Aretino, *Historiarum Populi Florentini Libri XII*, ed. E.Santini (*Rerum Italicarum Scriptores*, XIX, iii), pp. 5-26.

[2] E.Santini, 'Leonardo Bruni Aretino e i suoi "Historiarum Florentini Populi Libri XII"', *Annali della R.Scuola Normale Superiore di Pisa*, XXII, 1910, with many other examples of Bruni's use of evidence. Cf. Baron, *Crisis of the Early Italian Renaissance*, ch. 3.

of contemporary Florence, the *Parte Guelfa* (seen by him primarily not as a pro-papal institution but in its more recent colour as a club of staunch republicans) had roots in ancient Florence;[1] he believed, as others did, that the twelfth-century Florentine Baptistry was a Roman temple of Mars adapted to Christian use.[2] These errors have in common an exaggerated desire to assimilate the Florentine present to the Roman past, and vice versa, which could be just as serious a hindrance to historical accuracy as any other presupposition. They do not, however, destroy the novelty in Bruni's work which is that historical evidence has gained a large and sudden advantage over mythological appropriateness as a standard for interpreting the past. This was a result of the intense interest in classical civilisation which drove its devotees to get the true facts because they really wanted to know about the classical world for its own sake.

The novelty of Bruni's *History* is also due in part and perhaps more strikingly to another feature. It is a panegyric of republicanism. Florence, in his interpretation, had its first age of prosperity under the Roman Republic, and it was Republican Rome not the emperors that created the empire. 'I judge that the beginning of the decline of the Roman Empire is to be put at about that time, when, having lost its liberty, Rome began to serve the emperors.' Augustus and Trajan had some good things to their credit but most emperors had been scoundrels. With the end of liberty virtue too was lost.

Soon, as the state came into the hands of one man, virtue and greatness of spirit began to be suspected by the rulers. Only those men pleased the emperors who lacked that force of mind which the concern for liberty can encourage. Thus the imperial palace received not the strong but the ignoble, not the industrious but the flatterers, and the government of affairs put into the hands of the worse people gradually brought about the ruin of the empire.

Similarly in medieval times the rivalries and internal discords of the Tuscan cities were largely due to the malevolent intervention of emperors and popes. This republican interpretation was not

[1] Santini, op. cit., pp. 45-6.
[2] See below, p. 176.

merely a change of detail; it altered the perspective of history completely. Medieval Florentines, though proud of their city, had also been proud of its associations with emperors, popes and kings. Bruni established a new pattern in which the admirable part of classical civilisation was not its imperial tradition but its republican city life, and its best legacy was the revived republicanism of the Italian cities. The providential Christian view of history was not necessarily confronted in this account because Bruni was writing a history of Florence, not of the world. In presenting the background to the Florentine past, however, he ranged so widely that his first book was in effect an essay on world history conceived on the pattern of the decline and rebirth of secular republican virtues. It contained the germ of a novel view of history as the history of secular civilisation, which was eventually to grow into Gibbon's *Decline and Fall*.

The first stirring of this new interpretation is probably to be found in a piece of Florentine political propaganda composed by Salutati sometime between 1397 and 1403, his *Invective against Antonio Loschi* (*Invectiva in Antonium Luschum*). The *Invectiva* was a reply to a piece written by Loschi in defence of the mission of Florence's great enemy, Giangaleazzo Visconti the tyrant of Milan, to unify Italy and exclude the French. Salutati supported the contrary mission of Florence to defend the tradition of *Libertas*. Part of his case was the historical argument, based roughly on the evidence used later by Bruni, that Florence was the true inheritor of the traditions of Rome, but republican Rome not Caesar's. The remains of buildings in the city demonstrated its Roman origin, and its foundation by Sulla was proved by Sallust and Cicero.[1] A similar argument was developed about the same time in an early work of Bruni, a panegyric of the city of Florence on the model of Aelius Aristides' *Panathenaicus*, the *Laudatio Florentinae Urbis*, probably written more than ten years

---

[1] *Invectiva Lini Colucii Salutati . . . in Antonium Luschum Vicentinum* (Florence, 1826), pp. 24-9. H.Baron (*Humanistic and Political Literature in Florence and Venice*, pp. 51-61) discerns two strata fused in the final version, one of 1397-8, the other of 1402-3. B.L.Ullmann (*Humanism of Salutati*, pp. 33-4) reasserts the view that it was all written in 1403.

before his *History* in about 1401.[1] The interest of Bruni's *Laudatio* is that it not only asserted the historical connection of Florence with Roman republicanism but also dwelt at some length on the virtues of the contemporary Florentine republican constitution. The argument is as follows. He begins by describing the physical excellence of Florence and its buildings. Then he passes to the qualities of its people, resulting from the fact that they are descended from Romans and, moreover, from the Roman republic in its prime, when it had won its great military victories and not yet started on the decadent path of imperial government. The Florentines had retained their attachment to liberty in the tradition of the Roman republican heroes and were always the enemies of tyranny. He then proceeds to an analysis of the Florentine constitution as a mechanism carefully designed to protect right and freedom. He describes the magistracies, colleges and councils, limiting and balancing each other's powers, preserving liberty and justice because 'nothing can be decided out of the wilfulness of one man or another against the opinion of so many'. He digresses on the thirteenth-century origins of the constitution, likening the Florentines who left the city after the defeat at Montaperto to the Athenians who left their city to preserve their freedom in the Second Persian War. The Florentine magistracy had been set up to do the work of the *censors* at Rome, the *Areopagus* at Athens and the *ephors* at Sparta: to safeguard the individual so that the lesser man oppressed by the greater could immediately cry '*ego quoque Florentinus sum civis*'. The final catalogue of Florentine virtues includes the superiority of its speech and its cultivation of letters.

Niccoli, according to Guarino, 'did not cease to attack and execrate his native Florence, despised the state and inveighed against the most prudent counsels of the city'.[2] Bruni at any rate,

[1]For the date see Baron, *Humanistic and Political Literature*, ch. 4; Seigel, ' "Civic Humanism" or Ciceronian Rhetoric'; Baron, 'Leonardo Bruni'. Extracts from the *Laudatio* are printed in T.Klette, *Beiträge zur Geschichte und Literatur des Italienischen Gelehrtenrenaissance*, II (Greifswald, 1889), pp. 84-105; in G.Kirner, *Della Laudatio Urbis Florentinae di Leonardo Bruni* (Leghorn, 1889), pp. 29-32; and at various points in Baron, *Crisis of the Early Italian Renaissance*. An Italian version was printed by F.P.Luiso, *Le vere lode de la inclita et gloriosa città di Firenze* (Florence, 1899).

[2] *Epistolario di Guarino Veronese*, I, p. 39.

whatever may be thought of Niccoli and Poggio, was not guilty
of the indifference to politics and political thought which Rinuccini professed to see as a characteristic of the new humanists. But
he was also a youthful alien who would not in any case have had
any political rights in the city. Before assuming a natural connection between humanism and republicanism one must beware.
For one thing it is particularly difficult to be sure of the sincerity
of professional humanists when they write about politics. As the
servants of despots, communes and popes, they lived by writing
political propaganda to order and their political pronouncements
were therefore of a different kind from their statements about
literature and philosophy, which were not so obviously related to
the vested interests of their employers and therefore need not be
suspected for the same reasons. When Loschi extolled the mission
of Giangaleazzo, or Vergerio defended the policy of Innocent VII,
they were earning their bread by exercising their professional
skill in putting opinions into the most effective literary form; it
did not necessarily mean that they agreed with what they wrote.
Salutati's official correspondence involved him in flattering politicians of every kind and colour.[1] Bruni was not here writing
to order but it is very likely that he hoped to improve his standing
in Florence by praising its institutions, and Florence's defence of
liberty was a well-established motif in its everyday diplomatic
correspondence. The other great source for humanist insincerity
was of course the imitation of classical models, and in this case
Bruni was copying a classical panegyric of a city state, which to a
considerable extent dictated his theme. Many years later, in a
letter written in 1440, he apologised for the *Laudatio*. Exaggeration and even untruth in a *Laudatio* were justified by ancient
exemplars. It had been done simply as an exercise. 'That oration
was written when I was a mere youth, when I had just completed
the study of Greek. It was a juvenile exercise in composition.'[2]

When these allowances have been made the fact remains that,
whatever the source of his inspiration, Bruni was inventing for

---

[1] The wide range is suggested by P.Herde, 'Politik und Rhetorik in Florenz am
Vorabend der Renaissance', *Archiv für Kulturgeschichte*, XLVII, 1965.

[2] Bruni, *Epistolae*, VIII, iv.

the modern world a new type of political literature in which the inspiration of humanist ideals was linked with republicanism. It was in a sense an easy and obvious marriage. Nothing could be more natural than that a clear-sighted admirer of classical literature should come to think of politics in terms of the republican city state. But the form in which the marriage took place was entirely new. Medieval thinkers had carried out the feat of absorbing Aristotle's *Politics* into a political philosophy directed primarily towards monarchical forms of government. This was a testimony to the prevalence of monarchy and to their lack of historical perspective rather than to their classicism. One great Italian thinker of the early fourteenth century, Marsilius of Padua, had used Aristotle lavishly to construct a republican political theory for Italian communes. His defence of the commune however was embedded in a philosophical justification of the state on the scholastic model. Bruni's approach owes nothing to this tradition. His political ideas were not a modification of scholasticism as Marsilius's had been but a departure along an entirely different road. Bruni admired and translated Aristotle, but he did not write political philosophy on the Aristotelian model and his politics were divorced from the philosophical structure which scholasticism had drawn from Aristotle. His inspiration was not philosophical but literary; it was drawn from the historical and political attitudes of Cicero, Sallust and Livy. The nature of the inspiration can be seen clearly in the life of Cicero, loosely based on Plutarch, which he wrote about 1415. He saw Cicero's particular excellence in the combination of literary and political ability, a mixture of talents which Bruni also had.[1] Cicero, for Bruni, was the man who introduced philosophy into Latin literature and raised the literary level of the language and yet was deeply involved in affairs. More generally, Bruni saw in ancient Athens and Rome the union of high literary culture with republican polity. He evolved a simplified, secularised attitude to politics out of this, which ignored scholastic interests in the philosophical basis of the state, or the relation between state and church.

Among Rinuccini's charges were complaints that the human-

[1] Bruni, *Schriften*, pp. 113-15.

ists were scornful of traditional philosophy, especially logic, that they undervalued Aristotle and finally, that they preferred the pagan gods to the Christian God. It is not easy to discover how much truth there was in these charges, partly because the humanists after Salutati were not much given to systematic statements of belief, and partly because any really anti-Christian opinions would have been unlikely to find open expression. A view of philosophy consistent with Rinuccini's remarks was put into the mouth of Niccoli in Bruni's *Dialogi*, which, although only a rhetorical exercise, expresses some opinions that were actually held. Consider philosophy, says Niccoli when defending his belief in the inferiority of modern times, consider philosophy from which all our *'humanitas'* is derived. Antiquity produced the schools of Stoics, Academics, Peripatetics and Epicureans, and their works were available to Cicero. Now their books are lost. We have philosophers, but – Niccoli's scorn for them is boundless. They teach philosophy when they do not know their letters. They 'utter more solecisms than words when they speak'. They lay down the law in the name of Aristotle, without understanding him, as if it was the edict of Apollo. He had no quarrel with Aristotle, he says, but this use of him is unbearable. Cicero rebuked his contemporaries for not understanding Aristotle properly; now the situation is much worse. The books which pass for his works are travesties. The art of dialectic has been ruined by British thinkers (Oxford philosophers in fact) whose very names – Farabrich (Richard of Ferribrigge), Buser (possibly William of Heytesbury), Occam (William of Ockham), proclaim the barbarity of their thought.[1] Some years later Niccoli was accused by Bruni, at a time of enmity when he was more outspoken than usual, of despising St Thomas himself: 'even Thomas Aquinas, a man endowed, immortal gods, with what *scientia* and *doctrina*, whom I do not hesitate to link with Aristotle and Theophrastus, this clownish fool so condemns that he openly announces to all those listening that he lacked letters or brilliance or intelligence.'[2] These opinions of Niccoli or pseudo-Niccoli might be summarised as approval for the philosophical traditions

[1] *Prosatori Latini del Quattrocento*, pp. 54-8.
[2] Zippel, *Niccoli*, p. 78.

conveyed by Cicero's *De Officiis* and disapproval of modern philosophy, both because it is obscurantist and because it is based on insufficient knowledge of the Greek originals. They are very much in line with Petrarch's earlier outspoken assertion of the merits of the Ciceronian combination of eloquence with wisdom against the Aristotelian logic-chopping which invaded Italy from the northern universities in the fourteenth century. One of the factors that assisted the reception and expansion of this attitude in Florence was the fact that it was not a great university town. In striking contrast to Padua and Bologna, with their long established schools enjoying a European reputation, which could become centres for the dissemination of scholastic philosophy, the *Studio* at Florence was founded late, in the mid-fourteenth century, and never became a powerful independent influence.[1] In 1400 Florence was unusual if not unique in being a city with impressive intellectual resources and a weak university. It was therefore easier in Florence than elsewhere to point out the absence of the emperor's clothes and treat the whole subject of scholasticism with derision.[2]

The humanists found medieval philosophy frankly tedious and, from a literary point of view, barbaric. They preferred the more elegant and less abstract sub-philosophy embedded in the rhetorical literature, which they admired, by Cicero and Seneca and, to a lesser extent, the originals of Plato and Aristotle. Bruni had translated Plato's *Phaedo* by 1405 and *Gorgias* by 1411. For both translations he wrote dedications to the popes whom he was serving at the time excusing himself on the grounds that Plato's doctrines were so much in conformity with Christianity as to be a support to it.[3] But it was not for the purpose of Christian

[1] C.Morelli, 'Discorso' in *Statuti della Università e Studio fiorentino*, pp. xxxiii-xlviii; H.Rashdall, *The Universities of Europe in the Middle Ages* (ed. F.M.Powicke and A.B. Emden, Oxford, 1936), II, pp. 47-51.

[2] C.Vasoli, 'Polemiche occamiste', *Rinascimento*, III, 1952; E.Garin, 'La cultura fiorentina nella seconda metà del 300 e i "barbari Britanni"', *La Rassegna della Letteratura Italiana*, LXVI, 1960.

[3] Bruni, Schriften, pp. 3-4; L.Bertalot, 'Zur Bibliographie der Übersetzungen des Leonardus Brunus Aretinus', *Quellen und Forschungen*, XXVII, 1936-7, pp. 181-2. Cf. E.Garin, 'Ricerche sulle traduzioni di Platone nella prima metà del sec. xv', *Medioevo e Rinascimento Studi in Onore di Bruno Nardi*, I, pp. 361-3.

apologetic that he had undertaken the translations. Just as it was the attraction of style rather than ideas which had first encouraged Petrarch to adopt Cicero's outlook on life, so the main impulse towards Plato was probably the literary attractiveness of the dialogues to one who had passed the barrier of learning Greek. Bruni wrote to Niccoli around 1403-4 about '*your* Plato, for so it pleases me to call him for whom you have always fought against the ignorant crowd', whose works he had now begun to translate: 'he has the greatest elegance, the highest powers of argument, subtlety; the rich and divine utterances of the disputants are set forth with a wonderful liveliness and an incredible wealth of expression. In the language there is the greatest facility and much to be admired of what the Greeks call *charis* (grace). No straining, no violence; everything is said as if by a man who has words and their laws in his power.'[1] In addition to being susceptible to literary charm Bruni also shared a taste for moral philosophy with Petrarch and Salutati. In December 1407 he wrote to Niccoli complaining that he was bored with history and would more willingly give his time to philosophy, 'that I might understand on what basis our life must be established and how conducted, how much virtue should be valued, how great is the splendour of justice, how fitting is integrity, how praiseworthy modesty, what glory there is in fortitude, how much these things are their own fruits and how much store is to be set by wealth or power'.[2] The man who wants encouraging information on these topics will naturally turn to Plato, Aristotle and Cicero if he can rather than to scholastic philosophy. The humanists found that ancient philosophy, particularly as explained by Cicero, suited both their literary tastes and their urbane moral interests. They did not explore its metaphysical basis or its relationship to Christianity, and therefore the more easily came to think largely in its terms.

At least one contemporary critic did see in humanism even at this early stage a serious threat to Christian belief. The book in

[1] Bruni, *Epistolae*, 1, p. 16. On the date, Baron, *Humanistic and Political Literature*, ch. 5.
[2] Bruni, *Schriften*, p. 112.

which the accusation was elaborated, *Lucula Noctis* (the glow-worm), was written, probably in 1405, by Giovanni Dominici, a prominent Dominican Friar.[1] Dominici was a powerful and extremely successful conservative puritan. He became prominent at Venice in the last decades of the fourteenth century as a leader of the rigorous wing of the Dominican Order, working with Catherine of Siena's disciple Raymond of Capua, and as a popular preacher. In 1399, when opposition to his extremism both in the city and in the order drove him away, he moved to Florence and continued his work there. He was spoken of by a lay observer as a preacher who could 'draw souls out of the living body', and was so highly regarded that the commune went to considerable trouble to secure his services as lecturer on the Bible in the university. It was at this point in his career that he became involved in a controversy about humanism and religion with Salutati.

The occasion for the dispute[2] was a letter written by Giovanni da Saminiato, a friar at the Camaldolese convent of S.Maria degli Angeli, to a young member of Salutati's circle, Angelo Corbinelli, urging him that the reading of classical poets was vanity and blasphemy and that Seneca and Aristotle, though harmless, were no substitutes for the Bible. Salutati took up the dispute and replied at great length with Petrarchan arguments in favour of the study of ancient poetry. Poetry was essential to theology because God could not be described in ordinary language and to dismiss poetry would be to dismiss all scriptural statements about God from Moses onwards, which are clearly poetic in form. The attitude of the Fathers was not entirely hostile to the use of the classics whose study was obviously at the very least necessary for anti-pagan apologetics. Finally he argued that poetry was in fact good in its effects and that poets were rarer and more valuable people than philosophers.[3]

Lucula Noctis is a full-scale reply to these arguments. During

[1] A.Roesler, *Cardinal Johannes Dominici O. Pr. 1357-1419* (Freiburg-im-Breisgau, 1893).

[2] Summarised in the introduction by R.Coulon to *Beati Iohannis Dominici Cardinalis S. Sixti Lucula Noctis* (Paris, 1908). There is another edition of the text by E.Hunt (*University of Notre Dame Publications in Mediaeval Studies*, no. 4, 1940).

[3] Salutati, *Epistolario*, IV, pp. 170-205.

his stay in Florence Dominici had been able to observe with severe disapproval the humanist antics which had been reported with sympathy by Bruni in his *Dialogi* and with some amusement by Rinuccini in his *Invective*. Dominici exposed their worship of classical manuscripts and authors. 'This school of Christians – or should I say pagans – will be indignant because I say they should not have their manuscripts. Sacred writings are neglected, books of faith uncared for; the writings of pagans are bound in silk, decorated with gold and silver, read as precious things, and all the schools of Christians – Christians in name only – resound day and night, holy days included, with the words of pagans. . . . It is not even permitted that this evil of secret infidelity should be bewailed amongst Christians publicly.'[1] He laughed at the prevalent assumption that government could not be carried out successfully without the aid of the rhetoricians' knowledge of Cicero and Virgil.[2] He lamented the confusion of belief bred by classicism.

Would that our friends who reek of dialectic, physics, poetry and the Ciceronian font would not make such a muddle of many opinions. I know, alas, what they propose in secret, what they say when there is no independent witness present; in how many the Christian religion flourishes externally in name only when Christ is not present in their minds by faith, still less by grace. What one finds is not people who are Ciceronian in friendship, moral like Seneca, abstemious like Epicurus, despisers of the world like Diogenes, reasoners like Aristotle, theologians like Socrates, awaiting death like Cato, or like Christ perfect in all things. What one finds is everything returning confused into a sort of false ancient chaos, including some good things but also obvious evils mixed with them. I venture to say that all this springs from immoderate love of secular knowledge.[3]

These are asides. The main argument of *Lucula Noctis*, pursued relentlessly through every objection, is the fundamental incompatibility between Christianity and pagan literature. All the standard arguments for the study of the classics – that they support the Christian religion, that they are a product of the

[1] *Lucula Noctis*, cap. 13.
[2] Cap. 18.
[3] Cap. 20.

same one God's world, that they help the understanding of scripture, that they must be studied by opponents of paganism, that many pagans were good men, etc. – are taken up and decisively rejected. No study of the classics which is not quite clearly subordinated to a Christian purpose is permissible. A Christian is generally better occupied in tilling the soil than in reading pagan authors. Dominici was not ignorant of the classics; on the contrary his book was packed with evidence of familiarity. It is all the more impressive as a statement of the irreconcileable opposition between Christian and pagan ideals. It makes far more convincing reading than Salutati's embarrassed efforts to give the reading of Virgil a Christian purpose.

There is some irony in the fact that Salutati, the immediate object of Dominici's onslaught, had a horror of unconventional religious opinions and was himself anxious to protect humanism from some of the dangers which Dominici perceived. In Bruni's *Dialogi* Salutati is made to defend the superiority of modern Christian literature against Niccoli's assertion of the absolute superiority of the ancients. 'In these dregs of time and with so great a lack of books,' Niccoli says, what cultural hope could there be? Mankind had lost crucial works of Varro, Livy, Sallust, Pliny and Cicero while the mediocre works of Cassiodorus and Alcidus had been preserved – precisely the attitude to literature which Dominici attacked.[1] Salutati tried to counter this, pointing out that a good deal of ancient literature had in fact survived and that Dante, Petrarch and Boccaccio among the moderns were themselves excellent, but Niccoli rejected this argument with scorn. To approve these authors was merely to follow vulgar opinion. Dante was a poor classicist: he misunderstood a line of Virgil, portrayed Cato the Younger who died at forty-eight as a greybeard and placed Brutus the defender of the republic in hell. Petrarch was continually advertising his *Africa* in his letters but what emerged was a work which any friend of the poet would wish unwritten or burnt. The *Dialogi* are at least partly imaginary but we happen to know that Salutati did in real life feel bound to counter similar opinions held by Poggio. Salutati had always

---

[1] *Prosatori Latini del Quattrocento*, p. 54.

maintained that Petrarch was the equal of the greatest writers of antiquity because, although they might surpass him in poetry or prose, none had his command of Latin composition in a variety of forms and none combined his literary skill with the true faith. In September 1404 or 1405 Poggio wrote a letter from the papal court to Salutati challenging this view. Unfortunately it is known only from Salutati's reply. The most specific indication of its contents is this: 'You and your friend show yourselves to be malicious critics of modern times in that you prefer not one man to another but one age to another as if you were their judges.'[1] Poggio had apparently expressed a wholesale preference for antiquity over modern times. It called forth from Salutati a renewed defence of Petrarch. As far as wisdom went, he said, some ancients were Christians, some pagans were nearer to the truth than others, but pagans were necessarily inferior to Christians. In March 1406, after another letter from Poggio, Salutati again wrote reprovingly. He was delighted with the evidence which Poggio gave of his gifts for *studia humanitatis*, but he wished that Poggio and others unspecified, whose well-being was close to his heart, would make the same progress in other virtues, in wisdom, piety and charity. 'I still do not see that you acknowledge the perfection of Christian doctrine.'[2]

Nobody of course could reject Christianity in the fifteenth century, but Salutati had bred a school of humanists whose devotion to the classics was so absorbing that they were setting up an independent secular scale of values. If this scale of values was to be taken seriously it threatened not only common medieval views of philosophy and politics but also the priorities of conventional Christianity itself. Its distinctness from scholasticism and theology made its rapid development much easier. Dominici, the first prophet of the Counter-Reformation, was essentially right.

[1] Salutati, *Epistolario*, IV, pp. 126-45. The defence of Petrarch to which he and Poggio refer was in a letter written in 1379 (*Epistolario*, I, pp. 334-42).

[2] *Epistolario*, IV, pp. 159-60. Salutati went on to reprove him for some highly indiscreet revelations to Niccoli, unfortunately not specified.

2

The Environment of the Avant-garde

The most obvious part of the humanists' environment was their link with the Florentine upper class and their dependence on the wealth, security and sophistication of life in the city of Florence. Salutati, although not a Florentine originally, never left the city in the last thirty years of his life and owed his living and standing to the fees which he commanded as chancellor, which put him financially on the fringes of the wealthiest Florentine society.[1] Chrysoloras was supported in Florence by a stipend of 150 florins, later raised to 250, and presumably augmented by the admiring wealthy circles in which he moved: a later imaginary dialogue portrays him taking part with other humanists in a discussion on the theme of the tranquillity of the soul at the villa of Palla Strozzi, to which they had moved during an outbreak of plague in the city.[2] The most famous portrayal of the humanist discussions of this period is the one in Giovanni Gherardi da Prato's *Paradiso degli Alberti*. This was probably written in the 1420s and therefore may well be inaccurate in the details of some of the arguments which it attributes to 1389.[3] There is no reason to doubt that it reflects truly the kind of social milieu in which Salutati and Marsigli moved. The *Paradiso*, at which they were honoured guests, was the suburban villa of Antonio degli Alberti, the leading member of the most successful banking and trading family in Florence in the second half of the fourteenth century, which had

---

[1] Martines, *Social World of the Florentine Humanists*, pp. 105-8.
[2] Cammelli, *Manuele Crisolora*, pp. 41, 47, 61.
[3] Baron, *Humanistic and Political Literature in Florence and Venice*, ch. 1.

formerly enjoyed a commanding position in papal finance of the kind which the Medici were to have in the next century.[1] Bruni and Poggio in their early days at Florence were men without private means. We do not know how they survived before they went off to seek their fortunes at the papal court, but it is likely that they had received some sort of assistance, perhaps in return for copying, from the well-to-do Florentines with whom they were intimate. The professional humanists were linked with the wealthy amateurs. Niccoli was one of six brothers who inherited the estate of their father, a successful wool manufacturer. Niccoli himself paid no attention to the business and during his lifetime the family fortune went downhill, but he was prosperous enough to live in cultivated idleness until Cosimo de' Medici began to help him.[2] Roberto Rossi, another character in Bruni's *Dialogi*, pupil of Chrysoloras and translator of Aristotle, seems also to have been a man living on inherited wealth without himself engaging in any business activity, independent but not particularly affluent.[3] Angelo Corbinelli, whose devotion to the classics Salutati was defending in his controversy with Dominici, and Antonio Corbinelli, patron of Guarino and later collector of a great manuscript library, were brothers and members of a cloth manufacturing and landowning family.[4] Palla Strozzi, socially the most distinguished of Chrysoloras's known pupils and a prominent humanist patron and collector, belonged to one of the very wealthiest trading families and was reckoned later to be the richest man in Florence.[5]

The humanists recognised and enjoyed this background. When Bruni was with the papal court at Viterbo in the autumn of 1405, shortly after leaving Florence, he fell ill and wrote back to Salutati

---

[1] G. Mancini, *Vita di Leon Battista Alberti*, 2nd ed. (Florence, 1911), ch. i, pp. 3-14.

[2] Martines, op. cit., pp. 112-16.

[3] Martines, op. cit., pp. 108-10; A. Manetti, 'Roberto de' Rossi', *Rinascimento*, ii, 1951.

[4] Martines, op. cit., pp. 51-2, 318-20; Idem, 'Addenda to the life of Antonio Corbinelli', *Rinascimento*, viii, 1957.

[5] Martines, op. cit., pp. 316-8; P. J. Jones, 'Florentine Families and Florentine Diaries in the Fourteenth Century', *Papers of the British School at Rome*, xxiv, 1956, p. 187.

a nostalgic letter about the miseries of being sick in a rough country town where there were no decent doctors or food.

There flowed before my eyes the delights and conveniences of the city of Florence: the wealth of doctors, the exquisite and delicate foods created to suit the tastes of invalids by the most expert cooks, the abundance of the smoothest wines. A thousand times a day came into my mind the fame of the Val di Greve and the nymphs of the grape-harvest ... I thought and I still think that you are blessed to live in Florence where nothing is lacking to living well. When I was there I lived in the greatest happiness and tranquillity of mind both because of the amenity and delights of the city and because of the polished manners of my acquaintances. . . . Of course I understand those who live according to nature, in case you should think I have become an epicurean given up to pleasure. But I add: especially if they are devoted to the study of humane letters which seems to me to have deserted all other cities like shabby houses and betaken itself to our Florence as to some shrine of the muses, some choice dwelling. There is no place in the world to compare with the splendour of Florence or the urbanity of the Florentines.[1]

This self-indulgent plea of the exile from the city lights earned a sharp rebuke from the austere Salutati.[2] One would not indeed naturally think of the papal court, even out of Rome, as an insufferably provincial place. Yet this is evidently how it appeared during the Great Schism to an exile from the metropolis of Florence. Salutati himself, writing in a propagandist vein against the Milanese around 1400 could ask, 'what town, not only in Italy but in the whole world, has safer walls, more superb palaces, more ornate churches, more handsome buildings ... has more inexhaustible wealth, more cultivated fields ... what city lacking a harbour imports and exports so much ... where is there greater trade, a richer variety of goods?'[3] For the humanists Florence was the summit of wealth and refinement and its wealthiest class provided the material background for their lives.

The Florentine upper class was dependent on the wealth of the

---

[1] L.Bertalot, 'Forschungen über Leonardo Bruni Aretino', *Archivum Romanicum*, xv, 1931, pp. 321-3.

[2] Salutati, *Epistolario*, iv, 113.

[3] *Invectiva . . . in Antonium Luschum*, p. 125.

city's industry and commerce. Though its members did not necessarily participate in trade they generally had some family connection with it. A famous Florentine canon lawyer of the late fourteenth century, Lapo da Castiglionchio, who claimed rather snobbishly to be himself essentially a landowner, admitted that members of his family had been merchants, 'but of noble and honest not base merchandise, voyaging to France and England and trading in cloth and wool as do all the greater and better men of the city: which activity is deemed fine and undemeaning.'[1] Though individuals might derive their incomes from land or from investment in the state debt, the prosperity of the city and of their class depended ultimately on industry and commerce. A good indication of the sort of economic activity on which Florence depended is provided by the biography of the best documented of all medieval merchants, Francesco di Marco Datini, who flourished roughly in the period 1382-1410. Although he lived at Prato, a subject city fifteen miles away, his trade was essentially within the Florentine orbit. His earliest interest was a trading and banking firm at Avignon in the last years before the Great Schism. When he returned to Prato in 1382 he formed a partnership in cloth-making and another in dyeing, his own function being in both cases to supply the capital for the enterprise and to import the raw materials. He thus became involved in the import of wool from England and Spain. To facilitate this he founded a new branch at Pisa. In 1383 he formed a partnership at Florence to trade in wool, cloth, hides and spices, and another in 1387 to export silk and cotton veils. He became a member of the silk gild and opened a big shop in Florence. Later he established branches at Genoa, Valencia, Barcelona and Majorca. He dealt in wool from Spain, alum, iron, spices, slaves from Byzantium, silk, and an endless variety of other merchandise according to the opportunities of trade. He had a bank at Florence and dealt in international exchange as well as goods. He died a very wealthy man.[2] Datini was an outstandingly successful mer-

[1] Quoted by P. J. Jones, op. cit., p. 191.

[2] I. Origo, *The Merchant of Prato* (London, 1957) is a portrait of Datini. Full investigation of his records has been begun by F. Melis in *Aspetti della Vita Economica Medievale*, 1 (Siena, 1962).

chant but the character of his enterprises was not peculiar. For instance, Goro Dati, who wrote a famous history of Florence's wars against Giangaleazzo Visconti, left a book of memoranda which shows him to have been a merchant in the western Mediterranean orbit, like Datini on a smaller scale.[1]

The growth of Florence into a city of perhaps 90,000 inhabitants by the mid-fourteenth century had been due partly to the fact that it was one of the chief European centres of the cloth industry. Giovanni Villani, the historian, who was himself a partner in a cloth manufacturing firm, said that in the year 1338 'the workshops of the wool gild were 200 and more and they made 70 to 80,000 cloths of the value of more than 1,200,000 gold florins of which a good third and more remained in the land to be worked.'[2] The industry was so highly developed that various quarters of the city concentrated on the manufacture of cloth of varying qualities, using different grades of raw wool. Most of the cloth-making was done in smallish workshops scattered about the city owned by masters who were members of the wool gild, the *Arte della Lana*. Their employees constituted a substantial proletariat, highly organised and subdivided and rife with incipient trade-unionism. Each gild quarter had a bell which summoned the day labourers to their workshops in the early morning. Early fourteenth-century Florence was in fact a medieval fore-runner of early nineteenth-century Lancashire, concentrated into a small urban area.[3]

The other major economic activity for which Florence was particularly famous was banking. Florentine banking was essentially international finance; its techniques developed out of the need for the transfer of money from one city to another and its gild was known as the *Arte di Cambio*. The Florentines were not the only Italians who practised this art but in the fourteenth century they were its foremost exponents. For most of the period of the Avignon papacy the transfer of papal moneys from all parts of Europe was undertaken by Florentine banks. In 1357 there was

[1] *Il libro segreto di Gregorio Dati*, ed. C. Gargiolli (Bologna, 1869).
[2] *Historie Fiorentine di Giovanni Villani* (Muratori, XIII), col. 827.
[3] A. Doren, *Die florentiner Wollentuchindustrie vom vierzehnten bis zum sechzehnten Jahrhundert* (Stuttgart, 1901), esp. chs. 3, 5.

a regular postal service, an unusual thing in the medieval world, between Avignon and Florence, maintained by twenty Florentine companies who presumably found it essential to have good communications with the centre of ecclesiastical finance.[1] Another aspect of Florentine society which illustrates its degree of financial sophistication is the state debt. Hundreds of years before this happened in Northern Europe, the Italian cities had established permanent debts funded by taxation and held by large numbers of the more prosperous citizens. The consolidated state debt of Florence, the *Monte Comune*, was established in 1345. By 1378 it amounted to over 2,300,000 florins and it grew considerably during the expensive wars of the late fourteenth and fifteenth centuries.[2] The *Monte* offered an alternative form of investment to land and money. It was normal for a proportion of Florentine fortune to be held in this way.

Some aspects of this commercial society suffered severe shocks in the later fourteenth century. There was a sharp decline in population. Giovanni Villani, who seems to have been a reliable statistician, claimed that there were 90,000 mouths in the city in 1338. A decade later Florence, like the rest of Europe, was struck by the Black Death and, as it happens, produced the most famous of all literary accounts of the plague, the preface to Boccaccio's *Decameron*. A set of tax records compiled in 1380 suggests that the population at that time could not have been much above 60,000 and the births registered at the Baptistry from 1450 onwards are consistent with a population of about 50,000.[3] Accurate figures of medieval population are impossible to obtain but the probability is that Florence in 1400 was much reduced in size from its medieval height. At the same time the cloth industry seems to have been passing through a prolonged crisis. The revolt of the *Ciompi* in 1378, though connected with other

---

[1] *Miscellanea Fiorentina di Erudizione e Storia*, I, 1886, pp. 150-3.

[2] G.A.Brucker, 'Un documento fiorentino sulla guerra, sulla finanza e sulla amministrazione publica (1375)', *ASI*, cxv, 1957, p. 169; M.B.Becker, 'Economic Change and the Emerging Florentine State', *Studies in the Renaissance*, xiii, 1966.

[3] E.Fiumi, 'La demografia fiorentina nelle pagine di Giovanni Villani', *ASI*, cvii, p. 19. K.J.Beloch, *Bevölkerungsgeschichte Italiens*, ii, (Berlin, 1940), pp .137-9.

troubles, in particular the War of the Eight Saints against the papacy and internal political rivalries, was in part a proletarian revolution of cloth workers against their masters and a symptom of decline in the industry. The *Ciompi* demanded that cloth production should be maintained at a level of at least 24,000 cloths a year, probably much lower than it had been a generation earlier; and there are other indications of this contraction. Even in the market at Pisa Florentine cloth was losing ground to the cloth of England and Languedoc.[1] In spite of these changes, however, there is no evidence that the commercial character of the city was undermined or that the relative wealth of the city had been reduced in the general contraction of European population. The efforts of the commune to ensure the supply of wool from England in the fifteenth century show that the wool industry remained important.[2] If the export trade in woollen cloth was declining, silk manufacture was probably becoming more important.[3] Florentine bankers controlled the finances of the papacy after the Schism much as they had done before it.

Since Florence was so obviously and characteristically a commercial society there is a temptation to regard its humanism as an emanation of the spirit of its bourgeoisie. Florentine humanism is indeed unthinkable without its urban background. Secularisation of values, republican political ideals and identification with the manners and morals of Cicero and Seneca, though they were closely connected with the profession of the rhetorician which might be exercised in a seignorial court, were more easily compatible with the life of a gentleman of the city, enjoying wealth and education but freed from the hierarchical links of the seignor-

[1] R.Davidsohn, 'Blüte und Niedergang der florentiner Tuchindustrie', *Zeitschrift für die gesamte Staatswissenschaft*, LXXXV, 1928; F.Melis, 'Uno sguardo sul mercato dei panni di lana a Pisa nella seconda metà del Trecento', *Economia e Storia*, VI, 1959.

[2] A.Grundzweig, 'Le fonds du Consulat de la Mer aux Archives de l'Etat à Florence', *Bulletin de l'Institut Historique Belge de Rome*, x, 1930, e.g., p. 15.

[3] F.Edler de Roover, 'Andrea Banchi, Florentine Silk Manufacturer and Merchant in the Fifteenth Century', *Studies in Medieval and Renaissance History*, III, ed. W.M. Bowsky (Lincoln, Nebraska, 1966).

ial world, than with that of a nobleman or a bishop.[1] One can go further and say that the economic maturity of a well-established rather than incipient urbanism was needed to produce patrons like Palla Strozzi and Cosimo de' Medici, who had both the ingrained values of a commercial society and the educated detachment of a leisured class living on inherited wealth. But attempts to go beyond this very general suitability of the background and to explain particular developments in humanism in social and economic terms have not been convincing. Historians have not yet identified any social and economic peculiarities which made the Florentine bourgeois of 1400 especially fitted to revive this particular brand of humanism rather than those of Genoa or Venice. Nor have they explained why it should be the Florentine of this moment rather than his countrymen of the early fourteenth or the late fifteenth centuries – who produced radically different ideologies. This may be because the facts of Florentine economic history are not clear.[2] The truth is probably that explanations of this kind are misdirected rather than imperfect, and that the economy of Florence must be regarded as no more than a part of the background; an essential aspect but one in which Florence did not differ significantly from other cities in other times and places. To find the peculiarities of the environment of Niccoli and Bruni we must look elsewhere.

Another factor which certainly had some influence on the form of Florentine humanism was the background of political events. There were many other heroic periods in the history of Florence but the years at the end of the fourteenth century and the beginning of the fifteenth were remarkable, if not unique, for the combination of resistance to the threat of political annihilation and expansion of territorial power. These events produced an

[1] Ideological developments within bourgeois society at this period have been most fully examined by C.Bec, *Les Marchands Écrivains; affaires et humanisme à Florence 1375-1434* (Paris – The Hague, 1967).

[2] Hence the possibility of finding almost opposite explanations in recent literature: one writer suggests that the Florentine bourgeoisie became more suitable because it was tending to turn from commerce to industry (H.Baron, 'A Sociological interpretation of the Early Renaissance in Florence', *South Atlantic Quarterly*, XXXVIII, 1939), another that they were more suitable because they were becoming more remote from industrial activity which was declining (F.Antal, *Florentine Painting and its Social Background* (London, 1948), pp. 25-31, 55-8, 86-8, 105-9).

enhanced consciousness of republicanism. Florence in the later fourteenth century was a city republic ruling a surrounding subject territory. Its sovereign government, the *Signoria*, was a group of nine priors who held office for two months only, without the right to immediate re-election, and were selected from a list of eligible citizens who were members of gilds. The *Signoria* lived in the *Palazzo* and conducted the day-to-day government of the commune. On important matters they normally consulted two colleges whose members also held office for limited periods, the sixteen *gonfalonieri* and twelve *buonuomini*; and sometimes a specially summoned council of notables, a *Consiglio de' Richiesti*. In matters of legislation, as opposed to administration and diplomacy, they were limited by the obligation to pass their proposals through two councils containing several hundred citizens, the *Consiglio del Popolo* and the *Consiglio del Comune*. The *Signoria* was assisted by a staff of permanent notaries, and justice and police were also in the hands of permanent, not elective, officials; but there were a number of particular commissions controlling various aspects of city life which were also composed of citizens elected for short terms of office. In times of crisis such as a dangerous war, a *balìa* was appointed, a special commission of chosen citizens with temporary but wide powers independent of the normal communal constitution. By this time a considerable subject state stretched beyond the city walls, the *contado*, whose boundaries were in most directions 25 miles or more from Florence and enclosed once independent cities like Volterra and Pistoia. The *contado* had no representation in the government of Florence. The relations of its various parts to the capital were determined by arrangements made when they had been subjected, so that their government was partly in the hands of their own citizens, and partly in the hands of commissioners sent out from Florence. Florence itself was nowhere near being a democracy. At no time was more than a small proportion of its population effectively engaged in government.[1] It was a republic in which a considerable proportion of power was in the hands of a fairly

[1] P. J. Jones, 'Communes and Despots: the City State in Late Medieval Italy', *Transactions of the Royal Historical Society*, 5th ser., xv, 165, p. 76.

small group, whose names constantly recur as members of advisory councils and as ambassadors, limited by the rapid turnover of office holders and by the legislative powers of the big councils which gave some political influence to, at most, a few thousand men. It was, however, a genuine republic in which the more prosperous citizens assumed the duty and responsibility of political service, and in which there was a constant process of voting and consultation.

The period in which the new humanist group emerged was an age of repeated political crisis which made the Florentine upper class intensely conscious of its republican tradition and of the difficulty of preserving it.[1] During the years 1375 to 1378 the Florentine patriciate endured two crises, one internal, the other external, which shook the city to its foundations: the War of the Eight Saints against Pope Gregory xi, and the Revolt of the *Ciompi* which, for a few weeks in 1378, overthrew the normal constitution. In the 1380s limited republican government had been effectively restored, but the integrity of the city was threatened by the armies of the two contenders for the throne of Naples, Charles of Durazzo and Louis of Anjou, moving up and down the peninsula. By a mixture of diplomacy, bribery and employment of mercenary troops Florence weathered this storm and emerged with its territory enlarged by the purchase of Arezzo. This was followed, however, by the greatest threat of all, the expansion of Milan under Giangaleazzo Visconti. Giangaleazzo was not content with the hegemony which he acquired in Lombardy; he had his eyes on Tuscany as well. In 1390 his interference in a dispute between Florence and her southern neighbour Siena led to a full-scale war lasting until 1392, in which Florence survived by paying for a French invasion of Lombardy from the west and by the operations of her own mercenaries in the east. In 1397 Milanese intervention in Tuscany, this time with the help of Siena and Pisa, provoked the War of Mantua which lasted a year and again

[1] The best account of the politics of the period remains F.-T. Perrens, *Histoire de Florence . . . jusqu'à la domination des Medicis*, vi (Paris, 1883). There are modern accounts of the War of the Eight Saints in G.A. Brucker, *Florentine Politics and Society 1343-1378* (Princeton, 1962) and of the struggle with Giangaleazzo in D.M. Bueno de Mesquita, *Giangaleazzo Visconti* (Cambridge, 1941).

Florence survived ingloriously, partly through French intervention at her instigation. Giangaleazzo's actions again became serious in 1399. In 1398 he had finally bought Pisa. In 1399 he accepted the lordship of Siena and stretched his hand even further over Florence to accept that of Perugia. In 1402 he won over Lucca and Bologna. Florence tried to counter his policy by paying for an expedition to Italy by the German King Rupert in 1401; he was ignominiously defeated by Giangaleazzo. It seemed as if the ring was tightening inexorably when, as if by a miraculous intervention, Giangaleazzo died of the plague in September 1402 and the threat was suddenly removed. Released from this danger Florence turned to the offensive. Recent events had driven home forcibly the awful danger to a commercial republic of isolation from the sea. The years 1403 to 1406 were occupied by a series of tortuous and discreditable manoeuvres by which Florence finally reduced the city of Pisa to subjection and so prepared the way for her emergence as a sea power. Strengthened in territory and prestige she then faced the next serious threat, the aggressive activities of King Ladislas of Naples between 1408 and his providential death in 1414.

The ruling Florentine politicians who guided the city through these vicissitudes regarded their state, understandably, as a frail bark tossed upon the stormy seas of Italian politics and kept afloat only by their unceasing vigilance, their skill and their wealth. They also regarded themselves, with some justice, as the champions of republicanism. To say this is not to attribute any particular altruism to Florentine policy in these years. The fourteenth-century slogan *Tuscis Tuscia*, 'a Tuscan Tuscany', expressed not a policy of benevolence to surrounding peoples but a determination to maintain her own predominance in that part of Italy. The events of the struggle with Giangaleazzo showed that there was much jealousy and fear of Florence in the neighbouring communes of Pisa and Lucca, and indeed within her sphere of influence Florence was as willing as Milan to suppress independent cities. It remained true, however, that in the most dangerous episodes of this period Florence was a republic fighting against a tyrant with all the disadvantages and the glories of that role. The speech which Leonardo Bruni put into the mouth of Rinaldo Gianfigliazzi in his description of a meeting held in 1399, when the final crisis of the duel with Giangaleazzo was approaching, if not authentic in its words at least expresses a genuine attitude of the times and also evokes the genuine dilemma of the free society.

When indeed the dangers are on our very threshold and can now by no means be evaded, then at last we consult in agitation, then we summon the Council of the two hundred and of the hundred and thirty-one, we enter on interminable discussion. And I would not think this serious if our struggle were with another people; for then conditions would be the same, or almost the same, on both sides. But now our struggle is, not with another people, but with a tyrant, who watches continually over his own affairs, who has no fear of cavillers, who is not hampered by petty laws, who does not wait for the decree of the masses nor the deliberation of the people.[1]

The heightened consciousness of the republican tradition of the city had a profound influence on humanism for two reasons. First, the leading propagandists employed on both sides in the Florentine-Milanese struggle were humanists so that the themes of Florence's republican mission, and the opposing Visconti mission to unify and protect Italy, were enshrined in humanist writings. Secondly, much classical literature and history was concerned with the problems and vicissitudes of republican city states; these were easily and not unreasonably seen as analogous to the trials of Florence, so that it was natural to identify the Florentine experience with the experience of Athens and Rome. The impact of the war is seen in Salutati's *Invectiva* (*c.* 1397-1403) and Bruni's *Laudatio* (*c.* 1401).[2] Salutati wrote as the defender of a *civitas libera*, a 'free city', the natural inheritor of the traditions of republican Rome, against the propagandist of a tyranny. Bruni similarly ascribed the justice of the Florentine cause and its success against the tyrant's onslaughts to the virtues of the republican inheritance and constitution of the city. It has even been suggested that the marriage of humanism and republicanism

[1] Bruni, *Historiarum Florentini Populi Libri* XII, p. 277; translation by Bueno de Mesquita, op. cit., p. 254.

[2] The relationship is one of the main themes of H.Baron, *Crisis of the Early Italian Renaissance*, to which this argument is much indebted.

is a result of the particular crisis of 1402. This is hardly convincing,[1] but there is little doubt that Florence's struggle as a whole encouraged humanists, both in their professional capacity as propagandists and in their more private capacity as connoisseurs of literature, to embrace a republican political philosophy as something with a special humanist significance. For the duel with Giangaleazzo coincided with the blossoming of classical scholarship in the city under the aegis of Salutati and Chrysoloras. If Bruni had not lived through the war it is unlikely that he would have written his *History* with the crucial emphasis on the cultural implications of republicanism. This did not mean that humanists stopped writing works praising monarchs or monarchy. It did mean that within the Florentine environment they invented a new attitude to political philosophy and history based on republicanism. The political situation of Florence around 1400 therefore does help to explain one prominent aspect of the new humanism.

But the background of city-state warfare does not help very much in explaining the intenser classicism which embraced other, non-political features of the ancient world. There is another aspect of Florentine society which is perhaps more illuminating for the wider problem of explaining the acceptability of transmuted classical values; this is the relation of Florence with the church and the papacy. There are two fairly obvious reasons for emphasising this side of the situation. First, humanism displayed some paganising tendencies which did not pass unnoticed at the time and which naturally direct one's attention to the attitude of the ecclesiastical authorities. Secondly, the Florentine humanist group developed a conspicuously strong connection with the papal court which, considering their intellectual tendencies, seems at first sight paradoxical. The position of the church locally and the relationship with the papacy were inseparable in Florence. This was true, to some extent, of all medieval Europe, but it was more obviously and acutely true in Florence than elsewhere because of the unusually close links – political, financial and intellectual – with the papal court, resulting from Florence's

[1] Seigel, ' "Civic Humanism" or Ciceronian Rhetoric', has shown the weakness of this interpretation; but cf. Baron, 'Leonardo Bruni'.

geographical position, its banking and its intellectual prestige. The relationship with the papacy was one aspect of Florence's position which did undergo a crucial and significant transformation at the time when the new humanism was developing.

In the background of the relationship between Florence and the popes still loomed the awful and complex crisis of the years 1375 to 1378. For three years Florence had been involved in the War of the Eight Saints, a bitter, expensive and occasionally bloody conflict with the papacy. This war temporarily exhausted the resources of the city and left deep scars on the Florentine mind. The effect of the same years on the papacy was still more catastrophic. In the midst of the war, at the end of 1376 and the beginning of 1377, Pope Gregory XI made his painful journey to Rome to end the seventy-year residence of the papal court at Avignon. The stress produced by this change in the difficult circumstances of war was too great for the reluctant, mainly French court and when Gregory XI died in 1378 to be succeeded by a cantankerous Italian, Urban VI, the majority of the cardinals rapidly formed a schismatic Curia under the leadership of Clement VII and eventually moved back to Avignon, leaving a depleted court at Rome to be filled with Italian cardinals and officials.

The crisis of 1375-8 is of interest to the historian of humanism for two reasons. To begin with, it produced an early phase of humanist political propaganda in which anti-clerical motifs were very prominent. In 1376 Florence was placed under an interdict. There was a strong sense within the city of engagement in a deep religious conflict. A pro-papal waverer could say that Florence was fighting an invincible enemy. On the other side some people demanded that priests should be compelled to maintain divine services in spite of the papal ban. Early in the war officials were appointed to levy forced loans upon the clergy and to sequestrate their property if necessary and, as the pressure of war expenditure grew more intolerable, a preliminary inventory of ecclesiastical property was made and some seized and sold.[1] Anti-papal feeling

[1] On confiscation of church property see M.B.Becker, 'Church and State in Florence on the Eve of the Renaissance (1343-1382)', *Speculum*, XXXVII, 1962, pp. 522-3; P.J.Jones, 'Le Finanze della Badia Cisterciense di Settimo nel XIV secolo', *Rivista di Storia della Chiesa in Italia*, X, 1951, pp. 109-110.

was not a new thing in Florentine history. With the exception of the kingdom of Naples, Florence was the closest powerful neighbour of the papal state, and therefore extremely sensitive to the popes' repeated efforts to consolidate their territorial power.[1] Indeed suspicion of this kind was probably the main reason for the outbreak of the war in 1375. There was also a tradition in the city of radical religious sentiment associated with the *Fraticelli* which tended to attach itself to anti-papal politics. The War of the Eight Saints was therefore in a sense the culmination of a long history of political and ideological conflict between Florence and the papal court.[2] But it also introduced a new form of expression which superseded the old ones. Official propaganda during the war was in the hands of the new chancellor, Salutati, and the terms in which he conducted it were not the terms of religious dissent but those of Petrarchan evocation of the glories of the Italian classical inheritance. The papal armies in the war were partly English, mainly French; the administration of the papal state at the highest level was in the hands of French ecclesiastics. In the eyes of Salutati it was a war in defence of Italian liberty, in the tradition of the Roman republic, against barbarian tyrants. He wrote to the reluctant citizens of Rome on behalf of the commune of Florence in January 1376 urging them in ringing tones to remember the love of liberty which had inspired their ancestors Horatius Cocles and Mucius in the establishment of the republic and the overthrow of tyrants. This spirit was the reason for the Roman conquest of the world. They must not now be seduced by the blandishments of priests which would lead only to the oppression of Italy by the Gauls.[3] Salutati's future ally, Luigi Marsigli, wrote a famous letter in the same year in less elegant but even more specifically Petrarchan terms:

[1] P.Partner, 'Florence and the Papacy 1300-1375', *Europe in the Late Middle Ages*, ed. J.Hale, R.Highfield, B.Smalley (London, 1965).

[2] M.B.Becker, 'Florentine Politics and the Diffusion of Heresy in the Trecento: a Socio-Economic Inquiry', *Speculum*, XXXIV, 1959.

[3] *Archivio di Stato*, Florence, Missive 15, fol. 40. Much of Salutati's official correspondence in these years is printed in *Lini Colucii Salutati Epistolae*, ed. J.Rigacci (Florence, 1741-2). There is a private defence by him of the Florentine position in a letter of November 1375 (*Epistolario*, I, pp. 213-18).

Would that my lord [Petrarch] were here that he might have seen the Italians revenge themselves for the torment of the dissolute, hungry Limousins. . . . Look at the churches of Rome. The altars are better covered by the dust than by the roofs maintained by those [the cardinals] who derive their titles from them. . . . This is because all the offerings of St Peter and St Paul do not suffice for the expenses of Avignon. The riches that Crassus gathered in India would not suffice nor those that Julius Caesar gave in Rome, nor everything that Nero destroyed there. . . . How pleased my lord would have been with this holy enterprise you may know if you read three of his sonnets inspired not by earthly love but by love of God and grief and holy indignation, of which one begins 'l'avara Babilonia', the second 'Fiamma del Cielo' and the third 'Fontana di dolore'.[1]

All this is interesting in the context partly because it is an early example of political humanism, and partly because it shows how humanism, in the stress of certain political circumstances, might develop a specifically anti-clerical significance. Anti-clericalism, indeed, remained a common characteristic of humanists, but in the changed circumstances of Florence in the later Schism period it became a relatively unimportant and inoffensive feature of their thought.

The other great importance of the period 1375-8 is the transformation which it wrought in the position of the papacy. Gregory XI's conscientious determination to return from Avignon to Rome was perhaps the most disastrous decision ever taken in the history of the papacy. The popes did return to their natural place in the see of St Peter but in harrowing circumstances of conflict and bloodshed, and to a scene of desolation. The three years of war were notable, at least in the Italian memory, for the furious atrocities of the English and Breton mercenaries employed by the pope – the most memorable was the 1377 massacre of the citizens of Cesena at the orders of the future Avignon Pope Clement VII, then Robert of Geneva and vicar-general in the papal state. When the humanist Giovanni da Ravenna visited Rome in 1400, and rhetorically addressed the 'wretched city once lord of the world', he could still attribute a large part of its long ruination to the events of twenty-five years earlier. 'Gregory XI,

[1] F. Tocco, 'I Fraticelli', *ASI*, 5th ser. XXXV, 1905, pp. 349-50.

all too different from the first of that name, some time ago gathered together Britons from the ends of the earth and laid waste all Italy and in particular the Roman part. Once flourishing cities, fine towns whose citizens, tillers of the soil and wealth had been the glory and strength of the papacy, were emptied and destroyed by the fury of the Britons.'[1] The main disaster which followed the return to Rome, however, was the Schism itself, the division of the Christian world between two obediences. This meant in effect that two curial organisations had to be maintained with no more resources than had been previously needed for one. This would at any time have been a ruinous state of affairs. It was doubly so because it happened at a period in which the old resources themselves were declining rather sharply. The financial system of the fourteenth-century papacy had depended on the taxation of the clergy all over Europe. In the second half of the century the system was undermined by opposition from both the clergy and the laity. This was stimulated, at least in part, by the losses which rural landlords everywhere suffered from the decline in rents and the rise in wages in the period of falling population initiated by the Black Death of 1349. Gregory XI, the last pope to rule over a united church at Avignon, made the last successful attempt to reactivate the papal financial system by levying taxes on a large scale in North-West Europe to feed his armies in Italy. The ultimate effect of this effort in the circumstances of crisis and Schism was to destroy the credit of the papacy beyond the Alps irreparably. England, for instance, which was loyal to the Roman obedience and, according to the reported words of one of the popes, its most fruitful source of income,[2] never again allowed taxation of the clergy for papal needs on the old scale after Gregory XI's efforts had produced the violent reaction which brought John Wycliffe into prominence.[3] In the decline of seig-

---

[1] R.Sabbadini, *Giovanni da Ravenna* (Como, 1924), pp. 168-9.

[2] A.Esch, 'Bankiers der Kirche im Grossen Schisma', *Quellen und Forschungen aus Italienischen Archiven und Bibliotheken*, XLVI, 1966, p. 292.

[3] The decline in English contributions can be worked out from the evidence in W.E.Lunt, *Financial Relations of the Papacy with England 1327-1534* (Cambridge, Mass., 1962).

norial society which resulted from the population fall, the papacy, the grandest seigneur of all, depending largely on the collection of taxes and dues from rent-collecting institutions, was the largest sufferer. The division in its organisation served to make its losses immediately apparent and reduced its power of resistance to its taxpaying subjects. Eventually in the fifteenth century the popes were painfully to rebuild their position on a new, Italian basis; the Roman popes of the Schism had lost their northern empire and not yet acquired a new one.[1]

The Roman papacy which confronted Florence after 1378 therefore rapidly became a much less powerful and alarming rival than its Avignon predecessor.[2] Instead of being a dangerous neighbour inspiring radical anti-clericalism largely through fear of its potential aggressiveness, it became, as the difficulties of the Schism deepened, a relatively harmless institution, a useful ally in some circumstances but never terrifying for its material strength. The Florentines were often frightened by lay powers during the Schism period, sometimes by the armies of the Duke of Anjou and the King of France advancing the claims of Avignon, or by those of Charles of Durazzo and Ladislas of Naples advancing the claims of Rome; they could hardly be frightened by Rome itself. On the eve of the Council of Constance which was to end the Schism the most determined of the Schism popes, John XXIII, was a suppliant ally sheltering gratefully in the suburbs beyond the Arno. The seeds of humanism took root and flourished in a city which regarded ecclesiastical authority without subservience and with equivocal disillusionment.

[1] The general situation is indicated by E.Delaruelle, E.R.Labande and P.Ourliac, *L'Eglise au temps du Grand Schisme et de la Crise Conciliaire* (*Histoire de l'Eglise*, ed. A. Fliche and V.Martin, XIV), I, pp. 295-306; P.Partner, 'The Budget of the Roman Church in the Renaissance Period', *Italian Renaissance Studies*, ed. E.F.Jacob (London, 1960).

[2] Florentine realisation of this contrast is apparent in Dati's fifteenth-century chronicle in his account of the War of the Eight Saints. The war is attributed to the viciousness of the Avignon popes and ends with the election of Urban VI, 'who was Italian and who immediately pardoned the Florentines ... because he had known that they had acted with good reason and ... since then the pastors of the church have held them to be good sons.' (*Istorie di Firenze*, ed. Pratesi, p. 125).

The communal government was concerned to minimise the political dangers resulting from the Schism: aggression by armies supporting either side in the peninsula and commercial difficulties produced by the division of Europe into two ecclesiastical organisations. Between 1378 and 1408 Florence officially acknowledged the Roman papacy, at first with some enthusiasm because Clement VII, the pope at Avignon, was an old enemy.[1] But the enthusiasm was short-lived. By 1387 Urban VI was suspicious of Florentine tendencies to listen to the arguments of Clement.[2] A German commentator wrote in 1408 that 'the Florentines ought to fear the King of France more than any other single king because in one day by closing their banks in his kingdom he can lose them 500,000 florins'.[3] This was an exaggeration but it reflected a vital Florentine concern. As the idea of an agreed settlement of the Schism by the voluntary abdication of both popes, the *Via Cessionis*, gained popularity in Europe in the 1390s Florence found it far more attractive than the weak sentiment of obedience to the canonically elected pope. Florence listened willingly to the envoys of the Avignonese Benedict XIII in 1394,[4] and wrote respectfully to him in March 1395: 'Restore to your most devoted Florentines henceforth the trade by which a great part of the world and especially the Roman court used to abound in all things.'[5] Contact with, and influence at, Avignon were never quite lost because of the presence there of the Florentine Piero Corsini, known as the Cardinal of Florence, a defector from the Roman obedience, from 1381 to 1405.[6] As the day of reckoning

[1] See the letter of 5 February 1380 in which Florence tried to persuade Piero Corsini, the Cardinal of Florence, to adhere to Urban VI (Salutati, *Epistolae*, ed. Rigacci, I, p. 39).

[2] M. de Bouard, *La France et l'Italie au Temps du Grand Schisme d'Occident* (Paris, 1936), pp. 112-4.

[3] *Deutsche Reichstagsakten, Ältere Reihe*, VI, p. 405.

[4] N. Valois, *La France et le Grand Schisme* (Paris, 1896-1902), III, p. 88.

[5] 'Reddite devotissimis florentinis hinc inde commercia quibus consueverat magna pars orbis et presertim romana cuira rebus omnibus abundare' (Archivio di Stato, Florence, Missive 24, fol. 117-18 (12 March 1394), addressed 'Pape', presumably Benedict XIII, since it speaks of 'predecessor vester sancte recordationis Clemens septimus').

[6] F. Novati in Salutati, *Epistolario*, II, pp. 480-1.

drew nearer, in the years before the Council of Pisa (1409), Florence was therefore well prepared to adopt a neutralist attitude.

This equivocation was reflected in the chequered history of the main ecclesiastical office in Florence itself, the episcopal see. The bishop who had lived through the War of the Eight Saints, Angelo Ricasoli, was removed by the pope in 1383 and saved only by a Florentine embassy from deprivation of his episcopal order.[1] When his successor, Angelo Acciaiuoli, was made a cardinal in 1385 the commune recommended that he should be replaced by the native humanist Luigi Marsigli, now permanently resident in Florence at the Augustinian convent of S.Spirito.[2] The pope appointed Bartolomeo Oleari.[3] When the see again fell vacant in 1389 Florence again pleaded for Marsigli.[4] Another man, not unwelcome in Florence, Onofrio Visdomini, was chosen.[5] He fell under papal disapproval and was finally translated in 1400, but he had been defended by the commune and apparently remained for some time in office in defiance of the pope while his successor, Alamanno Adimari, who was *persona non grata* at Florence, never effectively assumed control of the see.[6] Episcopal authority therefore probably reflected in its weakness the uncertain links between Florence and the Roman court. Perhaps the strangest aspect of these proceedings is that the commune several times advocated the appointment as bishop of a man whose personal allegiance to the Roman papacy was suspect. Marsigli, who was prominent in the Augustinian Order, was in 1387 officially threatened with excommunication if he did not take the expected oath of allegiance to Urban VI. The commune intervened to protect him in the disorders at S.Spirito which resulted from his attitude. There is no evidence that he ever did declare himself for Urban. It is not surprising that the papal court did not want him,

[1] F.Ughelli, *Italia Sacra* (Venice, 1717), III, p. 156.

[2] Wesselofsky, *Paradiso degli Alberti*, I, i, pp. 305-12.

[3] *Italia Sacra*, III, 159.

[4] Casari, *Luigi Marsigli*, p. 94.

[5] *Italia Sacra*, loc. cit.

[6] E.Sanesi, 'Episodi Fiorentini dello Scisma d'Occidente', *La Scuola Cattolica*, August 1935, pp. 447-51.

and the commune's advocacy of his claims seems to imply a very cool detachment on the part of the Florentine government.

Until his death in 1394, when the commune commissioned a sculptural monument for him,[1] Marsigli was at the centre of the humanist circle. This was the man whom the humanists remembered as 'always speaking of Cicero, Virgil, Seneca and the other ancients'.[2] His neutralism, the reaction of the independent intellectual, impatient of obstinate ecclesiastical legitimism and the obstacles which it appeared to present to spiritual and material well-being, became typical of humanist opinion. As the arguments for the *Via Cessionis* became more popular and the power of the Roman papacy declined still further the humanists sometimes became outspoken in their comments. Salutati made a private approach to the Avignonese Benedict XIII, connected with an exchange of manuscripts in 1395.[3] In 1397 he was personally advocating the *Via Cessionis*.[4] Unlike the Curia of the Avignon period, the Roman Curia during the Schism was largely Italian; not only were the popes Italian but also most of the cardinals and a larger proportion of the officials. They were susceptible to the prestige of the humanists of the Florentine school. In December 1404 Salutati wrote a lengthy private letter to Innocent VII exhorting him in rather patronising terms to do his duty by accepting the *Via Cessionis*. Instead of being ignored or rebuked he received a courteous, defensive reply, composed on the pope's instructions by Vergerio, by this time employed at the papal court, who also wrote privately to Salutati apologising for the circumstances which had obliged him to advocate opinions which were not entirely his own.[5] Before the conclave in which Gregory XII was elected in 1406 Vergerio himself addressed an oration to the college of cardinals, exhorting them to do their duty by ending the Schism. If the text which has come down to us is a faithful one he spoke in graceful but blunt Latin with little

[1] G.Gaye, *Carteggio Inedito d'artisti dei secoli XIV, XV, XVI*, I, (Florence, 1839), p. 537.

[2] *Prosatori Latini del Quattrocento*, p. 50.

[3] *Epistolario*, III, pp. 53-7.

[4] *Epistolario*, III, pp. 197-217.

[5] *Epistolario*, IV, pp. 42-69, 370-75.

regard for the susceptibilities of sincere believers in the Roman position. The Schism would never have happened, he said, if the spirit of the early Church had still been abroad. The present ambitions of the Roman court had little relevance to the ordinary or proper concerns of Christians. He deplored the procrastination which had defeated all hopes of action to end the Schism in the pontificate of Innocent VII. The cardinals should forget the justice of their cause and negotiate wholeheartedly with the envoys of Avignon. Christians were not interested in the rights and wrongs of the two obediences but in seeing who was the readier for reunion.[1] This is the clearest statement of a humanist attitude to the Schism. Judging by their letters it was probably shared by Salutati and Bruni. It fitted their detached liberal-humanitarian view of the Church. It also fitted the ordinary political interests of Florence.

In 1405, when Dominici's *Lucula Noctis* was composed, Europe was moving towards the dramatic climax of the period of the Schism. Since 1378 there had been two rival popes, one at Avignon supported, roughly speaking, by France and the Iberian kingdoms, one at Rome supported by the greater part of Italy and by Germany and England. Though both popes claimed authority over the whole of Christendom neither was secure even within his own obedience. Benedict XIII at Avignon had come into severe conflict with the French clergy and court; Innocent VII at Rome, like his predecessors, had never been without opponents in the Italian peninsula. At the beginning of the fifteenth century there were growing forces in both camps demanding the ending of the Schism by the *Via Cessionis*. Florence was as keenly as ever convinced of the desirability of reconciliation when the opportunity for advance in this direction was suddenly presented by the death of Innocent in 1406. At the time of the election which followed, Dominici was dispatched, possibly at his own suggestion but certainly with the enthusiastic backing of the commune, as an official envoy from Florence to the papal court to urge the adoption of the policy of reunion. The new pope Gregory XII was in

[1] C.Combi, 'Un discorso inedito di Pier Paolo Vergerio il seniore', *Archivio Storico per Trieste, l'Istria e il Trentino*, I, 1881-2.

fact elected with an undertaking that he would embrace the *Via Cessionis*. At the beginning of 1407 Florence suggested that Dominici should be made a cardinal and entrusted him with another embassy to advocate the claims of Florence to be the meeting place of the two popes. In April envoys from both sides agreed that the popes would meet at Savona on the Italian Riviera. Shortly after this Dominici, possibly because he had failed in his mission, was rather unceremoniously dismissed from his employment by the commune.[1]

In 1407 and the early part of 1408 the two popes moved hesitatingly towards their meeting, each desperately anxious not to put himself into the power of the other. The cockpit in which the events moved to their climax was the area between Genoa, controlled at this time by French troops, Florence and Pisa, a Florentine possession since 1406. In the spring of 1408 Gregory XII was at Lucca, unable to make up his mind to the final step of meeting Benedict. In that city in May 1408 he quarrelled with the majority of his cardinals who abandoned him to join eventually with renegades from the Avignon obedience in organising the Council of Pisa in 1409 which led to the election of a third pope.

Florence's attitude throughout these events was one of careful detachment. She was the most influential power in the corner of Italy in which they took place. She was noticeably unmoved by ecclesiastical allegiance. Her policy was to promote the resolution of the Schism, to help her European position, so far as this was compatible with her political position in Italy. At certain points her influence was used decisively in favour of the movement towards the Council of Pisa. In March 1408, though officially still in the obedience of Gregory XII, she was willing to declare neutrality if France and Venice would also do so, and entirely sceptical of the intentions of the two popes. 'God knows the secrets of their consciences,' the *Signoria* wrote in a letter to its envoys with Gregory. Before the break the envoys were instructed to make secret promises of support to Gregory's cardinals.[2]

[1] Roesler, *Dominici*, pp. 121-9.
[2] Valois, *La France et le Grand Schisme*, III, pp. 602-4.

The cardinals fled from Gregory's court with the hope of finding refuge on Florentine territory, and their political position was ensured by a Franco-Florentine alliance. In June they were admitted to the Florentine city of Pisa and in August Florence agreed that Pisa might be used as the seat of a council independent of the popes. Dominici was in the opposite camp. The immediate antecedent of the secession of the cardinals in May 1408 was the creation of four new cardinals by Gregory in violation of a promise which he had made at the time of his election. One of them was Dominici who remained faithful to his master throughout the rest of his humiliating pontificate and wrote extensively in his defence. Many years later Dominici was enshrined in Poggio's book on hypocrisy as a shining example of that vice because of his abrupt change of allegiance from the party of cession to the party of Roman legitimism.[1] This was humanist spite: Dominici was consistent in his refusal to coerce the man whom he regarded as the true pope and there is no reason to doubt that he acted from conscientious motives. Dominici's career has a different significance. It shows a rigorous adherence to conservative ecclesiastical principles, in contrast to the opportunism which characterised the policy of the Florentine state, and in contrast to the indifferent humanist liberalism which fitted so well with that policy.

A further stage in the relationship between Florence and the papacy was reached in the pontificate of John XXIII, elected by the Pisan obedience in 1410 and deposed at the Council of Constance in 1415. Before his election John XXIII had been Baldassare Cossa, cardinal-legate at Bologna. In this role he had been an ally of Florence and had had particularly close connections with one group of influential politicians in the city.[2] He established himself in Italy at the expense of Gregory XII by means of an alliance with France and Florence, who had a common enemy in Ladislas of Naples, and with the financial help of Florentine bankers.[3] When his power declined and he was

[1] Poggio Bracciolini, *Contro l'ipocrisia*, ed. G.Vallese (Naples, 1946), pp. 104-6.

[2] *Cronica di Buonaccorso Pitti*, ed. A.Bacchi della Lega (Bologna, 1905), pp. 155-7.

[3] G.A.Holmes, 'How the Medici became the pope's bankers', *Florentine Studies*, ed. N.Rubinstein (London, 1969).

driven out of Rome by Ladislas in 1413 it was in the suburbs of Florence that he took refuge, and his career was watched with friendly interest by an influential section, at least, of Florentine opinion through his misfortunes at the Council of Constance until his return to die in Florence in 1419.

The political alliance was accompanied by strong intellectual ties. During this pontificate the papal court became a centre of Florentine humanism to rival if not surpass Florence itself. The humanists of the new generation had already been gathering at the papal court for some years. Jacopo d'Angelo da Scarperia became a *scriptor* in 1401.[1] Poggio obtained the same position in 1403. Bruni and Vergerio became secretaries in 1405. When the Milanese humanist Antonio Loschi visited Rome in the autumn of 1406 as an envoy from Venice to the pope the occasion was celebrated in two pieces of humanist verse which have survived. Loschi wrote how he had been reconciled to the horrors of the journey by the prospect of seeing, apart from the pope, Cardinal Bartolomeo Capra, an amateur humanist, an older poet called Francesco da Fiano, and the two illustrious men from Capodistria and Arezzo, Vergerio and Bruni, who had been called by the pope to adorn the papal household.[2] Vergerio himself wrote describing a poetry competition in a meadow by the Tiber in which the con-

---

[1] Weiss, 'Jacopo Angeli da Scarperia', p. 813.

[2]
    'Sunt duo praeterea diversis partibus orti:
    Hunc super Adriaco tulit urbs Justina profundo;
    Alter habet patriam Tuscis in finibus, in qua
    Natus et ipse fuit profuga de matre Petrarca.
    Docti ambo sunt, ingenuis praestantibus ambo;
    Optima uterque colit studia et pulcherrima rerum,
    Illustresque ipsis quas nos infundimus artes.
    Hos, ut Apostolicam claris virtutibus aulam
    Ornaret, pius Antistes ad honora vocavit
    Officia, et pedibus sanctis assistere jussit.'

(*Antonii de Luschis Carmina quae supersunt fere omnia* (Padua, 1858), pp. 57-8). Francesco da Fiano was the author of a defence of poetry rather like the one by Salutati mentioned in the previous chapter (M.L.Plaisant, 'Un opuscolo inedito di Francesco da Fiano in difesa della poesia', *Rinascimento*, ser. 2, I, 1961) and showed some other intellectual tendencies similar to those of the Florentine school (Baron, *Crisis of the Early Italian Renaissance* (1955), I, pp. 270-84; II, Appendix 4; (1966), pp. 295-314.)

testants were Francesco da Fiano, Loschi and Bruni.[1] A few years later however John XXIII collected the most impressive gathering of humanist talent that had yet been assembled outside Florence. Bruni, Vergerio, Loschi and Poggio were all secretaries. Chrysoloras arrived at the court on another mission from the Byzantine emperor, this time to Alexander V. He found that pope already dead but was persuaded to stay by his successor John.[2] He found there also a favourite pupil in the Roman humanist Cencio da Rusticci who became a *scriptor* at the end of 1411.[3] Some at least of the humanists were not only employees of the pope but also intimate counsellors.[4] John was not ultimately a successful pope but the temporary brilliance of his pontificate owed much to the Florentine political alliance, Florentine money and the Florentine mind.

John XXIII's court also included one major ecclesiastical personage who was especially close to the humanists in outlook, Cardinal Francesco Zabarella. After the deposition of the three rivals at Constance there were hopes in humanist circles that Zabarella might be elected pope. If this had happened it might indeed have ushered in a humanist millennium. Zabarella is best known as the author of *De Schismate*, perhaps the greatest canon lawyer of his time and one whose moderate views on papal authority were in line with the ecclesiastical liberalism expressed by Salutati, Bruni and Vergerio. He was unique among the cardinals in being not only a patron of humanists but himself a minor humanist writer closely associated with Florentine circles. After his early training at Bologna he had lectured on canon law at Florence from 1383 to 1390 and become highly regarded in the

---

[1] L. Smith, 'Note cronologiche Vergeriane', *Archivio Veneto-Tridentino*, 1928, pp. 134-7.

[2] 'A praesente domino nostro pontifice, cum vellem tunc statim posteaque recedere, manere persuasus maneo . . .' he wrote in a letter to Uberto Decembrio when the Curia was at Florence in August 1413 (R. Sabbadini, 'L'Ultimo ventennio della vita di Manuele Crisolora', p. 331).

[3] Bertalot, 'Cincius Romanus', pp. 208-10.

[4] 'Communicaverat mecum Pontifex arcane mentem et cogitationem suam,' Bruni said later (*Rerum suo tempore tempore gestarum commentarius*, p. 442); cf. Manetti's funeral oration on Bruni (Bruni, *Epistolae*, I, p. xcv).

city.[1] There is some evidence that in 1386 at the age of 26 he was already regarded by the commune as a possible candidate for the episcopal see.[2] He left Florence, however, for Padua where he built up a very high reputation as a canonist. He also became a close friend of Vergerio. About 1395 they published together a treatise on Latin poetry, De Arte Metrica. In 1400 he dedicated to Vergerio a short treatise De Felicitate in memory of their discussions of the theories of the philosophers out of which the book had arisen. The ostensible purpose of the book is to refute the philosophy of Epicurus,[3] which seems to have been a common talking point between them, and to establish the orthodox position that felicity is ultimately union with God. On the way he managed to bring in a good many quotations from Virgil, Horace and Terence and the work is very much suited to a classical taste. Another record of his classical interests is a letter written about the same time to Salutati, criticising the latter, rather curiously, for underestimating the value of the Stoic teaching on the death of the body as set out by Cicero. Like other humanists he acknowledged in Salutati a generous intellectual father.[4] Zabarella was at the Council of Pisa in 1409 and finally obtained from John XXIII an office in the church to match his academic reputation. In 1410 he was given the see of Florence. Poggio remarked characteristically that he accepted it not so much for the sake of the office as for the glory of association with the city.[5] In 1411 he was made a cardinal and later went to Constance to take a major part in the council. The 'refuge of all the learned' as Poggio called him[6] died in September 1417, just before the council at long last proceeded to the decisive step of election.

[1] A.Kneer, Kardinal Zabarella 1360-1417 (Münster, 1891), pp. 6-10. On Zabarella as a canonist see B.Tierney, Foundations of Conciliar Theory (Cambridge, 1955), pp. 220-37.

[2] Vergerio, Epistolario, pp. 364-5; A.Zardo, 'Francesco Zabarella a Firenze', ASI, ser. 5, XXII, 1898.

[3] Francisci Zabarellae ... De Felicitate libri tres (Padua, 1655), cap. 6; cf. Smith, Archivio Veneto-Tridentino, 1928, p. 103.

[4] Salutati, Epistolario, IV, pp. 350-61.

[5] Poggio, Opera, p. 254.

[6] A.C.Clark, 'The Literary Discoveries of Poggio', Classical Review, 1899, p. 125.

Oddo Colonna, elected Martin v in November of that year, was a very different kind of man who had much less use for Poggio and his like. Bruni had already returned to Florence, Chrysoloras was dead, Poggio and Vergerio went into the service of other masters. For the time being the humanist circle at the papal court was dispersed and the intellectual axis between Rome and Florence was weakened.

The gathering at Constance was the climax and end of the heroic period of humanism, if that adjective can be used of so un-heroic a movement. The Schism period had begun with Floren-tine politicians believing themselves the victims of papal persecu-tion, continued by producing an attitude of detachment and ended with Florence in a position of friendly superiority to the pope who was most widely recognised in Europe. This relation-ship helped to create an atmosphere which was peculiarly favour-able to the growth of humanism. The characteristic of humanist thought was not to quarrel with traditional Christian ideas but to bypass them, erecting another different structure of values. This would have been impossible in circumstances in which intel-lectuals were encouraged to come into conflict with ecclesiastical authority. Censure breeds revolt; ecclesiastical oppression, or the belief that ecclesiastical authority is oppressive, breeds heresy, not scepticism. Florence around 1400 had the ideal circumstances of a political climate which positively encouraged a certain degree of detachment from the church, and implied an absence of effect-ive ecclesiastical disapproval. Florentines neither yearned for reformation nor feared papal authority. In other circumstances the hostility of people like Dominici, who took the threat of humanism seriously and reaffirmed traditional religious values, might have been effective, as it was to be at various times in the next two centuries.

That was the first, purely Florentine stage of the movement, up to about 1405. In the next few years the circumstances became uniquely favourable for a penetration of the papal court by humanists and for the development of a Florentine-Curial in-tellectual axis which took its ideas from Florence. The signifi-cance of this is not merely that the court provided profitable

employment, though this was important in that it gave the professionals like Poggio a much better economic position than they
could have enjoyed at Florence. It is further significant that the
acceptability and prestige of the humanists in the circles closest to
the heart of the church was securely established. Humanists were
accepted at the Curia partly because they were useful embellishments; but partly also because an Italian Curia was susceptible to
the sheer intellectual prestige in Italy of the Florentine classicism
which had developed under the aegis of Salutati. The result was
the strange phenomenon of a humanist movement, cultivating
classical ideals with little regard for their religious implications,
sheltered and venerated at the heart of the Christian church.

In the eyes of the Christian world the Council of Constance was
a solemn gathering of prelates brought together to resolve the
Great Schism. The letters which Bruni, Poggio and Cencio wrote
from it are products of an altogether different world of thought.
Poggio and Cencio protested at the iniquity of those who had
concealed or destroyed classical manuscripts. Bruni wrote to
Niccoli that he would spare him the details of the Council's
activities because, 'if I know you, your attitude will be not only
that you do not care to hear about these things but that you
positively prefer to be ignorant of what you call the mischiefs and
absurdities of men'.[1] Poggio playfully transposed the factions in
the council into the terms of Roman republican history, ending
with a despairing comment based on a quotation from Terence,
'salvation itself could scarcely save this gathering'.[2] These are not
anti-Christian sentiments; they suggest rather a comfortable
detachment from the concerns of the Christian assembly at
which they were written, whose antics the writers seem able to
regard with the amused superiority of visitors from another,
classical planet.

Behind the playfulness there was a certain amount of plain anti-
clericalism. It comes out strongly in a piece written by Poggio at

[1] Bruni, *Epistolae*, I, p. 102.
[2] 'Nam ipse salus si cupiat hanc familiam saluare vix potest', A. Wilmanns,
'Ueber di Briefsammlungen des Poggio Bracciolini', *Zentralblatt für Bibliothekswesen*,
XXX, 1913, pp. 459-60.

Constance, published with the title *Exhortacio in Clerum Saluber-
rima*, but really a rather bitter denunciation of ecclesiastical
vices.[1] Simony and ecclesiastical pride come under attack. The
most effective passage is an attack on the whole ceremonial way
of life of prelates. Why the crowds of servants, the lavish clothes,
the horses, the kneeling postulants? Why the concern about your
estates when you ought to be distributing them to the poor? No
doubt the Council of Constance was a good place to observe the
grosser manifestations of ecclesiastical competition and self-
seeking, but these are of course quite unoriginal anti-clerical
sentiments of a kind common to all periods and places. Their
significance in the mouth of a Lollard hedge-preacher is however
different from their significance when they come from the pen of
a humanist papal secretary. If he has an alternative to offer the
prelates it will not be evangelical religion but presumably some
humanised version of Christianity which would be a good deal
further removed from orthodoxy. This contrast is the really
interesting thing about Poggio's most famous letter, his letter to
Bruni from Constance describing the burning of Jerome of
Prague, Hus's heretical colleague, in May 1416.[2] Poggio's experience, reflected in this letter, is one of the very few real meeting-
points of humanism and reformation in this period of which
record has survived. The chief impression which it leaves is of the
width of the gap separating them. The demeanour of the victim
through his trial and martyrdom evoked deep admiration and
comparison with Cato, Mucius and Socrates, but little suggestion
of sympathy with or indeed interest in the ideas for which he

---

[1] Printed in Albrecht von Eybe, *Margarita Poetica* (Nuremberg, 1472), fol. 410 seq.
It has been reattributed to Poggio by R.Fubini ('Un Orazione di Poggio Bracciolini
sui vizi del clero scritto al tempo del Concilio di Costanza', *Giornale Storico della
Letteratura Italiana*, CXLII, 1965) and republished by him in Poggio Bracciolini,
Opera Omnia, II. An anti-clerical piece by Bruni ('Oratio in Hypocritas', printed in
Fasciculus Rerum Expetendarum et Fugiendarum, ed. E.Brown (London, 1690), I, p. 307
seq.), which was probably written about the same time (Baron, *Crisis of the Early
Italian Renaissance* (1955), II, p. 613), seems to borrow some passages from it (cf.
Bruni, p. 308, and Poggio, fol. 411).

[2] Poggio, *Epistolae*, I, ii. The letter has recently been discussed by R.N.Watkins,
'The death of Jerome of Prague: divergent views', *Speculum*, XLII, 1967.

was dying. Since Jerome was an enthusiastic Wycliffite, steeped in scholastic philosophy, this is not surprising. They would have had very little in common except a critical view of the established church to which they would have attached widely different implications. The ideals for which Poggio himself stood were in the long run a more radical danger to Christian orthodoxy, but they were not an immediate danger to the Christian church. Conversely the atmosphere of ecclesiastical tolerance in which he lived at the papal court was as necessary to his urbane classicism as the atmosphere of intolerance and religious oppression was to heresy. Like other avant-gardists the humanists flourished best when they enjoyed the patronage of the old order.

To identify the environment which was favourable to humanism one has to look at it both in a very narrow and in a very wide perspective. Relations within Florence on a narrow personal scale between Salutati and Chrysoloras and their disciples were decisively important. So was the background of urban society. But Florence was not a self-contained world. The intellectual atmosphere depended also on a balance of power, prestige and influence which was Italian rather than Florentine and which was much affected by movements in other parts of Europe. So far as we know Florentine urban society was not, in respects significant for this argument, economically different from what it had been for the past century; but its external relationships were in some ways very different. The clear contrast between the isolated embattled republicanism of Florence and the great Lombard tyranny was a relatively new development. The relationship between Florence and the papacy which has been considered in this chapter was even more novel. The predicament of the papacy is comprehensible only in terms of general European history. The Roman papacy of the Schism period was more confined and Italian in its powers and connections than it had been since the early thirteenth century. It was weakened and isolated by forces which even the popes of the reunited church in the post-Schism period could not overcome. Historians have commonly and justly regarded Florentine humanism as an expression of attitudes appropriate to the more secular world of the Italian cities. These attitudes did not become independent and prominent at this moment because urban society was just developing – it had developed much earlier and this was in absolute terms probably a period of contraction at Florence – but because its relative importance within the network of European society had increased.

3

The Enlightenment in Florence and Rome, 1417-43

The intellectual innovations made at the beginning of the century were carried forward in the 1420s and 1430s by a group of humanists at Florence and Rome. The most prominent members of the group were Niccolò Niccoli, Leonardo Bruni, Poggio Bracciolini, Ambrogio Traversari and Leon Battista Alberti. They were not alike, nor were they altogether in agreement. They were men of diverse talents with differing and indeed often opposing inclinations. They belong together because they were caught up in the wave of humanist enthusiasm stemming from the school of Salutati, and because they had relationships and characteristics which were not shared by the many other eminent humanists in other parts of Italy. They exploited the humanist tradition in different, complementary and divergent ways. Their relationships included friendship, dependence, satire and enmity. They stimulated each other as men of contrasting talents and strong personalities within the loose framework of an intellectual movement in a common environment. They could not have developed their characteristics in isolation. For this reason they are best observed together as a school.

The circumstances which had been so favourable to the existence of the Florentine-curial group of humanists in the pontificate of John XXIII (1410-15) were recreated in that of Eugenius IV (1431-47). Once again a weak papacy found support in a political alliance in which a self-confident and defiantly republican Florence was the stronger partner and the curia accepted the hegemony of the Florentine intellect. This time the connection was still closer. It had been prepared by thirty years of contacts stretching back to the days of Salutati, and was cemented by a long period of actual residence in Florence by the papal court in flight from its own rebellious subjects. The purpose of this chapter is to indicate the circumstances and the nature of this continuation, or rather revival – it had been very much weakened in the intervening pontificate of Martin v (1417-31) – of the Florentine-curial axis. The main factors to be emphasised are, first, the continued existence of a strongly independent and republican Florence, secondly, the political dependence of the papal court, and thirdly, the high prestige enjoyed by humanism in this dual environment.

The decade following the death of Ladislas of Naples in 1414 has often been regarded as the golden age of republican Florence.[1] In the absence of serious threats to the independence of Tuscany and to Florentine preponderance there, either from Milan or from Naples, the republican oligarchy was able to enjoy and exploit the freedom which it had preserved at such cost in the wars of the preceding generation. This period also saw one of the most striking extensions of Florentine power. In June 1421 Florence purchased from Genoa the port of Leghorn. This completed the drive to the sea which had begun with the acquisition of Pisa in 1406, put an end to the worst dangers of a landlocked position and enabled Florence to fulfil her dreams of becoming a maritime power in imitation of Genoa and Venice. In 1422 Florence was able to begin sending her own galleys first to the eastern Mediterranean and then to north-west Europe.[2] She never in fact became a sea power to rival the great seaboard cities, but she increased her prestige, offered some new outlets to her merchants and safeguarded some of her commercial supplies.

When the first galleys left for Alexandria in 1422, however, the storm clouds to the north were gathering and Florence was about to begin another duel, of more than twenty years duration, with

[1] The best account of Florentine politics in this period remains F.-T.Perrens, *Histoire de Florence ... jusqu'a la Domination des Médicis*, vi (Paris, 1883); *Histoire de Florence depuis la Domination des Médicis*, i (Paris, 1888).

[2] M.E.Mallett, *The Florentine Galleys in the Fifteenth Century* (Oxford, 1967), ch. 2.

a tyrant of Milan, in which the conditions and emotions of the age of Giangaleazzo were faithfully repeated. Soon after the sale of Leghorn, Filippo Maria Visconti, the inheritor of the power and policies of Giangaleazzo, was in control of Genoa and interfering in Bologna, and Florentine leaders were coming reluctantly to the conclusion that they must fight another war to defend their position in Tuscany. In August 1423 they decided that the time had come to appoint the Ten of War and engage mercenary captains. The war which followed was dangerous and expensive and on the whole inglorious. The Florentine mercenaries were defeated in one of the main battles at Zagonara in the Romagna in 1424 and Carlo Malatesta, one of Florence's *condottieri*, went over to the Milanese side. The war was marked by an unusual amount of mercenary defection and treachery. In 1425 a series of distinguished Florentine ambassadors, including Rinaldo degli Albizzi, Palla Strozzi, Giovanni de' Medici and Lorenzo Ridolfi, finally succeeded in their desperate attempts to arouse Venice to a common effort – on unfavourable terms, for Florence was to pay two-thirds of the cost of the mercenaries. Milanese troops were finally defeated by the Venetian *condottiere* Carmagnola at Maclodio in October 1427 and peace was made in 1428.

This was followed by one of the most harmful and discreditable episodes in Florentine history, the War of Lucca. Lucca, thirty miles away, was an old commune, such as Pisa had been, which had not kept pace with the growth of Florence and which normally attempted to preserve a timid neutrality between Florence and Milan without questioning Florence's leadership in Tuscany. In 1429 Florentine public opinion was strongly in favour of teaching Lucca a lesson for the alleged favour which her tyrant Paolo Guinigi had shown to Filippo Maria in the late war. An incursion into Lucchese territory by a *condottiere* in Florentine pay started hostilities which were eagerly accepted by some politicians, who no doubt foresaw a cheap victory against a small enemy to recompense them for the miseries of the struggle against the Visconti. It did not turn out as they expected. Operations by a much superior army led by Rinaldo degli Albizzi were totally unsuccessful in conquering Lucca in 1430 and produced only a bitter war of accusations between the Florentine leaders themselves. Filippo Maria sent down his *condottiere* Francesco Sforza, who took over Lucca without difficulty. A perfidious attempt to buy off Sforza by offering him a part in the conquest of the other remaining free Tuscan commune, Siena, also backfired. Filippo Maria dispatched another *condottiere*, Niccoló Piccinino, who remained harrying the borders of Florentine territory until a wound temporarily removed him from active service at the beginning of 1433. The War of Lucca demonstrated again, and very painfully, the extreme unsuitability of the republican body politic for the waging of offensive war.

It was succeeded by another decade of intermittent conflict with Filippo Maria and the *condottieri* in his service from 1434 to 1444. Much of the fighting in this period was done by two of the greatest of the mercenary captains, Piccinino and Sforza, who acted in part as aspiring rulers in search of lordships, and in part as servants of the Italian powers which could afford to employ them. Behind them lay the continual ambition of Filippo Maria to extend his authority into the Romagna and Tuscany. Another dangerous force appeared on the Italian scene in the person of Alfonso v of Naples, who began his serious intervention to secure the Neapolitan throne after the death of Joanna ii in 1435, and became an even more disruptive force outside the kingdom when he finally acquired it in 1443. Florence responded to these dangers by seeking the alliance of Venice and by employing her own *condottieri*, but there was hardly a year when she was not exposed to the threat of hostile armies in the Romagna or Tuscany. In 1434 her forces were defeated by Piccinino at Imola. In 1436 and the beginning of 1437 Piccinino was again in northern Tuscany, not many miles from the city. In 1440 another approach by him to the north of Florence was diverted into the Casentino and there defeated by Florentine troops at Anghiari, in a battle which the city remembered with particular pride partly because its forces had been under the direction of two citizen commissaries, Neri Capponi and Bernardetto de' Medici. This period was ended by the diplomatic revolution effected by Cosimo de' Medici in the 1440s, as a result of which Florence came to rely on an alliance with Milan, eventually controlled by Cosimo's personal ally Francesco Sforza. However, this development, which entailed a radical change in the political relations between Florence and the rest of Italy, lies outside the period with which we are concerned here. Until the early 1440s it remained true, as it had been in the lifetime of Giangaleazzo Visconti, that Florence's natural enemy was the Milanese tyranny and that Florentine politicians saw themselves as the defenders of their republican liberty against the continual menace of a hostile despotism.

The menace was met as in the days of Giangaleazzo by the expenditure of huge sums of money raised by taxation. There are no official figures for the total costs of the armies at this period but there is no reason to question the outraged statements of politicians, for instance Rinaldo degli Albizzi's remark in 1425 that the commune was spending 60,000 florins a month.[1] The high cost of the war against Filippo Maria compelled the oligarchy in 1427, after prolonged debates, to carry through a serious financial reform. The institution of the *catasto* in that year involved a new and very elaborate assessment of citizens' income which had the effect of both increasing the amount of property available for taxation and also making the burden more equitable.[2] The introduction of this new machinery was a striking indication of the continued capacity of the Florentine republic to respond to the difficulties of the time. Florence was frequently in financial straits, but she did not find the problems insuperable as she was to do when faced by the wars at the turn of the next century. Her ability to command the resources needed for war meant that independence and the republican constitution could be maintained.

The most serious shock suffered by that constitution was the internal political crisis which followed the ending of the War of Lucca in 1433. The failure of the war had discredited some of the political leaders of the city, notably the one who had been most active in its early stages, Rinaldo degli Albizzi. One of the least

[1] *Commissioni di Rinaldo degli Albizzi*, ed. C. Guasti (Florence 1867-9), II, p. 324.

[2] P. Berti, 'Nuovi Documenti intorno al Catasto fiorentino', *Giornale Storico degli Archivi Toscani*, IV, 1860; O. Karmin, *La Legge del Catasto Fiorentino del 1427* (Florence, 1906); U. Procacci, 'Sulla Cronologia delle Opere di Masaccio e di Masolino', *Rivista d'Arte*, XXVIII, 1953, pp. 17-30.

enthusiastic about the war had been Cosimo de' Medici who had recently, on his father's death in 1429, succeeded to the headship of the family and to the enormous wealth and influence derived from its banking interests. Rightly or wrongly Cosimo was seen by some political rivals as an intolerable danger, and at the end of the war they determined to get rid of him. In the autumn of 1433 he was imprisoned, escaped death by bribery and went into exile at Venice. Albizzi and his friends, however, were not ruthless enough. They managed the war against Milan half-heartedly, they allowed a *signoria* favourable to Cosimo to be chosen in September 1434 and their coup d'état was abortive. In the following month Cosimo returned to become unquestionably the most powerful politician in the city.

In retrospect the return of Cosimo has seemed to mark an epoch, the beginning of the long process by which the republic was destroyed and the Medici eventually became Dukes of Tuscany. In the early years of his ascendancy, however, serious interference with the republican political system was still far off. Cosimo was certainly in some respects more ruthless than his predecessors. In the last months of 1434 the wholesale banishment of his political opponents, including Albizzi and Palla Strozzi, made a gap in the Florentine patriciate. But banishment was an old feature of republican politics, and after once securing his own safety Cosimo did not extend his persecution. He was also probably more influential, and certainly influential for a much longer period, than any of his predecessors. In the contemporary history of Giovanni Cavalcanti, which reflects the political gossip of the city, both in those sections written when he was an admirer and those written when he was an enemy of Cosimo, there is no doubt that he regards Cosimo as the man who pulled the strings of Florentine policy. But his influence though greater in degree was not very different in character from that exercised by individual citizens before. It was applied indirectly through the traditional republican forms of government without Cosimo himself holding office very frequently, and in the face of normal political opposition. The formal alterations of the constitution in the decade after 1434 – the chief ones were a restriction of the use of election by lot for major offices and the institution of a large nominated *balìa* with wide powers (and both of these were in abeyance from 1441 to 1443)[1] – were marginal changes of a kind which had not been unknown before and were assumed to be temporary. Down to the 1440s in fact the most spectacular result of Cosimo's policy was the diplomatic revolution which ended the struggle with Milan, not his tampering with the constitution. Florence remained unquestionably in form and in fact a republic.

The history of the papacy during this period is divided sharply between the very different policies and circumstances of the pontificates of Martin v and Eugenius iv.[2] Martin v, elected pope at the Council of Constance in 1417, was a member of the great Colonna family of Rome. He came back to Italy in 1418 determined to restore the papacy to its lost spiritual authority in Christendom and temporal rule in the papal states. His efforts in the first sphere on the whole failed; though he staved off the repeated threat of a major council like Constance, which was urgently demanded by some national churches, he could not recover the multifarious powers which the Avignon popes had exercised throughout Europe. His Italian policy, considering the weak foundations on which it was built, was brilliantly successful. It resulted in the rapid creation of a temporal papacy, based on the Italian state, foreshadowing the sixteenth-century papacy, and strong enough to act quite independently of Florentine interests in the concert of Italian powers. The old politician Gino Capponi, in his deathbed *Ricordi* of 1420, said that 'the divided church is good for our commune and for the maintainance of our liberty but it is against our conscience'.[3] For a decade Florence was to suffer the harsher effects of a papacy ruling over a reunited church before it was happily divided again under Eugenius. The new pope spent over eighteen months in Florence from February 1419

[1] N.Rubinstein, *The Government of Florence under the Medici (1434 to 1494)* (Oxford, 1966), pp. 1-87.

[2] Accounts of the pontificates of Martin and Eugenius in N.Valois, *La Crise Religieuse di XVᵉ Siecle: Le Pape e le Concile (1418-50)* (Paris, 1909); L.Pastor, *The History of the Popes*, 1 (London, 1899); P.Partner, *The Papal State under Martin V* (London, 1958).

[3] Muratori, *Rerum Italicarum Scriptores* (Milan, 1723-51), xviii, col. 1149.

to September 1420 preparing the ground for his return to Rome. While the curia was installed in a temporary palace at S.Maria Novella some leading Florentines were able to secure his forgiveness for an abject though still wealthy Baldassare Cossa, no longer John XXIII, whom they regarded as an old ally. He recovered the cardinal's hat a few months before he died. But Martin was quick to make agreements with Joanna of Naples, his neighbour to the South, and with the *condottiere* Braccio da Montone who held the balance of power in central Italy. Soon he was standing firmly on his own feet in a largely recovered papal state and playing a quite independent political role. From the Florentines' point of view the most conspicuous and irksome aspect of his policy was his stubborn refusal to embroil himself on their side in the quarrel with Milan. As the chronicler Morelli put it in traditional Florentine terms, 'after he had been settled in Rome a few days Pope Martin decided to raise up the Ghibellines and to bury the Guelfs and therefore he came to an understanding with the Duke of Milan'.[1] In reality Martin was adopting a wise policy of neutrality rather than partiality for Milan, but he showed no friendship for Florence and created the prevalent impression frequently repeated by Florentine politicians that 'the pope is greedy and seeks his own advantage more than anything else'.[2] Throughout the decade after 1420 the relationship between Rome and the Curia was distant and suspicious. In 1431 the Ten of War noted with pleasure the rumour that Martin had died without the sacraments.[3]

The election of Gabriel Condulmer as Eugenius IV was greeted with delight at Florence partly because, like John XXIII before him, he had been a friend of the city as legate at Bologna in the early years of the previous pontificate. Eugenius was a Venetian ecclesiastic, not a Roman nobleman, and his political ineptitude and bad luck were to throw him in a few years completely into the arms of Florence. He quickly succumbed to

---

[1] 'Ricordi ... di Iacopo Moregli', *Delizie degli Eruditi Toscani*, XIX, (Florence, 1785), p. 51.
[2] Rinaldo degli Albizzi in 1425, *Commissioni*, II, p. 327.
[3] *Commissioni*, III, p. 515.

difficulties on both the Italian and conciliar fronts which created a situation reminiscent of the later years of the Schism. In the papal states his reign started with a severe conflict between the Colonna and Orsini families, both represented in the college of cardinals. The states became increasingly a prey to the *condottieri* Fortebraccio, Sforza and Piccinino. The Council of Basle, to which Martin had reluctantly agreed, began to assemble in the summer of 1431. It was supported by the usual desires of the national churches to diminish papal authority and, more urgently, by the hopes of some central European powers that it would provide a means of dealing with the menace of the Hussites operating from Bohemia. Martin might have been able to handle the situation; Eugenius adopted a fluctuating policy of acquiescence and resistance which widened the gap between himself and the council and alienated a number of his cardinals, who believed that cooperation with the council was unavoidable. His failure to dissolve it or move it to Bologna in 1432 was followed by his trial at the council for contumaciousness. After he recognised it again in 1433 the council demanded his submission. By this time there was talk of his deposition and the council had been joined by several of his cardinals feeling varying degrees of sympathy with its extremists. Eugenius's humiliation was completed by a rebellion at Rome which forced him to flee the city in disguise. In June 1434 he arrived at Florence, a refugee pope with a depleted curia who had lost control both of the papal state and of Christendom.

One Florentine, Cosimo de' Medici, who was soon to be master of the city and was also as it happened a central figure in the Florentine humanist circle, had a particularly close relationship with the pope. The Medici bank, in which Cosimo was now the chief partner, had over the past quarter of a century built up a position of great importance in papal finance. The founder of this position and of the wealth of the family was Cosimo's father Giovanni di Bicci de' Medici. The apostolic chamber had always used Florentine bankers for the vast business of transferring its revenues from all parts of Europe to the Curia. The papacy, even in its diminished post-Schism condition, was one of the largest financial organisations in Europe and its legal jurisdiction in the western church also involved a continuous traffic in money on behalf of litigants between Rome and other parts of the continent. This field of business demanded the expertise of the Florentine bankers; it had been one of the main links between the city and the Curia and had contributed to the wealth of many prominent citizens. Giovanni di Bicci was the latest and perhaps the most successful of them. He established a special relationship with John XXIII which gave him a dominant position among the bankers serving the papal chamber. The slanderous, and no doubt inaccurate, stories about the money extorted by Giovanni di Bicci from John XXIII, later written down by the humanist Francesco Filelfo, show that the connection quickly became legendary. (One of them was that the pope bequeathed the money for the great Medicean enterprises of rebuilding S.Lorenzo and S.Marco.)[1] Legends apart however it was probably Giovanni's activity in the years of John XXIII's affluence and power, from 1410 to 1412, which first made the Medici outstandingly wealthy. It was also incidentally probably the reason why the young Cosimo, then twenty-four, went with John's court and its train of humanists to the Council of Constance to deepen his acquaintance both with ecclesiastical politics and with native humanism.[2]

After John XXIII's deposition the special relationship temporarily collapsed. Martin V was not keen to show favour to the intimates of Baldassare Cossa. Giovanni di Bicci was one of the executors who commissioned the tomb of Cossa from Donatello and, true to their old friend, assented to the inscription offensive to Martin describing Cossa as 'formerly pope'. But Martin too came to accept the financial power of the Medici as a desirable ally. In 1421 the manager of the Rome branch of the Medici bank, Bartolomeo de' Bardi, was appointed 'depositary of the papal chamber', which meant that all papal revenues were to pass through his hands. Cosimo was at this time beginning to take over the management of the bank from his ageing father. After

---

[1] R.Sabbadini, 'Notizie di Alcuni Umanisti', *Giornale Storico della Letteratura Italiana*, v, 1885, p. 167; C.Errera, 'Le "Commentationis Florentinae De Exilio" di Francesco Filelfo', *ASI*, ser. 5, v, 1890, pp. 207, 211.

[2] G.A.Holmes, 'How the Medici became the Pope's bankers'.

the appointment in 1421 his partners held this position continuously for over twenty years. One result of this was that Cosimo became incomparably wealthy. 'I think you are richer than many kings,' Aeneas Sylvius wrote to someone in 1445, 'I would not say richer than Cosimo de' Medici.'[1] The largest source of his wealth and the crux of his banking system was the branch at the court of Rome.[2] Another result was that it gave Cosimo a constant and influential relationship with the papal court. His employees were constantly in control of papal moneys and repeatedly required to lend money to the pope to tide him over difficulties. Martin v, for instance, used a Medici loan for his conquest of Bologna in 1428-9,[3] and the Medici managers in Rome advanced the expenses both of Martin's funeral and of Eugenius's coronation.[4] When the monk Ambrogio Traversari wanted to secure a purely ecclesiastical favour from the pope in 1430 – it was a question of allowing the revenues of a church to be used to pay the debts of a bishop who had died unexpectedly – he asked Niccolò Niccoli to persuade Cosimo to use his influence with the pope.[5] The Medici bank therefore had remained a link between Florence and the curia and between their humanists (Poggio was a friend of both Cosimo and his manager Bartolomeo de' Bardi) through the pontificate of Martin v. The connection was as strong as ever in 1434.

At the moment when Eugenius came to Florence, Cosimo was in exile at Venice. He was to return in triumph a few months later. In the critical days of September and October 1434, when the Albizzi faction nearly carried through a coup d'état to secure their position in the city, the pope used his influence against violence and thus helped, perhaps decisively, to prepare the way

[1] *Der Briefwechsel des Eneas Silvius Piccolomini*, ed. R.Wolkan (Fontes Rerum Austriacarum), i (Vienna, 1909), pp. 590-1.

[2] R. De Roover, *The Rise and Decline of the Medici Bank 1397-1494* (Cambridge, Mass., 1963), p. 47.

[3] K. A. Fink, 'Martin V und Bologna', *Quellen und Forschungen*, XXIII, 1931-2, p. 203.

[4] *Istorie di Giovanni Cambi* (*Delizie degli Eruditi Toscani*, xx, Florence, 1785), pp. 182-3.

[5] F.P.Luiso, 'Ricerche cronologiche per un riordinamento del epistolario di A. Traversari', *Rivista delle Biblioteche e degli Archivi*, x, 1899, pp. 77-9.

for Cosimo's return.[1] The union in one man's hands of so much financial influence at the Curia and so much political power at Florence was unprecedented, and moreover, until April 1436 and then for another four years from February 1439 to March 1443, Eugenius and his court resided in the city where his banker was the principal citizen. Cosimo apart, the entente between the pope and Florence was based primarily on a political situation in Europe and Italy which threw them into alliance.[2] Eugenius was fighting a war in two connected political arenas, in Italy and at Basle. In Italy, where he had already lost control of the papal state, his position became still more difficult after the death of Joanna II of Naples in February 1435. Her throne was disputed between two candidates, Alfonso V of Naples and René of Anjou, whom the pope wished to support and did support until 1442, partly because he seemed to have the stronger claim and partly because Eugenius required the friendship of France at Basle. Alfonso was far more successful. He quickly acquired control of a substantial part of the kingdom of Naples and thereafter presented the main obstacle to the recovery of the papal state. Because of his enmity with the pope in Italy he gave his support to the pope's opponents at Basle. Partly because of the alliance between Florence and the pope, there tended to be an understanding between Alfonso and Filippo Maria of Milan, both in Italy and at Basle. This basic pattern persisted through the years 1435 to 1442. The Schism was formally revived in 1439 when the extremists at Basle procured the deposition of Eugenius and the election of an anti-pope Felix V. For several years Eugenius's prospects seemed little better than those of Gregory XII and John XXIII in the evil days before the Council of Constance.

This relationship between Florence, the Medici and the pope reached its climax at the time of the council of the Catholic and Orthodox churches which was held at Florence from February to July 1439. The council and the curia had been competing to arrange such a meeting for some years. Florence had tried to

[1] *Istorie di Giovanni Cambi*, pp. 194-7.

[2] Valois, op. cit.; E. Preiswerk, *Der Einfluss Aragons auf den Prozess des Basler Konzils gegen Papst Eugen IV* (Basel, 1902).

persuade the council to move to Florence for this purpose, presumably because of the money and prestige which the city would derive from such a gathering. In 1436 the commune had even offered the inducement of an advance of 70,000 florins and the manager of the Basle branch of the Medici bank, Roberto Martelli, had been involved in an abortive attempt in 1437 to forge a decree, which did not represent the will of the majority in the council, announcing that it would meet with the Greek church in Italy.[1] The council did not decide to move to Italy but Eugenius had his first meeting with the Greeks at Ferrara in 1438. At the end of that year, however, he was persuaded to move his council to Florence. The main reason for this seems to have been that he was finding the expenses, including the support of the large Greek delegation, too great for his resources. Florence was willing to contribute and Florence was also the headquarters of the Medici who could smooth the financial path with loans to cover pressing needs.[2] The negotiations between the city and the pope were carried out appropriately by Cosimo's brother Lorenzo.[3] The combined financial efforts of the commune and the Medici thus made possible the brilliant gathering later commemorated in Gozzoli's frescoes in the Palazzo Medici. The decree of union between the two churches which was agreed upon at Florence was, of course, as ineffective as it was spectacular; the Greek delegation could not persuade its church to accept its concessions

[1] E.Cecconi, *Studi Storici sul Concilio di Firenze* (Florence, 1869), pp. ccxxxviii-xcii; Valois, 11, p. 63; cf. a letter from Martelli to Cosimo about the conflicting opinions on this issue at Basle, Cecconi op. cit., p. cclxx. The Medici continued to lend money to the council as well as the pope until the final breach in 1437 (P.Lazarus, *Das Basler Konzil* (*Historische Studien*, c, 1912), p. 255).

[2] J.Gill, 'The Costs of the Council of Florence' in *Personalities of the Council of Florence And Other Essays* (Oxford, 1964); *The Council of Florence* (Cambridge, 1959). pp. 171-9. Even before the members of the Council had reached Florence, Cardinal Cesarini wrote to Cosimo from Faenza on 2 February 1439 saying that he was stuck there with the emperor and the Greek delegation and could not move unless Cosimo sent him animals and money (G.Hofman, 'Ein Brief des Kardinals Julian Cesarini an Cosimo von Medici', *Orientalia Christiana Periodica*, 5, 1939).

[3] *Acta Camerae Apostolicae et Civitatum Venetiarum, Ferrariae, Florentiae, Iannuae de Concilio Florentino*, ed. G.Hofman (Rome, 1950), pp. 48-9; *Epistolae Pontificiae ad Concilium Florentinum Spectantes*, ed. G.Hofman, (Rome, 1940-46), 1, pp. 70-71.

and the pope gained only a little temporary prestige. For the humanists of Florence and the curia, however, the days when the Emperor of Byzantium rode through the streets were more than a picturesque carnival. When the Florentine monk Ambrogio Traversari composed the Greek version of the decree of union, and Cosimo and his friends discussed philosophy with cardinals of the Roman Church and the best Platonists of the hellenic world, Florentine humanism reached the summit of prestige and ecclesiastical favour.[1]

There is no indication that Martin v cared much about the enthusiasms of the humanists. The single-minded pursuit of the obvious political interests of the papacy and of his own family seems to have been combined with relatively little interest in intellectual and doctrinal issues. He encouraged Traversari's work of translating the Greek fathers but otherwise he seems neither to have helped nor to have hindered humanist effort.[2] Nor is there much evidence of personal interest from Eugenius iv. In their court, however, the prestige of the new humanism was by this time high and unquestioned; even among the cardinals, including the most powerful, there were keen amateur humanists and patrons. Giordano Orsini, a veteran of Pisa and of the court of John xxiii, cardinal since 1405, who was Eugenius's firmest supporter in the quarrel with Basle until his death in 1438, was also, apart from Cosimo de' Medici, perhaps the most prominent patron of the period. He collected a large library, engaged actively in the hunt for manuscripts and in the 1420s nourished the ambition of publishing the newly discovered manuscript of Plautus.[3] The ascetic Niccolò Albergati, an indefatigable diplomatist for both Martin and Eugenius, was remembered by Poggio as a kind

[1] A Florentine tradition, later set down by Giovanni Rucellai, credited Bruni, who had no official standing in the council, with a decisive influence in persuading the Greeks to accept the union (*Giovanni Rucellai e il suo Zibaldone*, i, ed. A.Perosa (London, 1960), p. 48).

[2] A.Thomas, 'Extraits des Archives du Vatican pour servir à l'histoire littéraire du Moyen-Age', *Mélanges d'Histoire et d'Archéologie*, iv, 1884, pp. 51-2.

[3] E.König, 'Cardinal Giordano Orsini', *Quellen und Darstellungen aus dem Gebiete der Geschichte*, v, 1906, pp. 82-108.

benefactor.[1] In 1438 Eugenius promoted Gherardo Landriani, an old friend and correspondent of the whole Florentine circle.[2] Giuliano Cesarini, perhaps the most remarkable ecclesiastical politician of the age, president of the Council of Basle by papal nomination and architect of victory against the Hussites, was a close friend of the humanists. When his old teacher Traversari came to Basle as general of the Camaldolese Order and papal envoy in 1435 they returned to the study of Greek in the intervals of debating the fate of Christendom. Poggio corresponded with him during his long absence at Basle, offering him news about Italian events and advice which sometimes bordered on the impertinent about the ecclesiastical politics of Basle and Bohemia. When Cesarini sent a scathing reply to a letter which had gone too far in anticlerical witticism Poggio admitted that he had fathered bastards himself, 'but I wish that the rest of the clergy (Poggio had taken minor orders to be eligible for benefices) were no worse than I am. If they were, believe me the Bohemians would be quiet.'[3] With the exception of Alberti the humanists themselves might have said that their most important work was to follow up the manuscript discoveries made by Poggio at the time of the Council of Constance. They did not go to Northern Europe themselves but they had the influence necessary to make repeated use of the contacts with the North which flowed through the Curia. Cardinal Giordano Orsini's legation in central Europe, when Nicholas of Cusa served him as secretary and first became known as a manuscript collector, was one such contact. Orsini however was interested in the manuscripts himself, and seems to have been rather secretive about the Plautus which he unearthed. Poggio had high hopes in 1427-8 of the German monastery of Hersfeld which was pleading a case at Rome and gave him the opportunity to ask for manuscripts in return for pulling strings. Niccoli's list of manuscripts and libraries in Northern Europe, the only piece of Latin from his hand, was prepared for Cardinals Cesarini and Albergati to

[1] Poggio, *Epistolae*, IX, iii.

[2] Voigt, *Wiederbelebung des Classischen Altertums*, II, p. 30.

[3] Poggio, *Epistolae*, IV, xx; V, vii; *Poggii Bracciolini Florentini Historiae de Varietate Fortunae Libri Quatuor*, ed. Dominicus Georgius (Paris, 1723), pp. 207-11.

take on their diplomatic missions in 1431.[1] Not much came of these efforts. The fruitless search for the lost decade of Livy and other imagined treasures is interesting for its motives rather than its results; but it also gives an indication of the sympathetic interest of busy prelates in the characteristic humanist field of research.

Poggio spent almost the whole of this period at the papal court. His exile in England ended in 1422. In 1423 he was once again a papal secretary and held this position until he left the Curia thirty years later. He enjoyed the society of the Curia but he remained essentially a Florentine, keeping up a steady correspondence with Niccoli, Cosimo, Traversari and Bruni, with whom he was reunited when the court moved to Florence in 1434. While Florence was the source of ideas and of Cosimo's money, the Roman court, because of the large secretariat which it required, offered the best opportunities of employment for the professional humanist. When the chancellorship at Florence was vacant in 1427 Poggio told Niccoli that he would not take the job (it was eventually accepted by Bruni after the conditions had been improved): 'I am in the most famous place in the world, I have the greatest freedom, I earn enough for a modest life with little work, I do not care who goes up or down, I have no ambition.'[2] The most enthusiastic portrayal of the curia as a paradise for humanists is to be found in a little dialogue with the title *On the advantages of the Roman Court* dedicated to Cardinal Condulmer in 1438 by Lapo da Castiglionchio, a second-rank humanist who had managed to get employment there in 1436 after hammering on the door for some time. For him, as for Poggio, the curia was a scholars' haven, a humanist research institute which gave its members both leisure and the opportunity to converse daily with experts in every field. Lapo listed the luminaries of the court who

[1] R.Sabbadini, *Le Scoperte dei Codici Latini e Greci ne' secoli XIV e XV* (Florence, 1905); Idem, *Storia e Critica dei Testi* (Catania, 1914), pp. 2-7, 49-50, 263-74, 327-9; E. Vansteenberghe, *Le Cardinal Nicolas de Cues* (Lille, 1920), pp. 16-23; L. Pralle, *Die Wiederentdeckung des Tacitus* (Fulda, 1952), pp. 16-39; N.Rubinstein, 'An unknown letter by Jacopo di Poggio Bracciolini on discoveries of classical texts', *Italia Medioevale e Umanistica*, I, 1958.

[2] A.Willmanns, 'Ueber di Briefsummlungen des Poggio Bracciolini', *Zentralblatt für Bibliothekswesen*, xxx, 1913, pp. 305-6.

made it an incomparable centre of humanist brilliance: Traversari (not an official but very much about the court in those days), Garatone da Trevigi, Poggio, Cencio da Rusticci, Flavio Biondo, Giovanni and Andrea Aurispa, Rinuccio da Castiglione and Leon Battista Alberti. The only two people needed to make the galaxy complete were Filelfo and Bruni.[1]

Employment at the Curia was a common ambition of humanists. Lapo himself had expended much effort on translations dedicated to Pope Eugenius and to various cardinals before he got the position he was aiming at.[2] Leonardo Dati has left records of his efforts to get a place through the influence of his friend Alberti, of Cosimo and of Archbishop Zabarella of Florence, to name only the most eminent, strengthened by direct appeal to the pope in Latin verse. This was in 1443-6, a bad period for Florentine influence, and Dati, though a humanist of some distinction who had been secretary to Cardinal Orsini as early as 1432, had to wait several years for employment.[3] The great Valla was excluded from the curia for years before he gave up the quest and turned to anti-papal propaganda instead. Influence and professional jealousy clearly played a large part in curial appointments; still as Lapo indicated the secretaries were an impressive group. Of Poggio's old friends, Loschi survived the Council of Constance to serve Martin and Eugenius, though he was an old man by this time, until his death in 1441; and Cencio went on long enough to get an inappropriate bishopric from Pius II.[4] Martin V gave a secretaryship to Bartolomeo da Montepulciano, a lawyer with humanist tastes who was another close friend.[5] Giovanni Aurispa, one of the greatest Greek scholars of the period, joined the curia as secretary sometime in the 1430s.[6]

[1] R.Scholz, 'Eine Humanistische Schilderung der Kurie aus dem Jahre 1438', *Quellen und Forschungen*, XVI, 1914.

[2] F.P.Luiso, 'Studi su l'Epistolario e le traduzioni di Lapo da Castiglionchio juniore', *Studi Italiani di Filologia Classica*, VII, 1899.

[3] F.Flamini, 'Leonardo di Piero Dati', *Giornale Storico della Letteratura Italiana*, XVI, 1890, pp. 11-22.

[4] Voigt, II, pp. 19, 22.

[5] Voigt, II, pp. 25-6.

[6] Voigt, II, p. 37.

Flavio Biondo who was later to become the founder of Roman archeology became a secretary in 1434.[1]

The greatest literary genius of the age, Leon Battista Alberti, also belonged to the curia and in a curious way to Florence as well. Leon Battista was born in 1404, the bastard son of a member of one of the greatest Florentine families of the fourteenth century.[2] The Alberti had been an outstandingly rich family of cloth merchants and bankers, in some respects the predecessors of the Medici; in the last years of the Avignon popes they had controlled the transfer of papal moneys throughout Europe and one of them had been reckoned the richest man in Florence. But they failed in city life at the point where Cosimo decisively succeeded. In the years 1387 to 1401 they were banished by their political enemies and not allowed to return until many years later when their influence had disappeared. Leon Battista was not only a bastard but a bastard born in exile. The family retained much of its banking wealth and some contacts with the papacy. Leon Battista's father was a banker employed by popes and a rather remote relation became a cardinal in 1439. The first relaxations in the Florentine ban on the Alberti were made in the 1420s in response to papal requests, one of which was carried to the city in 1424 by Giuliano Cesarini.[3] Leon Battista's early life is obscure but he probably acquired a humanistic education at Padua and Bologna where he took a law degree in 1428. His entry into the papal court is also obscure. He was employed there as an *abbreviator* by 1432, and in 1433 procured a letter from the commune of Florence to Cardinal Francesco Condulmer asking the cardinal to speak for him to the pope. Thereafter his fortunes were to some extent linked with the curia and it was for this reason that he spent much time in Florence in the years 1434 to 1443.

Alberti's relationships with other humanists were perhaps never very close. Poggio, a fellow employee, mentions him in 1437 as 'a

---

[1] B.Nogara, 'Scritti Inediti e Rari di Biondo Flavio', *Studi e Testi*, 48, 1927, p. lxiii.

[2] Life in G.Mancini, *Vita di L.B.Alberti* (second ed., Florence, 1911); more recently by C.Grayson in *Dizionario Biografico degli Italiani*, 1 (1960).

[3] Mancini, *Vita*, 66.

man of outstanding gifts and my very good friend',[1] and Lapo da Castiglionchio listed him in 1438, attributing to him already the character of universal genius which was later to become legendary: 'He is such a man that to whatever branch of study he applies his mind he easily and quickly excels beyond others in it.'[2] He must have enjoyed some degree of celebrity in humanist circles already in the late 1420s for he was one of the persons to whom Panormita addressed verses in the *Hermaphroditus*, but his contacts and contemporary reputation remain obscure until after the time when he had written some of his major works. Alberti was in no respect ordinary or conventional and he probably always maintained a reserve from the rest of the world. Unlike most humanists of the period his activities are not chronicled in the voluminous epistolary literature. Personal contact with individual Florentines is revealed only by the dedications of some of the works which he composed in the 1430s. The Italian version of his treatise on painting was dedicated to Filippo Brunelleschi. A few years later he dedicated three books of Lucianesque satires, the *Intercoenali*, respectively to Paolo Toscanelli the physician and mathematician, to Bruni and to Poggio, and an Italian translation of one of them to Cosimo's son Piero. In the last dedication he also claimed Cosimo's friendship.[3] The main reason, however, for including Alberti within the Florentine group is the relationship of his major writings to it. Before 1433 he had written a variety of minor works to suit the humanist taste ranging from imitative plays to a topographical survey of the city of Rome. The period from the mid-thirties to the mid-forties, when he was most closely in contact with Florence, saw the composition of a series of major works which are all in different ways reactions to Florence. The books on art (*Della Pittura* and *Statua*) are both partly inspired by the achievements of the Florentine art world and addressed to it; *Della Famiglia* is inspired by the social attitudes of Florentines; *Tranquillità dell'Animo* and *Momus* by the revival of interest in

---

[1] Poggio, *Epistolae*, VI, xxiii.

[2] R. Scholz, 'Eine Humanistische Schilderung', p. 132.

[3] *Opera Inedita*, ed. G. Mancini (Florence, 1890), p. 122; *Alcune Intercenali Inediti*, ed. E. Garin (*Rinascimento*, N.S. 4, 1964), pp. 127, 140; *Opere*, II, p. 303.

ancient schools of philosophy. In spite of the ironical and detached view of Florentine thought which these works reveal they reflect unmistakably the fascination which the Florentine world exercised over Alberti, and they themselves contributed to the intricate pattern of contrasting humanisms which made up that world.

Poggio's *Facetie*, the book of jokes which he put together in old age, grew, he tells us, out of the story-telling sessions of the papal secretaries in the chancery of Martin v. Loschi and Cencio were apparently among the good raconteurs. The stories are generally irreverent and frequently obscene.[1] A hilarious Roman dinner party involving Loschi, Cencio, Bartolomeo da Montepulciano and Bartolomeo de' Bardi, the local manager of the Medici bank, is described in a letter by Poggio in 1424,[2] and some of the atmosphere of these gatherings is preserved in his dialogues. The more serious side of the daily intercourse of the curia, which the dialogues also recall, is suggested again in Flavio Biondo's account of how the famous dispute about the origin of the Latin language arose in 1435. The curia was in Florence. Bruni, the chancellor of the republic, was waiting to go in to an audience with the pope. While he waited he was chatting with some of the secretaries, Loschi, Poggio, Cencio, Andrea Fiocco and presumably Biondo. His impassioned defence of the theory that Italian had existed at the same time as classical Latin was cut short by the *Cubicularius* coming to tell him that the pope was ready to see him.

In retrospect the most remarkable aspects of the humanist group at the curia are their closeness to the heart of papal power and the respect and influence which they enjoyed in that august environment. The papal court of the post-Constance period and especially that of Eugenius iv was a poor thing in comparison with what it had been in the Avignon days, but it was still the capital of the *respublica Christiana* as the humanists liked to call it. Lapo da Castiglionchio could boast justifiably in favour of the curia as a resort for humanists that there was no better place for making money – the constant traffic in benefices involved so much

[1] Poggio, *Opera*, p. 491.
[2] Poggio, *Epistolae*, ii, viii.

spending – or for meeting well-informed visitors from all over the world. One of the points he makes is that this central and international position gave an exceptional sophistication and freedom to the intercourse of the curia:

> If conversation about lighter matters passes to jokes and banter everyone in the curia exercises great freedom and licence of abuse and slander; no one absent or present is spared, everyone is attacked equally with great laughter and amusement; dinners, taverns, pimping, bribery, theft, adultery, debaucheries and misdemeanours are discussed freely. This is not only delightful but also instructive . . .[1]

At the same time, as the framers of papal policy,[2] in a literary sense, and as venerated scholars, the secretaries were always close to papal decision-making and even exercised a degree of influence over it. In 1433 Poggio wrote to Niccoli about some unexplained episode connected with a monastic house:

> I read the part of your letter dealing with the nuns to the pope. He laughed and bewailed the iniquity of things. He asked me what I thought ought to be done. I said that the affair ought to be put into the hands of some good man. 'Where is he to be found?', he said. Finally I arranged that if you can find a sound man what you ask will be done, that is, the place reformed. So write again saying to whom you think the job should be entrusted. . . . The general of the order is expected here soon. He is a good friend of mine and when he comes I will discuss the matter with him and urge him to pluck out the thorns from that overgrown field.[3]

It would be easy to pick out other cases of Poggio pulling quite important strings at the curia. The joking humanists carried weight in strictly ecclesiastical affairs as well as in matters of literary taste. They were comfortably installed in an easy relationship with the highest ecclesiastical authority. Poggio said in 1429

[1] Scholz, 'Eine Humanistische Schilderung', pp. 137-8.

[2] In 1429 Martin v wrote in explanation of a passage in a papal brief: 'Scio fuisse nobiscum ferentini tres secretarios, quorum Cincius et Poggius asserent se illa brevia non scripsisse. Melchior de Scribanis (uncle of Lorenzo Valla) qui erat tertius et junior defunctus est, et is forsan illa scripsit.' E.v.Ottenthal, 'Die Bullenregister Martin v und Eugen iv', *Mittheilungen des Instituts für Oesterreichischer Geschichts forschung*, Ergänzungsband I, 185, p. 475.

[3] Poggio, *Epistolae*, v, viii.

that he would not publish his dialogue on avarice while Martin V was still alive because the pope was sensitive about the common belief that he was himself avaricious.[1] In general the humanists show very little sense of restraint in the expression of ideas. They were in the saddle and more likely to be accused of persecuting the ecclesiastical rigourists than suffering persecution themselves.

At the Florentine end of the axis we are faced again by the greatest problem in the history of humanism, the mystery of the career and personality of Niccolò Niccoli. Only three writings by his hand have survived into modern times. One is a brief set of instructions for a manuscript search in northern Europe; one was a letter, now lost, asking someone to arrange a loan of a manuscript from the Bishop of Arezzo; the third is a letter, also about manuscripts, written to Cosimo de' Medici in 1425.[2] Both the letters were written in Italian. This immediately indicates the strangeness of his position. At a time when brother humanists poured out streams of Latin compositions Niccoli, the intellectual tyrant whose judgments they valued and feared, wrote little or nothing in that language and may not have been very proficient in it. His biography can only be reconstructed from the letters and recollections of his friends. Niccoli lived in Florence until his death at the age of 73 in 1437. At one time in 1420 he had plans for visiting Greece,[3] but they came to nothing and he remained the most confirmed stay-at-home, hardly leaving the city except in times of plague in spite of his burning interest in manuscripts and antiquities all over the world. The reason for this may have been partly his relative poverty, resulting from his obstinate determination to ignore money making and devote himself entirely to scholarship. Without the financial support of Cosimo de' Medici this might not have been possible. A precious entry in his tax return in 1433 said that he was 'debtor to Cosimo and Lorenzo de' Medici for some years for 355 florins which they have paid for my extreme needs . . . and if I had not been supported by their

---

[1] Poggio, *Epistolae*, III, xxxv.

[2] R.P.Robinson, 'The Inventory of Niccolò Niccoli', *Classical Philology*, XVI, 1921; *Traversari/Mehus*, I, pp. l-li; C.S.Gutkind, *Cosimo de' Medici* (Oxford, 1938), p. 228.

[3] Poggio, *Epistolae*, I, x.

liberality I would have been forced many years ago to go begging and wandering through the world'.[1]

There is enough concordant evidence in the funeral oration which Poggio wrote immediately after his death and in the life which Giannozzo Manetti wrote some time in the middle of the century to give some idea why his friends valued him as a scholar.[2] He had an absolute devotion to everything connected with antiquity, its literature, history and art. His temperament was such that this expressed itself not in an outpouring of writings but in an extreme fastidiousness about the minutiae of classical scholarship which was a positive obstacle to literary expression. The combination of personal elegance and meticulous scholarship is not rare among intellectuals, and the personality which emerges from the writings both for and against Niccoli is a credible one. Manetti has a famous passage describing the elegance of his life: 'He clothed his body in fine red garments. His senses, especially those of sight and sound from which instruction was to be obtained, were so delicate that he could not bear to see or hear anything unpleasant. He would not hear a braying ass, a rasping saw or a squeaking mouse and he admitted nothing to the sight of his eyes unless it was finely made, fitting and beautiful.'[3] Manetti and Poggio agree about the perfectionism which prevented him from writing. It is possible that he was in fact a shaky classicist. There are indications that his knowledge of Greek was not good in spite of his devotion to it[4] and if, as seems to have been the case, he started his classical studies as an adult, it is quite possible that he never acquired the proficiency even in Latin composition of those with a proper rhetorical education. This may be the reason why his fastidiousness turned towards what seemed to some of his contemporaries to be an eccentric concern with peripheral minutiae, handwriting, orthography, art, coins. This characteristic was pilloried in Guarino's attack on him in 1413. It comes out again in another diatribe

[1] Martines, *Social World of the Florentine Humanists*, p. 116.
[2] Poggio, *Opera*, p. 270 seq; *Traversari/Mehus*, I, p. lxxvi seq.
[3] *Traversari/Mehus*, I, p. lxxvii.
[4] Zippel, *Niccolò Niccoli*, p. 19.

written by one Lorenzo di Marco Benvenuti in 1420.[1] One of Benvenuti's points was that his interest in diphthongs and manuscripts was a substitute for the real scholarship which he did not possess. Paradoxically, and this is not an unknown occurrence in intellectual history, the eccentric passion for trivia which seemed insignificant to many scholars was a sign of original genius which inspired other people to fruitful efforts in archaeology, manuscript-hunting and art. Guarino's judgement that the mountain of his eccentric interests bore a ridiculous mouse turns out in the light of history to have been a singularly misplaced gibe. But the poverty of his own literary output did not prevent him from having a very wide knowledge of classical literature or from being accepted by literary men as the most august arbiter of literary matters. This is clear from many letters to him from Poggio and Traversari who clearly awaited his judgements with awe and admiration.

His interests extended also to theology. Manetti, who was a considerable theologian, mentions this; Poggio says he drew more from *sacrae scripturae* than many who devoted all their time to that study, and a prominent Franciscan of the day, Alberto da Sarteano, who was no indiscriminate admirer of classical humanism, wrote to him in praise of his devotion to *sanctae scripturae*.[2] One would like to know more about this side of him. It was linked in the minds of his friends with an austere moral authority and outspokenness. Another aspect of Niccoli's character is suggested by a letter of Bruni to Poggio in 1421 explaining why he had quarrelled with Niccoli. The trouble he says was caused by a woman called Benvenuta who came to Florence and was taken in by one of Niccoli's brothers. Niccoli spirited her away, she was quarrelsome and had made him so and the whole thing had become so scandalous that high-minded Bruni felt bound to rebuke his brother humanist.[3] Manetti's version of the same thing in his commemorative oration was that Niccoli, 'following the

[1] Ed. G.Zippel, 'L'Invettiva di Lorenzo di Marco Benvenuti contro Niccolò Niccoli', *Giornale Storico per la Letteratura Italiana*, xxiv, 1894; cf. Baron, *Crisis* (1955), ii, Appendix 5.

[2] Albertus a Sarthiano, *Opera Omnia* (Rome, 1688), p. 227 (in 1433).

[3] Bruni, *Epistolae*, v, iv.

example of the supreme philosopher Socrates and Ennius the poet and many other learned men, was attended by a single maid-servant and remained content with his books'. Niccoli did quarrel with his brothers and did have some sort of connection with a woman called Benvenuta.[1] At any rate we must assume that the moral authority exercised by Niccoli was of a highly individual-istic and eccentric kind. He had no taste for politics or interest in political life. He did in fact, like other Florentine citizens, hold some political offices[2] but his general indifference to politics con-trasts very sharply with Bruni's political humanism. Whatever the cause of their quarrel Bruni's complaint in an invective written about 1424[3] that he was a useless citizen does indicate a dividing line between them. The main external signs of his influence were the hunt for manuscripts of the classics and the collection of his library. According to Poggio, who was not inclined to underrate his own efforts even in a funeral oration, most of the manuscript discoveries were made as a result of 'Niccolò's persuasion, in-spiration, exhortation and verbal pestering'. Although not stir-ring himself outside Florence Niccoli kept up a constant corres-pondence with potential agents, which is known to us from their replies, including many letters from Poggio and Traversari. He acted as a clearing house for manuscripts and news about them probably rather more effectively than his papal namesake Nicholas v, who later imitated him with the weight of the pontifical see behind his efforts. Manetti tells us that he spent some part of each day in the copying of manuscripts. His incomparable collection of classical writings was bequeathed first in a will made in 1430 to the Camaldolese convent of S.Maria degli Angeli, where his friend Traversari lived, and then later in another will to be dis-posed of according to the judgement of a committee of sixteen Florentine citizens who included Traversari, Bruni, Paolo Toscanelli, Poggio, Marsuppini, Cosimo and Lorenzo de' Medici

---

[1] Martines, p. 115; Walser, *Poggius*, pp. 64, 90. Benvenuta is mentioned e.g. by Poggio, *Epistolae*, I, p. 151, and Traversari, *Traversari/Mehus*, II, col. 362, cf. I, p. lxi.

[2] Martines, pp. 161-2.

[3] Printed by Zippel, *Niccoli*. Cf. Baron, *Crisis* (1955), II, pp. 528-9.

and Giannozzo Manetti.[1] It eventually became the core of the library established by Cosimo in the rebuilt S.Marco. Niccoli's great importance, however, lies not in the creation of the library as a public collection but in the influence he exerted in his lifetime over those who entered the sanctum to fall under the spell of his personality and enthusiasm. As Poggio said in a letter to Marsuppini immediately after Niccoli's death, 'his house was always full of learned and important men who attended upon him every day. No-one with any knowledge visited Florence without giving priority to seeing Niccoli and his books'.[2] He was not universally liked and his friends admitted weaknesses but Poggio's delight in his company, as expressed in his letters, rings true and no-one was unimpressed. The paradox remains that perhaps the strongest personal influence exerted within the Florentine school was the one about which we have the least clear direct information and which must be reconstructed as far as possible from incidental scraps.

Leonardo Bruni, on the other hand, was a voluminous writer with an easily definable set of interests. It has only recently become clear[3] how extraordinarily successful Bruni's social and material career was. The son of the corn merchant from Arezzo had, by the time of the first *catasto* of 1427, become one of the rich men of Florence, economically on a par with many of the great families. The wealth acquired by the exercise of his rhetorical and administrative gifts during his career in the papal chancery before 1415 enabled him to begin a new, and as it turned out, longer life as a Florentine gentleman. Aeneas Sylvius, quoting him as the best example of the money to be made from humanism, said 'no prospector ever brought you as much gold as Quintilian procured for Bruni'.[4] Until we come to the humanist pope himself Bruni's

---

[1] *Traversari/Mehus*, I, pp. lxii-lxiii.

[2] Poggio, *Epistolae*, VI, 12.

[3] From the analysis of his wealth and official career by Martines, esp. pp. 117-23, 165-76, 241-2, 254-6. For his writings see Baron, *Crisis*; E.Santini, 'Leonardo Bruni e i suoi "Historiarum Florentini Populi Libri XII"' *Annali della R.Scuola Normale Superiore di Pisa*, XXII, 1910; Bruni, *Schriften*; L.Bertalot, 'Forschungen über Leonardo Bruni Aretino', *Archivum Romanicum*, XV, 1931; 'Zur Bibliographie der übersetzungen des Leonardus Brunus Aretinus', *Quellen und Forschungen*, XXVII, 1936-7.

[4] *Briefwechsel des Eneas Silvius Piccolomini*, I, p. 329.

career remains the greatest social success story among the humanist biographies. By 1427 he had lived for twelve years in Florence as a prosperous private citizen and had already helped the *Parte Guelfa* to revise its statutes (1420) and served as an ambassador. In 1427 he accepted the post of chancellor, which he held until his death in 1444. This in itself gave him a position of importance, but he seems also to have acquired real political as opposed to administrative power, especially after 1439 when his citizenship was renewed and enlarged on the ground of his services to the republic in writing the *History of the Florentine People*. He reached the heights of power in his membership of the Ten of War which managed the war against Milan in 1440-41. When he died the city gave him a funeral of a splendour which required a place in the contemporary histories. By the end of his life Bruni was one of the great, playing the political game on something like an equal footing with the Capponi if not the Medici.

It was in this period, much more than in his curial days, that Bruni became the expositor of political humanism. Those books of the *History of the Florentine People* written after he left the papal service are mainly concerned with the history of Florence since the mid-thirteenth century, the history of the modern republic, based on the Florentine chroniclers and on the very archives which he administered as chancellor. Much of his time must have been spent in composing official correspondence. There is no clear dividing line between works which he wrote as a private humanist and those, like the funeral oration on the death of the *condottiere* Nanni Strozzi, which he composed at least partly because of his official position. The uniqueness of Bruni is that in him the private and the public writer met much more even than in his master Salutati, who had a large interest in poetry and allegory of which there is not much sign in Bruni. His interests were no more typical of the Florentine school than those of the other main members who did not share his political and social success or his profound political concern. His early works of political interest (the *Laudatio* and the first book of the *History*) would not entitle him to be regarded as a predominantly political writer. It was after 1420 that he became passionately concerned with the theory and practice of contemporary politics. A large proportion of his work during this later period was history, written always with a sense of relevance to the contemporary Florentine situation. This applies not only to the *History of the Florentine People* but also to the *Commentarium de Bello Punico*, which he wrote using Polybius's material in imitation of Livy in 1418-21, the *De Bello Italico Adversus Gothos*, which is largely a translation of Procopius, done in about 1441, and the *Commentaria Rerum Graecarum*, this time mainly translation from Xenophon, done in 1439. His interest in these works was in the predicament of the city in a world of dangerous international politics, and the lessons which could be drawn from ancient authors to illuminate this problem. As he put it in the preface to the *Commentaria*, addressed to Angelo Acciaiuoli:

> There was never a city, however rich and flourishing, which did not fall into great dangers as a result of small errors. Some came to complete ruin in this way. Therefore if I seem to you and others to be hesitating and slow or even timid and diffident in these matters the reason is that I am deterred at the outset by examples from any conflict. A blessed and happy city should embrace peace and so avoid being exposed to fortune and mutability. But I think this is less dependent on the effects of fortune than on our own folly. Men who lack education and are not moderate in their attitudes can do a great deal of harm to their cities. They rule the state with more spirit than prudence and do not measure purposes or dangers. I have been persuaded by these considerations to write the *Commentaria* – for I prefer to tell of others' errors than our own – in which you will see the diverse calamities and downfalls and the wonderful turns of fortune of the most powerful cities of Greece.[1]

In spite of these substantial historical and political efforts, however, Bruni's energy was great enough for him also to keep up an interest in the translation of ancient philosophy. Between 1417 and 1439 he translated four dialogues of Plato and his *Letters* and Aristotle's *Politics*. These and some original works which will be discussed later made him the main exponent of a Stoic/Aristotel-

[1] Bruni, *Schriften*, p. 146. A similar attitude is expressed in the preface to the *De Bello Italico* (op. cit., pp. 147-9).

ian philosophy with a marked moral and political slant which was to a certain extent the common philosophy of the Florentine school.

Ambrogio Traversari practised another different kind of humanism.[1] Since 1400 he had been a monk of the Camaldolese convent of S.Maria degli Angeli in Florence. According to his own account he started to learn Greek not from the instruction of humanists but by comparing the Greek psalter and *New Testament* with the Latin versions, though he also says that he had from the first the encouragement of Niccoli.[2] From the time when he emerged as a considerable Greek scholar about 1420 he used his expertise primarily not for the revival of pagan antiquity but for the recovery and translation of the works of the Greek fathers. From 1420 to 1431 a series of translations of patristic works, writings of Basil, Chrysostom and Athanasius, came from his pen. There is no sign of friendship with Bruni and some suggestion of coldness between them, but his correspondence with Niccoli was voluminous. He entered fully into Niccoli's enthusiasm for the tracking down of manuscripts. In his last years, however, he was increasingly drawn into ecclesiastical politics. In 1431 he was made general of his order. Later on he was sent to Basle and then played a major part, as one of the few highly placed ecclesiastics with a knowledge of Greek, in the councils of Ferrara and Florence. He died in 1439. Ecclesiastical politics put an end to extensive literary work but not to his humanist enthusiasm. His *Hodoeporicon*, which is a diary of his travels from 1431 to 1434,[3] gives a fascinating insight into the life of a man who was genuinely both a devout churchman, not merely a holder of an ecclesiastical office, and a devoted humanist. We see him at the end of 1431 visiting Cosimo and Lorenzo to enlist their support for the order. In the first half of the next year he is in Rome to confer with the pope about the reform of the order. He finds time

[1] A.Dini-Traversari, *Ambrogio Traversari e i suoi tempi* (Florence, 1912); P.G. Ricci, 'Ambrogio Traversari', *Rinascità*, II, 1939; A.Sottili, 'Autografi e Traduzioni di Ambrogio Traversari', *Rinascimento*, ser. 2, V, 1965.

[2] L.Bertalot, 'Zwölf Briefe des Ambrogio Traversari', *Römische Quartalschrift*, XXIX, 1915, p. 102.

[3] Printed in Dini-Traversari, op. cit.

to translate the life of Chrysostom and present it to Eugenius who orders it to be read at his table. In a Roman church he finds a manuscript of Origen's *Homilies* translated by Jerome and immediately sends off a joyful letter to Niccoli. He has several meetings with the humanist secretaries at the papal court, Loschi, Cencio and Poggio, who are joined by Antonio da Pescia, one of the partners in the Medici bank. Traversari's Christian erudition has remarkably little in common with Bruni's use of the classics. His close friendship with Niccoli suggests that Niccoli sympathised. Traversari was not a creator, so his study of the Greek fathers produced no theological movement. It seems likely however that for both Traversari and Niccoli, and perhaps also for Poggio, following the tradition established by Petrarch's love of Augustine, the fathers offered a congenial approach to religion to be set against the scholasticism which they all disliked.

These were the men who contributed most to the Florentine school of thought. There were other more shadowy or peripheral figures, for instance Carlo Marsuppini a younger disciple of Niccoli who does not seem to have been an original writer or thinker but was much respected by the older men and belonged to their circle.[1] But Niccoli, Bruni, Poggio, Traversari and Alberti are the outstanding figures. Cosimo was an intimate and in some ways the focal point. Lapo da Castiglionchio, dedicating a translation from Plutarch to him about 1435, excused his offering 'especially as you have with you every day Leonardo Bruni, the prince of this age's eloquence, the ornament of the Latin tongue, Ambrogio Traversari, Poggio and Carlo Marsuppini.'[2] In large part no doubt this was based on Cosimo's money but he was also a patron with enough understanding to participate seriously in the enthusiasms of manuscript-hunting, copying and translating for which he paid. He possessed a number of classical manuscripts already in 1418[3]; he was interested enough in antiquities to

[1] P.G.Ricci, 'Una Consolatoria Inedita del Marsuppini', *Rinascità*, III, 1940.

[2] F.P.Luiso, 'Studi su l'Epistolario e le traduzioni di Lapo da Castiglionchio juniore', p. 266.

[3] F.Pintor, 'Per la Storia della Libreria Medicea nel Rinascimento', *Italia Medievale e Umanistica*, III, 1960, pp. 197-9.

accompany Poggio on an archaeological jaunt to Ostia in 1427[1] and it was he who compelled Traversari to undertake the distasteful task of translating Diogenes Laertius.[2] Cosimo's patronage did not create the humanist group, nor did its members depend solely on his patronage, but it was of great importance to them that a man with his unique wealth and influence at Florence and Rome was their close friend and keen supporter.

The importance of personal relationships within the group, and their jealousy of outsiders, is illustrated by the experience of Francesco Filelfo. Filelfo, one of the best classicists of the day, but a man with no previous Florentine connections, was invited to the city in the spring of 1429 to lecture at the *Studio* on the strength of the expertise which he had acquired in a visit to Constantinople extending from 1420 to 1427.[3] At first he was welcomed with open arms. Cosimo went to meet him and offered to pay his rent. In August he was able to write that he was getting on reasonably well with the whole group: Niccoli and Marsuppini attended his lectures, Bruni, Traversari, Cosimo and Palla Strozzi were all friendly. He was wary of Marsuppini and Traversari but relations were still good.[4] By the autumn of 1430, as we learn from a letter of Traversari, there was a severe breach with Niccoli.[5] The cause of it is not clear but it became bitter and irreparable. Things improved a little when Cosimo took Niccoli and Marsuppini away to Verona to avoid the plague at the end of 1430. In October 1431, however, a new board of governors of the *Studio*, including Lorenzo de' Medici, removed Filelfo from his post and replaced him with Marsuppini. He was restored in December. Two years later came the crisis of Cosimo's exile. Filelfo took the other political side enthusiastically and he was finally removed from his lectureship and replaced again by Marsuppini after Cosimo's return, and left Florence in December 1434. The dispute dragged on for many years in bitter invectives

[1] Poggio, *Epistolae*, iii, xii.

[2] Below, p. 124.

[3] On the episode in general G. Zippel, *Il Filelfo a Firenze* (Rome, 1899); C. De Rosmini, *Vita di Francesca Filelfo da Tolentino* (Milan, 1808), i.

[4] *Francisci Philelfi . . . Epistolarum familiarum libri XXVII* (Venice, 1502), f. 9.

[5] *Traversari/Mehus*, Letter vi, xxi.

by Filelfo against the whole Florentine school and replies by Poggio. A letter written in the spring of 1433 gives one the flavour of the situation. Filelfo recalled that he had complained to Cosimo about Niccoli's behaviour in 1430, 'and you replied calmly and smiling that I should not be surprised, that I should not take Niccoli's slander too hard, he being a man of genius who never left any scholar untouched by his sharpness, who did not spare even you, who always called that wise and great man Manuel Chrysoloras "lousy beard".' Cosimo had pointed out that Niccoli was always abusing even Traversari and had had rows with Bruni, Guarino, Poggio and Aurispa; an attack by Niccoli was really a mark of distinction, while Marsuppini, the other main offender, had no authority in the city and would only do himself harm by copying Niccoli's ways. Yet after the return from Verona, Niccoli and Marsuppini attacked him still more fiercely and Cosimo's relations did nothing to stop his salary being reduced. Why were Niccoli and Marsuppini preferred? 'If I do not frequent your house as they do daily that is because I am busy. You know that I have enough to do to earn my teaching salary.'[1]

Florence was only one of many centres of humanism. The Florentine school even with its curial extension did not contain all or indeed, from a strictly scholarly point of view, necessarily the best humanist talent in Italy. Guarino, Decembrio, Filelfo and Valla, who were largely outside it, were at least the equals of the Florentines in the study of Greek and the Venetian world, with its close commercial and political contacts with Byzantium, offered better opportunities for the study of Greek from which Guarino and Filelfo profited. Although the Florentines were inordinately proud of their scholarship their distinguishing characteristic, in retrospect, is not their command of classical learning but the thoughts of contemporary significance which devotion to the classics inspired in them. In that respect they formed a school without parallel, based on the friendships and contacts of a small number of men over a long period in an atmosphere congenial to intellectual originality.

Our knowledge of the thought of the humanists, to which we

---

[1] *Francisci Philelfi Epistolarum libri*, f. 12-12v.

shall pass in the next chapter, is derived mostly from their own writings. Before passing on to these ideas it is important to be as clear as possible about the scope and limitations of the writings, considered both as historical sources for us and as vehicles for the self-expression of the writers. The original compositions of the humanists, as opposed to simple copying or translation which took up a large part of their efforts, were mostly embodied in a small range of literary forms derived from antiquity. Even in their most original works the element of sheer imitation was very strong. This is important, as we have seen already in considering Bruni's early political thought, not only because it creates a special difficulty of interpretation (where does literary artifice end and self-expression of another kind, if there is another kind, begin?) but also because it imposed patterns and limitations, both aesthetic and intellectual, upon their imagination. All the more so, of course, because their chosen language was Latin not Italian, so that the gap between literary composition and ordinary expression was artificially maintained. The chief literary forms which they imitated from classical models were the letter, the dialogue, the oration and history. The use of these forms to some extent defines the limits of their creativity. Literary form was so important to them that they tended to accept the opinions and attitudes as well as the style of the authors whom they admired. This aspect of humanism is most predominant in the work of Bruni whose attitudes to philosophy and history, however epoch-making in the history of modern thought, were almost entirely derived from his classical authorities and found a ready hearing because those authors had a clear relevance to the contemporary situation. They did not imitate all ancient literary forms indiscriminately. It was not customary for instance, although it would have been possible, to imitate the poetry of Lucretius or the prose of St Augustine. The choice of forms was determined by the rhetorical origins of this brand of humanism, created by the professional rhetoricians Salutati and Bruni in obedience to the standards of Cicero, Seneca and Quintilian whom they regarded as their professional masters. The prevalence of prose is particularly striking. A perceptive correspondent writing to Francesco Barbaro in praise of one of

Poggio's dialogues in 1430 pointed out that it had not always been so, that there had been a poetic and especially Virgilian fashion in the fourteenth century which was now dead: 'to that age has now succeeded another in which the majesty of rhetoric which died under the Roman Empire, after its long exile, has been restored to its seat under the ciceronian banner.'[1] The whole humanist movement of this period was in a sense based on the happy historical accident that the authors whom the rhetoricians admired were appropriate to the circumstances in which they lived and did not lead them into a blind alley – like Petrarch's attempt to imitate Virgil. But at the same time the borrowing of external forms imposed severe limitations on their work, which are apparent in the contrast between their stunted philosophy and stilted history and the incomparable contemporary blossoming of the native visual arts, which they partly helped to inspire.

While Bruni was a happy slave to the inherited forms, however, Poggio and Alberti were both writers with stronger aesthetic instincts who tried to break out of them. A group of letters written by Poggio to his friends in 1429 about his first dialogue, *De Avaritia*, sheds a little light on his aims as he tried tentatively to develop a literary genre. He wrote to Niccoli explaining the thought which he had devoted to the choice of personalities in the dialogue. Loschi had been chosen to defend avarice because although he was not avaricious (Cencio was thought to be so and he had considered using him) he was at least *'prodigus'*. Andrew of Constantinople was put to take the other side because he was *'religiosus'*. Niccoli objected to the barbaric modern names, and also to the references to the contemporary S. Bernardino. Poggio explained that he did not intend a personal estimation of Bernardino but to use him for an attack on the mendicants. References to the writings of Isidore had gone in because it seemed a good idea to attack priestly avarice with an author whom priests constantly used. Niccoli had also objected to the lack of ornateness and elegance in the style, comparing it unfavourably with Poggio's letters. Writing to Traversari, Poggio defended himself by saying that Cicero's works showed that less ornament was required in

[1] Walser, *Poggius*, p. 434.

dialogues than in letters. To Bruni, who had evidently made similar criticisms, he said that he was not trying to compete with the ancients in eloquence: 'We ought to imitate, to read and absorb those (Cicero and others) who offer us not only eloquence but also wisdom; you may read my writings instead of them after dinner for a laugh.'[1] These comments show that Poggio's choice of personalities in his dialogues was not without meaning, that he expressed personal opinions artfully, not merely stock rhetorical talking points, and that he was willing to forgo the pursuit of ordinary rhetorical standards. They support the impression which the dialogues themselves give – they use a simpler more flexible Latin, closer to modern speech, and they have a liveliness which suggests that they are portraying real characters and opinions. Poggio's devotion to Cicero and Quintilian prevented him from abandoning Latin but he managed to turn the Latin dialogue into something like a living form of expression.

Alberti went very much further than this, almost to the extent of refounding Italian prose. Alberti's reaction against the prevailing humanist literary standards was of course possible only because he was himself an accomplished Latinist who, at an early stage, had passed through and seen through the discipline. His reaction against the literary standards of his contemporaries took two forms. First, he rejected the tyranny of Cicero. In the preface to one of the books of his *Intercenales*, written in the late 1430s, he put this point characteristically in the form of the fable of the lovers who tried to extinguish the inquisitive moon by imprisoning it in the wood from which it seemed to arise each night and then quarrelled about their inexplicable failure to pin it down. Modern rhetoricians competing in imitation of Cicero were fighting over something unattainable.[2] There are some compositions, notably the *Tranquillità dell' Animo* where Alberti, though writing in Italian, was reasonably faithful to the rhetorical tradition. There are others where he adopts a pose which is worlds away. One of the main factors making this possible was his discovery of Lucian. The characteristics of Lucian, wit, sophistica-

---

[1] Poggio, *Epistolae*, iii, xxxii, xxxv, xxxvi; Walser, *Poggius*, p. 429.
[2] *Alcune Intercenali inedite*, ed. E. Garin, pp. 179-80.

tion, irreverence, satire of conventional opinions, use of divine persons for satirical purposes, clearly appealed enormously to Alberti as they did to Erasmus a century, and to Giraudoux five centuries, later. Decadent hellenism suited his temperament better than Roman stoicism. The shadow of Lucian falls heavily over a number of the smaller works which Alberti composed in the thirties, especially those lumped together as the *Intercenales*, and over one important Latin composition of the forties, *Momus*, and the example of Lucian must also have fortified in general his naturally ironical and irreverent tendencies. He was least serious, this influence was strongest, at the period of his life when he was writing within the Florentine orbit, which makes the works of those years more revealing and interesting.

The other, less fundamental in some ways but more immediately shocking, divergence from the contemporary norm was his determination to use Italian. It is not at all clear why he took this stand. The famous passage in the preface to the third book of the *Della Famiglia*, in which he defends the use of the Italian language, treats it as a step which will meet with hostility from other Florentines but offers only the explanation that Italian is a language in which everything can be expressed and which everyone understands. The influence of Florence also played some part in his choice. He was writing Tuscan not Italian.[1] Whatever the motive, Alberti wrote several of his major prose works in Italian in the period 1433-43. The extent of his attachment to the language was shown by the curious episode of the *Certame Coronario* in 1441.[2] In October of that year Alberti and Piero, son of Cosimo de' Medici, who put up the money, arranged a public competition in Italian verses on the subject of 'friendship'. The

---

[1] The anonymous *Vita* (Muratori, xxv, col. 297) says that he wrote the *Della Famiglia* in Italian for the benefit of his relations who were ignorant of Latin; that it was difficult because exile had deprived him of the power of writing elegant Tuscan, but that he succeeded so well that 'his fellow-citizens who wished to be considered elegant in the Senate adopted many embellishments from his writings to adorn their discourse'.

[2] Mancini, *Vita di L.B.Alberti*, pp. 200 seq; F.Flamini, 'La Lirica Toscana del Rinascimento', *Annali della Regia Scuola Normale Superiore di Pisa*, xiv, 1891; A. Altamura, *Il Certame Coronario* (Naples, 1952).

The Florentine Enlightenment

competition pieces were recited before a distinguished audience
including the priors of the city and the archbishop. The judges
were ten secretaries of the Curia, including Poggio, Cencio,
Loschi, Aurispa, George of Trebizond and Biondo. The con-
testants included Alberti himself and one of his Florentine
relations. The judges decided that none of the entries deserved the
prize, and awarded it to the cathedral. Whether or not the verses
submitted were of such a low quality as to deserve this slap in the
face it was not taken as an impartial judgement and was probably
not intended as such. Alberti had made an error of judgement in
trying to enlist the support of the humanists for the revival of
Italian. They were hostile to it. A contemporary protest emanating from some Florentine citizens attributed the secretaries'
attitude to snobbery. Did the patricians sneer when Plautus came
on to the stage with his dirty clothes and calloused hands?[1] The
Certame Coronario had been preceded a few years earlier in 1435 by
an equally curious dispute among the humanists gathered at
Florence about the origins of the Italian language. Leonardo
Bruni, supported apparently by Cencio and Loschi, put forward
the hypothesis that there had always been two languages, Latin
for the educated and upper classes, Italian for the lower. Flavio
Biondo championed the other view, that Italian had evolved out
of Latin as a result of the barbarian invasions.[2] The dispute,
especially on Biondo's side, is interesting as an example of the use
of sources for fairly advanced historical analysis. Whether, apart
from the historical question, Bruni and his followers really
thought that the two languages must always run parallel, and
were opposed to any attempt to make Italian usurp the place of
the language of scholarship, is difficult to say. Bruni explicitly
allowed an excellence of its own kind to the Italian tongue as it
was used by Dante. They were not concerned to bridge the gap,
and probably accepted at least with equanimity the idea of a
separate language of scholarship and ornate writing, on which of

[1] G.Mancini, 'Un nuovo documento sul certame coronario di Firenze del 1441',
ASI, ser. 5, IX, 1892, p. 344.
[2] B.Nogara, 'Scritti Inediti e Rari di Flavio Biondo', *Studi e Testi*, 48, 1927, pp.
115-29; Bruni, *Epistolae*, VI, X; cf. Baron, *Crisis* (1955), I, pp. 303-6; II, Appendix 7.

course their professional position depended. Judging from the extremely cool tone of the one letter which Bruni is known to have written to Alberti, and which was about an exchange with Leonardo Dati arising out of the *Certame Coronario*, they were on opposite sides in that episode too.[1]

The incident of the *Certame Coronario* illustrates rather graphically the gap separating the humanists from even literate Florentines of superior rank. The dependence of the humanists on classical models made it possible for them to introduce radically new ideas suddenly; it also made it very difficult to integrate these ideas with vernacular thought. The peculiarities of humanist thought stem in part from these literary characteristics. They also stem, it will be suggested, from the close relationship with Florentine and Curial society which has been sketched in these chapters. The humanists expressed radical ideas with a confidence resulting from their secure social position. But security also limited their originality. It made them equivocal about their attitude to life and religion. Their ideas could be fruitfully creative only in those spheres where, in different ways, they engaged successfully with the native Florentine tradition: the spheres of politics and art.

[1] Bruni, *Epistolae*, IX, x.

4
Philosophy and Religion

The humanists of Florence and Rome did not write systematic treatises on philosophy or religion. It would have been entirely alien to their ways of thought to do so. They were comparatively unmoved by the more metaphysical aspects of Plato and Aristotle, and they regarded the logical architecture of the scholastics with positive distaste. Though they were professed Christians they showed comparatively little interest in theology and, though they were admirers of Aristotle, they had an intense dislike for logic. Nothing could have been further from their natural inclinations than the composition of a *Summa* or a *Philosophie*. This detachment from philosophical systems was not an accidental but an essential part of their outlook. Any attempt to deduce an embracing philosophy or religion from their works would misrepresent them seriously. Nevertheless they had certain fairly regular attitudes with important philosophical and religious implications, which, at the risk of giving an unreal impression of coherence, we must attempt to summarise and define. Since the forms in which they expressed their philosophical attitudes were largely derived from classical writers whom they admired for literary qualities and strove to imitate, it will be best to approach their beliefs first through works which are elaborate literary creations but also present a definable point of view. Two compositions which serve this purpose admirably are Carlo Marsuppini's *Consolatoria* addressed to Cosimo and Lorenzo de' Medici on the occasion of their mother's death in 1434, and Alberti's dialogue *Della Tranquillità dell' Animo* (*On the Tranquillity of the Soul*), composed in 1443.

At the beginning of his letter of consolation[1] Marsuppini justifies his grief (in part and rather incongruously by a reference to the behaviour of Niccolò Niccoli who, in spite of his unrivalled classical scholarship, was inconsolable at the funeral) and excuses his offering of consolation. What he offers is a summary of 'those things which were written by the most learned men about the defiance of death and about bearing misfortunes with a brave spirit'. As a gladiator becomes expert at parrying a variety of blows so we learn from philosophy how to deal with misfortune rationally. As the great Latin authors were not ashamed to learn from their Greek models and as the artists and architects of today copy the monuments of antique masters, so there is every reason for us to use the consolations of ancient philosophy. Turning to the burden of the argument, he first offers classical definitions of grief, then precepts about dealing with it. First we must know ourselves and the first article of self-knowledge is a realisation that we are mortal. The idea of death is repugnant but we must live with it. The condition of the temporal universe is constant change. We must learn therefore to expect ill fortune rather than good and to bear it without complaint. Even the goods of this life which we value, such as our bodies, bring us constant tribulation. Scripture forbids us to adopt the solution of some ancient philosophers who believed in the extinction of the soul at death, and ancient literature affords us many indications of the immortality of the soul and reasons to think of death as a good rather than an evil. There follows a eulogy of the virtuous life of the dead woman, which is the best preparation for death. The work ends with a string of classical examples of death confronted with fortitude.

The primary purpose of this little work is not philosophical analysis, least of all original analysis, but to exhibit elegantly an impressive acquaintance with classical literature. This passage will serve as an example.

Our body as Plato says gives us innumerable troubles because of the necessities of life (an allusion to *Phaedo*, 66 B). I pass over fevers, gout,

[1] Printed by P.G.Ricci, 'Una Consolatoria Inedita del Marsuppini', *La Rinascità*, III, 1940.

renal pains, colic, urinal and all other kinds of diseases. 'Even if some god had given me a hundred speaking tongues, genius and all the powers of Helicon I could not expound all the names of the diseases.' (An adaptation of Ovid, *Metamorphoses*, VIII, 533-5.) We are troubled by so many passions, worried by so many fears and griefs. Not only as our tragedian says do 'restless hopes and troubling fears storm through the cities' (adaptation of Seneca, *Hercules Furens*, 162-3) but battles, wars, enmities and seditions arise so frequently that in our life there is trouble without respite.[1]

This is a fair sample of the work of a not very inspired humanist showing off his command of the classics. The chain of quotations and allusions is typical. On the other hand the references to Christian authority are few: an apology for addressing the gods in the plural, an acknowledgement that in the last resort the Bible ensures immortality, a few references to the psalms; the other ninety-nine per cent is a flood of classicism. It might be thought that the absence of Christian authority is not significant in a literary exercise. But although the purpose is primarily literary the work also clearly enough presents an attitude to life, and one also derived from the classics: virtuous fortitude in the face of misfortune, Ciceronian stoicism.

Alberti's dialogue *Della Tranquillità dell' Animo*[2] is a more interesting work, no less devoted to the exhibition of acquaintance with classical literature but more seriously arguing the problems of moral philosophy. It was written in Italian but modelled on Cicero's philosophical dialogues. It takes the form of a debate in the presence of the author between two prominent citizens of Florence, Niccola di Vieri de' Medici and Agnolo di Filippo Pandolfini. They meet in the cathedral of Florence under Brunelleschi's dome and, after some graceful preliminary remarks on the therapeutic qualities of the architecture and music which they see and hear around them, settle down to a serious discussion of the ways in which the individual may meet the adversities of fortune. Niccola begins bitterly by complaining that the harmonies of

---

[1] References identified by Ricci, op. cit., pp. 417-18.

[2] Alberti, *Opere*, II, with the more correct title *Profugiorum ab Aerumna Libri III*. I have used the traditional title because of its familiarity.

music can do little to quieten the soul in the face of the injuries a man suffers and the sad memories which must remain in his mind. Agnolo counters this by saying that a man's will is strong enough to triumph over misfortunes, as is shown by the lives of Socrates, Pericles and other heroes of antiquity. As Hermes Trismegistus says, effective will is based on good counsel, and thus 'we men, well counselled, can accomplish as much by ourselves, with our mind, will and thought and emotions as we will and decide'. Niccola replies that no one in fact is strong enough to live up to these precepts. The advice of the Stoics was useless, for instance, to the mother of a soldier killed by Hannibal at Trasimene because the misfortunes which hurt come from outside us. Zeno, the 'father and expounder of this austere and horrible philosophy', was himself in practice anxious to avoid misfortune. What he asks of 'these philosophers, physicians of human minds and moderators of our souls' is that 'they should teach me, not to put a good outward face on things, but inwardly to avoid the perturbations and to purge the soul, with a certain reason and method, of whatever they think possible'.

Agnolo replies by lifting the discussion onto a higher plane. The individual must open himself to eternity by the practice of virtue. Life is movement, but there is also eternity, which 'I believe is nothing but a certain perfection and enviable continuation of life, and being always one and the same'. Immortal powers have given man understanding, reason and memory. Reason and society, as Seneca says, are given to us by God; we must use them for our own benefit. Man must use his higher inner powers to defend himself against adversity. This is the way to 'tranquillity of the soul'. In a long speech he sketches the way of life a man should follow in order to achieve this aim. He must be just to others. He must care reasonably for the health of his own body. He must use his leisure profitably, as advised by Aristotle and Epicurus, for reflection. His conduct must be open and above reproach. He must avoid the impediments to virtuous living. The art of living virtuously must be learnt and practised like other arts. An austere life is valuable. All this is expounded with a wealth of reference to classical examples such as Diogenes, who reacted to the loss of his slave by realising that he could live without a slave.

In Book 2 the trio meet again at mass in the cathedral. Agnolo is rejecting an invitation to advise the Priors of the city on a political issue because they want him to say something pleasing to them and not to speak his real mind. Instead he invites his friends to take a walk with him and continue the discussion. Agnolo's discourse this time springs from his distrust of the secure and honourable position which he holds in the city. Men should not glory in their good fortune. They should not hope for better things, nor should they fear worse. Turning to Alberti, who was smarting from recent injuries in Florence which may have been the immediate inspiration for the dialogue, he advises him to cultivate conscientiously the good of his fellow citizens without fearing their jealousy. The wise man must resolve to be himself the only arbiter of his life and deeds. The rest of the book is an exhortation with many classical examples, among which the trials of Ulysses figure prominently, to overcome injuries unjustly inflicted by others by cultivating reason and virtue unswervingly.

In Book 3 Niccola opens the discussion again by complimenting Agnolo on the splendid argument he has built up by fitting together fragments drawn from ancient writers, like a mosaic pavement made from chips of marble. He develops the metaphor. Unlike the mosaic-maker, who uses fragments left over from a building, we have to pillage the edifice of ancient philosophy itself. The Greek philosophers constructed a temple in their writings. 'They laid out the plan by the investigation of good and evil; set up the pillars by distinguishing the effects and powers of nature; and set a roof on it, to defend it from the tempests, which was made up of skill in avoiding evil, desiring and pursuing good, hating vice, choosing and loving virtue.'[1] We can only adapt pieces of this great structure to our own private uses. '*Nihil dictum quin prius dictum.*' You Agnolo have constructed a splendid edifice of argument of your own in this way. But you do not convince me. It is hard to carry out the precept of indifference to ill-fortune, and the fragile goods of this life are what men in reality

[1] Alberti, *Opere*, II, pp. 160-61.

live for. Agnolo replies to this with another string of exhortations to fortitude in the face of adversity, larded with classical examples. This life is certainly hard: 'fortune in itself always was and always will be capricious and destructive.' But if you turn to God he will give you wisdom and virtue to overcome adversity. The lesser comforts, wine, music, play, are not to be despised. But finally a good manner of life is a defence against all adversity.

These works by Marsuppini and Alberti, being primarily literary exercises, reveal the close connection between literary taste and the expression of moral attitudes. The most explicit discussions of philosophy for its own sake to emerge from this milieu are to be found in the writings of Bruni. The nearest thing to a manifesto of humanist philosophy is the *Isagogicon Moralis Disciplinae*, which he wrote in the early 1420s.[1] He begins this short treatise, which was addressed to a *condottiere* with Florentine connections called Galeotto de' Ricasoli, by making it clear that his interest is in moral philosophy not in natural science, 'which, although it is sublime and excellent, has less usefulness for life than those studies which descend to the manners and virtues of men'. The study of 'frost, snow and the colours of the rainbow' is therefore dismissed. The gesture represents a general humanist indifference to the study of physical nature, which played a much smaller part in the humanist culture of this school than in the scholasticism of the fourteenth century. It was discounted, like logic, because their attention was not directed to it by the Roman rhetorical tradition, and because its medieval flowering was embedded in repulsive treatises. The great exception to this generalisation was Alberti, whose interest in mathematics and optics bore fruit in the influential system of perspective sketched in his *Della Pittura*, and Alberti may have owed something to the Florentine mathematician and physician Paolo Toscanelli who moved in humanist circles. Apart from the crucially important artistic significance of this, mathematics and natural science seem to have had no organic role in the structure of ideas of the Florentine

[1] Bruni, *Schriften*, p. 20. There is a good analysis of Bruni's philosophy by J. Freudenthal, 'Leonardo Bruni als Philosoph', *Neue Jahrbücher für das klassische Altertum*, XXVII, 1911.

school. The philosophical questions which interest Bruni – and this again is a general humanist attitude – are the nature of the final good and the means of attaining it. For advice on the final good he turns to the philosophers of antiquity as summarised by Cicero. Aristotle and the Peripatetics thought it was to be found in virtuous and rational action. The Stoics thought the only good was virtue and that external fortune and the goods of the body were to be disregarded. The difference between them and the Peripatetics he thought, following Cicero, was more a matter of words than of realities. 'They both agree in fact that the arbiter and effective cause of a blessed life is virtue.' Even the Epicureans did not dissent as much as they might at first sight appear to do because the pleasure which they pursued also involved virtue. In deciding how the end was to be achieved Bruni turned to Aristotle and followed him fairly closely. The good life was to be pursued by the cultivation of virtues which were means between the extremes of conduct. The soul was to be divided into its rational and irrational parts. The virtues were classified into the moral virtues (fortitude, temperance, etc.) and the intellectual virtues (prudence, knowledge, etc.) and were variously appropriate to the active and contemplative ways of life.

Bruni did not regard philosophy as a live study to which original contributions might be made. All the possible variations had been stated in the different schools of classical philosophy. As the speaker in Alberti's dialogue put it, the modern moralist could only adapt parts of the edifice which had been created by the philosophers of the ancient world. The main sources of wisdom were Aristotle's *Ethics*, Cicero, Seneca and Plutarch's lives of the philosophers. Bruni's view was that the best system of ethics was to be found in Aristotle and the best exposition of it in Cicero.[1] The absurdities of this approach, to which in another facet of his personality he subscribed, were satirised by Alberti in one of his most remarkable works, *Momus*, probably written at Rome in the period 1443-50. *Momus* is the most substantial of his Lucianesque creations, and since it belongs to that genre it cannot be regarded as expressing a philosophical or, as has been even

[1] Bruni, *Epistolae*, VI, vi.

more incongruously supposed, a political doctrine. *Momus* is a large-scale satirical fable about the relations between gods and men. The central figure in the story is Momus, a rebellious and insolent god, displaying some of the characteristics of the author, who moves between heaven and earth in a series of pathetic and comic adventures (as a poet he undermines the authority of the gods by stories of their goings on; as a philosopher he argues that there is only one god, Nature).[1] Most of the story is moral fable. For instance, at one point Momus ravishes Laus (praise) who is a daughter of Virtue. She immediately gives birth to a chattering monster Fama (rumour) who spreads the news that Laus's sisters, Triumphus and Trophaeus, are not children of Virtue at all but of Chance and Fortune.[2] But the philosophers, encountered by Momus on his first descent to earth in Tuscany,[3] play a fairly large part in the story. At one point, at a divine dinner party in honour of Hercules, Momus describes the schools of philosophers which he has met on earth, including the rhetoricians who are more interested in winning arguments by eloquence than in finding the truth.[4] The gods, however, remain convinced that philosophers are important supporters of their terrestrial interests, and when Jupiter decides to make a new world they agree to seek the opinions of philosophers. As a result they have a highly unsatisfactory series of encounters with various schools in which only Socrates and Democritus make a favourable impression.[5] Later on, in another episode, Charon is shown round the world by a stupid philosopher called Gelastus (*gelastos*=absurd), who tries to explain things, in a parody of scholastic terminology, about matter and form.[6] Alberti makes the philosophers absurd in predictable ways. Virtue cannot be found in their company though they are always talking about her. Aristotle talks endlessly without allowing anyone else to speak. Alberti is not making any philosophical point but he does give one a satirist's view of a

---

[1] L.B. Alberti, *Momus o del Principe*, ed. G. Martini (Bologna, 1942), p. 21.

[2] *Momus*, pp. 37-40.

[3] *Momus*, p. 20.

[4] *Momus*, pp. 82-90.

[5] *Momus*, pp. 107-39.

[6] *Momus*, p. 162.

philosophical landscape in which the most conspicuous feature is a rather standardised bickering over points made by the ancient philosophical schools.

Plato seems to have had little influence in this circle, and Bruni again well represents the ambiguous way in which his works were regarded. There is no doubt about his admiration for Plato as a writer. His immense achievement of translation from Greek covered not only Aristotle's *Ethics* and *Politics* but also Plato's *Phaedo, Gorgias, Phaedrus* and *Crito* and the *Letters*. But he avoided translating the *Republic* on the grounds that the strangeness of its ideas would bring its author into disrepute.[1] Plato was too searching, too unconventional, too disturbing. Bruni expressed his own feelings in about 1429 when he dedicated a life of Aristotle to Cardinal Niccolò Albergati and ended it with a brief discussion of the differences between Aristotle and Plato.[2] On the really important things, the virtues, good and evil and the immortality of the soul, he believed that they agreed. But Plato held some offensive opinions on such matters as the transmigration of souls and the community of wives, and his ideas were not always clear; Socrates in the dialogues seemed to jump about from one opinion to another, more concerned with rebutting others than with making his own standpoint plain, which did not appeal to Bruni's straightforward mind. As a philosophical guide he thought the Platonic dialogues far inferior to the works of Aristotle.

The only serious attack on humanist philosophy from the scholastic camp which has come down to us was a rather distant complaint which had very little impact in Italian circles. It is nevertheless interesting both for the criticisms which it makes and for the reactions to it. In 1417 Bruni had completed a translation of Aristotle's *Ethics* to which he added, probably a year or two later, a preface which has been described with justice as a humanist manifesto against the medieval translators of Greek philosophy. The object of Bruni's scorn was probably William of Moerbeke, a mid-thirteenth-century translator of Aristotle. After denouncing

---

[1] Bruni, *Epistolae*, IX, 4. 'Multa sunt in iis libris abhorrentia a moribus nostris, quae pro honore Platonis tacere satius est, quam proferre.'

[2] Bruni, *Schriften*, pp. 41-9.

the ineptitude of the translation[1] he went on to explain his own method, which involved translating Aristotle into the ethical vocabulary used by Cicero and other ancient writers.[2] His translation and preface came into the hands of a learned Spanish ecclesiastic, Alfonso of Cartagena, Bishop of Burgos, who about 1430 wrote a courteous but highly critical reply, defending the old translation particularly on the grounds of its philosophical vocabulary.[3] Bruni had criticised the medieval translator for using the word *bonum* (good) when he should have used *honestus* (honourable, virtuous) on the grounds that Seneca and other stoics used *honestus* to make the crucial distinction from *utile* (useful) which also implied 'good' but in a different sense. Similarly the old translator had used the word *delectatio* when he should have used *voluptas*, the word used by Cicero, Seneca, Boethius, Lactantius and Jerome. In this case the precise authority of Cicero could be quoted: 'What the Greeks call *hedone* we call *voluptas*.' Alfonso objected that this raised the whole issue of philosophical dependence on Latin writers. 'How can we reply to this unless we first attack the root and consider whether Cicero, Seneca and other Stoics are to be followed so faithfully in questions of moral doctrines.' Cicero's pre-eminence in rhetoric was indisputable but not his philosophical competence. The *De Officiis* contained many defects and 'deviations from true doctrine'. His failure to distinguish *continentia* from *virtus* showed that he himself had not profited from the reading of the *Ethics*. Seneca also, though a writer with great moral authority, was careless in his ethical distinctions.

I have said this not for the sake of attacking those two illustrious orators who I think should both be admired but in order to cut off at its source the error, which I suspect is creeping in, of those who think moral teaching should be subordinated to eloquence .... Believe me,

[1] Above, p. 19.

[2] Bruni, *Schriften*, pp. 76-81; cf. E.Franceschini, 'Leonardo Bruni e il "vetus interpres" dell'Etica a Nicomaco', *Medioevo e Rinascimento, Studi in Onore di Bruno Nardi* (Florence, 1955), I.

[3] Printed by A.Birkenmajer, 'Der Streit des Alonso von Cartagena mit Leonardo Bruni Aretino', *Beiträge zur Geschichte der Philosophie des Mittelalters*, XX, 1922.

he who wishes to subordinate the strict conclusions of the sciences to the rules of eloquence does not realise that when it comes to adding or subtracting words for the sake of graceful persuasion the rigor of science shudders.... Our translation (Moerbeke's) should not be attacked on the ground that it diverges from the verbal usage of even the greatest orators; it should be examined to see whether it conforms to plainness and the strict meaning of words.

Bonum, Alfonso argued, was in one sense what all beings tended towards, but only in so far as they apprehended it, and they were fallible, otherwise there would be no distinction between good and bad men. *Honestas* was virtuous action which arises in pursuit of a true good as opposed to a false good. The two concepts should be kept separate: otherwise it would appear that virtuous action was itself the ultimate good, not the good for the sake of which it was done. Similarly *delectatio* was a better word than *voluptas* because *voluptas* had the connotation of bodily pleasure which was inappropriate.

Alfonso's critique came to Bruni's notice in 1436 through an intermediary who read it at the Council of Basle, and in the next few years he wrote several letters defending himself.[1] The interesting thing about his replies is that he entirely refused to face the issues raised by the critic. Alfonso had admitted that he knew no Greek: his point was that Bruni's Stoic vocabulary did not conform to moral philosophy as he understood it. Bruni in reply insisted that translation was simply a matter of fidelity to the original; he would not discuss the philosophical issues raised, according to Alfonso, by the vocabulary he had used. Bruni was not merely putting up a smokescreen in thus attempting to deflect the issue to the question of translation. The literary and historical problems involved in making a faithful rendering of a Greek author were a genuine preoccupation, part of his highly developed historical sense, and he had written a little treatise about the problem.[2] His refusal to discuss the philosophical implications of his translation must nevertheless have been deliberate. The argu-

---

[1] The longest is Bruni, *Epistolae*, x, xxiv, *circa* 1437-8.

[2] *De Interpretatione Recta* (Bruni, *Schriften*, p. 81); on the date see Baron, *Crisis of the Early Italian Renaissance* (1955), II, pp. 615-6.

ments of the two contendants therefore never really met. Both of course had weaknesses which made their positions untenable. The Spaniard, being ignorant of Greek, really had no idea how Aristotle should be translated. Bruni on the other hand had originally made no secret of the fact that he was using a Stoic vocabulary simply because it had the authority of Cicero and Seneca. The real issue between them was the validity of the Stoic as against the scholastic approach to moral philosophy. A more explicit stand in defence of humanist translation against ecclesiastical tradition seems to have been taken about the same time, in the late 1430s, by the Milanese humanist Pier Candido Decembrio, who was engaged in the philosophically much more dangerous project of translating Plato's *Republic*, which Bruni deliberately avoided.[1] Bruni however, characteristically both of himself and of the Florentine school in general, evaded any confrontation with traditional philosophy. He adopted Stoic attitudes on rhetorical authority, not only without defending them in Christian or scholastic terms but without acknowledging that the problem existed. This combination of actual philosophical radicalism with bland indifference to its philosophical implications was both the strength and the weakness of the Florentine approach.

In spite of his distaste for Socratic dialectic Bruni was, however, a man with some genuine philosophical interest. In the comments of his contemporary and friend, Poggio, the explicit reduction of philosophy to simple moral guidance was carried further and in a direction still more typical of humanist inclinations. The early part of his treatise *De Varietate Fortunae*, published in 1448 and mostly concerned with recent history, contains a discussion of the ubiquitous humanist concept of Fortune. The two speakers are Poggio himself and his colleague at the Curia, Antonio Loschi. Loschi put forward Aristotle's definition of fortune as *causa accidens* on human action – the causes being infinite and the fortune certain, a definition which, Loschi added, is accepted by Aquinas.[2]

[1] R.Fubini, 'Tra umanesimo e concili', *Studi Medievali*, ser. 3, VII, 1966, pp. 337-48.

[2] *S.Thomae Aquinatis in octo libros Physicorum Aristotelis Expositio*, ed. P.M.Maggiòlo (Turin-Rome, 1954), pp. 99-115.

Far be it from me, replies Poggio, to dispute the authority of Aristotle or Aquinas, but this does not seem to have any bearing on the common man's conception of fortune. For him it means for instance the fortune which Alexander the Great trusted and which contributed to his victories, or the fortune which gives a merchant a better return than he could reasonably have expected in his dealing. This is a 'divine power, turning and reversing human affairs capriciously, offering nothing firm and safe'. This is how fortune was seen by Cicero and Seneca and they seem right, though Seneca is mistaken in regarding it as a force affecting only external matters which can be disregarded by the wise man. But, complains Loschi, Seneca unlike Aristotle does not help us to define fortune. That is no more important, retorts Poggio, than the definition of food is to a starving man.

For that reason I have always considered Cicero's *De Officiis* more useful for the arrangement of our life than Aristotle's *Ethics*. Aristotle gives definitions of the virtues, investigating what they are and in what parts they are divided; Cicero brings the virtues themselves down into the battlefield and puts them in the front line, making them speak and instruct; he offers a way of life and precepts, tells us what virtue allows and forbids, what should be the office of a good man, and thus he finally directs our actions to a certain rule of life so that we seem to have a certain possession of virtues.[1]

This is the essence of the attitude to philosophy which the humanists had derived from their Latin mentors.

How did the humanists, as enthusiastic purveyors of an essentially pagan Stoicism, regard the Christian church and the papacy which most of them at one time or another served and counselled? Bruni is silent; Alberti almost equally so. In contrast to the late Schism period, which compelled employees of the Curia to take a stand over the issue of conciliarism, the distant machinations of the Council of Basle do not seem to have evoked much sympathy in the Florentine group. The only indications of a live attitude to religion and the church come from Poggio, Niccoli and Traversari, a group of close friends from whom Bruni stood a little apart and who may have had some ideas in common which he did

[1] *De Varietate Fortunae*, pp. 26-32.

not share. The indications are faint and tantalising but they reveal something of the humanist dilemma.

In the first place there was a good deal of anti-clericalism which, although it was not necessarily rationally connected with pagan philosophising, gave an added sharpness to their disregard for conventional Christian attitudes. Poggio's dialogues in particular are full of outspoken criticism of priests and prelates, spiced by his long and intimate knowledge of the Curia and the major ecclesiastical dignitaries of the Italian scene. *De Infelicitate Principum*, composed in 1440, is an imaginary dialogue in Niccolò Niccoli's library at Florence in which the speakers are Niccoli himself, Cosimo de' Medici and Carlo Marsuppini.[1] A sanctimonious remark by Marsuppini to the effect that the blessedness and holiness of bishops must ensure their happiness starts Niccoli on a diatribe in which he classifies them, together with other princes, as a useless race who 'do everything for ostentation's sake and very few deeds deserving true praise or glory'. The evidence which springs to his lips is the pope's indifference to Poggio's epoch-making manuscript discoveries in Germany, which still rankled in Poggio's mind, but this criticism was probably not meant to appear humorously trivial. Poggio gave his characteristic talent as an anti-clerical raconteur fullest scope in the *Contra Hypocritas* of 1449. This dialogue opens with Poggio visiting Marsuppini in his library and being asked hopefully whether the Roman Curia was as much besieged by hypocrites now, under Nicholas v, as it had been in the days of Eugenius iv. After a vivid picture has been painted of the crowds of clergy clamouring for benefices at the court of Eugenius, they are joined by Gerolamo Agliotti, a Benedictine abbot well known for his humanist interests. Poggio introduces him as an honest man who is expert in hypocrisy because of the circles in which he moves. Poggio and Marsuppini continue to pour out stories of clerical deceit and come round to a special attack on the Friars and finally to some notable individual ecclesiastics of the first half of the fifteenth century. (It is here that the denunciation of Giovanni Dominici occurs.) One of their victims is their old friend Traversari,

[1] Poggio, *Opera*, p. 392, seq.

recently dead. He is appropriately defended by Agliotti but the defence is only half accepted by Marsuppini.

> I praise his life and I believe that it was without hypocrisy while he devoted himself to the muses in the convent at Florence. But when he was made abbot he diverged somewhat from his previous way of life. He went about rather secretly so that he seemed to be seeking something higher. I remember that our Niccolò (Niccoli), who was free in speaking and very friendly to him, used often to reproach him for the useless affairs in which he voluntarily involved himself and repeatedly said that the nets were set for the red hat.[1]

In other words Traversari's humanism was praiseworthy but his high ecclesiastical career was useless.

Poggio was in one sense simply latinising the story-telling of Boccaccio, and he was himself the author of a popular book of bawdy and irreverent stories without the literary pretensions of the dialogues and letters, his *Facetie*. These things cannot be taken in themselves as representing any systematic criticism of Christianity or the church. Taken in conjunction with an embryonic philosophical attitude however they do represent a significant approach to religion even though it is a half-hearted and negative one. During the period from 1417 to 1443 the institutional background was particularly relaxed and no writer of the power and perceptiveness of Dominici arose to challenge the humanists. Nevertheless the nature of their position did occasionally become embarrassingly clear. One episode was appropriately connected with the activities of the Observant Franciscans who, under the leadership of the evangelical revivalist San Bernardino (1380-1444), were the most powerful popular religious force in central Italy at this period and in their extreme pietistic fervour natural enemies of the supercilious stoicism of the humanists. In 1429 an episode in the endemic conflict between the Observant and Conventual Franciscans led to a papal ruling that for the time being no more Observant houses were to be built. Poggio, as a papal secretary, was concerned in this decision. Visiting his own house at Terranuova near Florence later in the year, he noticed a new Observant convent being built in the vicinity in defiance of

[1] *Contro l'ipocrisia*, ed. G.Vallese (Naples, 1946), pp. 111-12.

the papal ruling and reported it.[1] It happened that one of the prominent Observants, Alberto da Sarteano, was a friar with some humanist interests who knew both Poggio and Niccoli and his correspondence with them about the Terranuova case survives. Alberto had been a keen student of the classics before joining Bernardino in 1423,[2] which suggests that Greek literature and evangelical religion might occasionally appeal to the same man. He wrote to Niccoli, whose views must have been well known to him, apparently expecting a sympathetic hearing for his complaint about the persecution of his order.[3] Niccoli took it seriously enough to write to Poggio and, though his letter does not survive, Poggio's reply, which does, implies that it required a justification of his action. Poggio denied that he had acted maliciously, but he did not conceal that, though he admired Bernardino and Alberto, he disapproved of the Observants in general and thought they included many disreputable people.[4] His moderate and reflective letter to Alberto himself, justifying his action, produced a long and withering attack on his whole preference for the urbane moralising of the pagans over the evangelical efforts of the friars. Alberto would not, he said censure Poggio's reading of pagan authors or his use of them in his writings so long as this implied no threat to the authority of scripture. But to put these authors and opinions above the actions of evangelical propagators of the Christian faith was unforgiveable. The teachings of the Observants, expressing the essential Christian hope of salvation, were infinitely superior to Diogenes's 'sharpness', Socrates's 'broken hope', Plato's 'unhealthy academy', Aristotle's 'subtleties', Epicurus's '*luxuria*', Democritus's 'stupid atoms' and all the rest of the panoply of ancient philosophy.[5]

To balance the anti-clericalism there are indications within the group of Niccoli's close friends of a serious interest in early Christian writers which would be a natural complement to their

[1] Walser, *Poggius*, pp. 114-21.

[2] Voigt, *Wiederbelebung des Classischen Altertums*, II, pp. 229-31.

[3] Martène and Durand, *Veterum scriptorum et monumentorum Amplissima Collectio* (Paris, 1724), III, cols, 755-7.

[4] Poggio, *Epistolae*, III, xxxiv.

[5] Poggio, *Epistolae*, IV, vii; *Amplissima Collectio*, III, cols. 757-73.

dislike of scholasticism and their appreciation of Greek and Latin literature. Niccoli may have gone further than the others in his criticism of contemporary Christianity. Filelfo accused him of atheism in one of his *Satyrae* composed in the 1430s and, though Filelfo's extravagant denunciations of his opponents deserve little credence, it may be significant that he chose that particular accusation for that particular enemy.[1] Among the many letters written to Niccoli is an undated one from Traversari in which, after asking for a loan of two books, he beseeches his friend to perform his Christian duty at Easter. 'I cannot tell you how much I desire and entreat you to it by right of old friendship. I cannot bear that such a close friend and especially one devoted to and learned in scripture should not for some years have received the holy nourishment for if our faith is not often aroused and confirmed it fades among the temptations of the flesh.'[2] This tells us two things about Niccoli: that he was negligent about religious observance and that he was a serious student of the Christian religion. When he and his friends did show an interest in Christianity it took the form of disregarding medieval and modern expositions and looking for guidance in the fathers. Poggio wrote to Niccoli in 1429 in reply to some criticisms which Niccoli had made of *De Avaritia*, saying that he could have inserted quotations denouncing avarice from St Paul, Augustine and St John Chrysostom whose works he knows that Niccoli approves.[3] Poggio himself had read Augustine and Chrysostom with great admiration during his stay in England in the early 1420s.[4] A recent analysis of the programme of *Old Testament* scenes executed by Lorenzo Ghiberti on the Gates of Paradise in the 1420s and 1430s has shown that it follows a novel pattern influenced by a reading of St Ambrose and Origen. As there is some evidence that Niccoli and Traversari, the outstanding student of the Greek Fathers, had a hand in it, it is a reasonable hypothesis that it

[1] *Traversari/Mehus*, I, p. lxi.

[2] G.Mercati, 'Ultimi Contributi alla Storia degli Umanisti, I, Traversariana' (*Studi e Testi*, XC, 1939), pp. 46-7.

[3] Poggio, *Epistolae*, I, p. 279.

[4] Poggio, *Epistolae*, I, vi-viii.

sprang from their theological interests.[1] A dislike for some of the paraphernalia of modern ecclesiastical life would go easily with a preference for the attitudes to religion expressed by pre-medieval writers. For an explicit statement of the literary basis of this attitude we may turn again to Bruni. In a work composed in the 1420s, *De Studiis et Litteris Liber*, a letter of advice to a lady of scholarly inclinations Battista de' Malatesti, he distinguished between the 'vulgar and confused erudition of those who now practise theology' and the legitimate and innate erudition which 'combines literary skill with understanding of things', as in Lactantius, Augustine and Jerome. Characteristically Bruni does not follow up the implications of his literary judgement. Earlier Christian writers are simply stated to be superior. But even they are not adequate. In the same letter he argues that, though much is to be learnt from Augustine, to understand moral problems it is essential to grapple with the ideas of Epicurus, Zeno and Aristotle.[2] Similarly Poggio in *Contra Hypocritas* makes Marsuppini quote the *New Testament* together with Cicero and Seneca when he is assembling texts critical of hypocrisy.[3] The available evidence will probably not allow us to define the humanists' attitude to Christianity much more clearly. They were not atheists or anti-Christians. They were sceptical of some aspects of modern ecclesiastical organisation and about the value of scholasticism. Their philosophical and religious instincts, such as they were, tended towards a simple moral system.

To imagine the potentialities of this attitude one has only to think of the Christian humanism of the early sixteenth century and its criticism of the contemporary church. The Florentine school of this period, however, produced neither an orthodox nor a heretical Christian humanism. The central group included the ecclesiastic, Traversari, who expressed uneasiness about Niccoli's laxity in religious observance. His own positive humanist activity, apart from his participation in the hunt for manuscripts, was mostly devoted to the translation of the Greek Fathers, notably

[1] R. Krautheimer, *Lorenzo Ghiberti* (Princeton, 1956), ch. 12.

[2] Bruni, *Schriften*, pp. 5-19.

[3] *Contro l'ipocrisia*, p. 82.

St John Chrysostom, St Gregory Nazianzen and St Basil. This was
an activity which could command the respect both of the most
enthusiastic classicists and of the most serious churchmen. In the
midst of these pious pursuits, however, he was persuaded by
Cosimo to translate Diogenes Laertius's *Lives of the Philosophers*,
an entirely pagan work of interest only to students of the pagan
world and its thought. In a letter written when he had finished the
translation he complained of the inappropriateness of the job for
a monk.[1] The letter of dedication to Cosimo is unusual and revealing because he used it to make plain his doubts about the undertaking. Only two considerations, he said, could justify it: first,
that a greater knowledge of the opinions of pagan philosophers
made clearer their hopeless discord and drove the reader more
firmly to the one clear truth of Christianity, and second that their
biographies included some inspiring examples of almost Christian
behaviour.[2] This is a consistent attitude as far as it goes. Traversari did not admit the independent value of pagan philosophy.
It is hardly consistent with his intimate involvement in the
humanist endeavours of Niccoli and Cosimo. Traversari no doubt
thought that his work for the Camaldolese Order was infinitely
more important than his promotion of Greek studies and saw his
expertise mainly as a contribution to knowledge of the Fathers
and to the promotion of union with the Orthodox Church;
Niccoli, according to Poggio, thought he deserted the muses for
the toils of ecclesiastical hypocrisy. Traversari was generally able
to keep his humanism and his Christianity in separate compart-
ments. In different circumstances humanist moralism could easily
have come into conflict with ecclesiastical institutions. On a
deeper level the philosophers whom the humanists admired were
in fact pagans whose attitudes could be reconciled with Christianity
only by a difficult effort of synthesis such as that which had been
made by thirteenth-century scholasticism or that which was to be

[1] *Traversari/Mehus*, VII, ii. Traversari mentioned the work of translation first in
1425 (VI, xxiii). If the dating of his letters proposed by F.P.Luiso ('Ricerche Cronologiche per un riordinamento dell Epistolario di A.Traversari', *Rivista delle Biblioteche e degli Archivi*, IX, 1898) is correct the work lasted until 1432; but this seems
unlikely.

[2] *Traversari/Mehus*, XXIII, x.

made by later Christian humanism. The precarious and unreal balance could only be maintained as long as peculiar circumstances allowed the humanists to keep up their detached and yet superior position, and did not drive them into submission to orthodox opinion or provoke them into conflict with it. Their comfortable position also dissuaded them from taking any positive stand.

As it happens we have an admirable instrument to help us see their ideas in perspective in the work of a contemporary humanist who commented on it. Lorenzo Valla knew the world of the Florentines intimately enough to understand them; but he was outside it and his life was deeply affected by quite different circumstances, and he observed them with an interesting mixture of sympathy and enmity. Also, unlike the Florentines, he had a serious interest in philosophy. Posterity remembers Valla for his book on the *Donation of Constantine*, an exposure of the forged document by which the fourth-century emperor Constantine was supposed to have granted the Roman Empire to the pope and a demolition of papal claims to temporal power. The forgery, however, was so blatant that even medieval critics had undermined it, and Valla's book, which has often been taken as a striking example of 'Renaissance' historiography, has in fact little originality. The sixteenth century remembered him for his *Elegantiae*, a textbook of latinity which went through an enormous number of editions in the first century of printing. Here we are concerned with another side of the man. He was the author of several daring philosophical works which had little historical effect apart from scandalising contemporaries. They deserve study for their own sake. One aspect of them, however, is the revealing way in which they indicate the implications and the limitations of the Florentine outlook.

Lorenzo Valla was born in 1405 or 1407 into a Roman family which had close connections with the papal Curia.[1] His father was an advocate in the papal courts of law; an uncle was a papal

[1] The details of Valla's life are derived from G.Mancini, *Vita di Lorenzo Valla* (Florence, 1891) and L.Barozzi and R.Sabbadini, *Studi sul Panormita e sul Valla* (Florence, 1891).

secretary under Martin V. His sister was later married to an official of the chancery. 'I was born and grew up in Rome and in the Roman Curia', he said himself. His education is obscure but it was presumably mostly Roman. Some time and somehow he got to know the Florentine circle, and he later claimed Bruni as one of his teachers. The acquaintance was no doubt made partly during visits of the Florentine luminaries to the Curia, but it seems likely that Valla also some time in the 1420s spent a period at Florence in which he got to know them more intimately. He was at any rate a Roman who knew the Florentine world. The turning point in his life came in 1429 when his uncle the papal secretary died. Valla had hoped to make a humanist career in the Curia and to begin by succeeding his uncle. But he was rebuffed and, according to his later complaints, excluded by the opposition of Poggio and Loschi. He gave up the Curia and went to look for a living elsewhere. He did not entirely lose contact with Rome. He knew Eugenius IV well enough to write him a letter of congratulation on his election to the papal throne in 1431 and to receive a present of two benefices from him.[1] But his occasional efforts to return to the Curia were ineffective for nearly twenty years, and he felt a grievance about it.

His search for a living took him first to Lombardy where he held a public lectureship in rhetoric at the University of Pavia from 1430 to 1433. Here he came into the orbit of a school of humanism which was in some respects very different from the one that he had known at Florence and Rome. The Lombard humanists, perhaps because the stronger university tradition forced it upon their attention, were much more interested than their Florentine contemporaries in the confrontation with scholasticism. This environment produced Catone Sacco's *Originum Libri*, which contains a direct attack on some Aristotelian concepts, such as the eternity of the world,[2] and also the first Renaissance defence

---

[1] Mancini thought that Valla even visited Eugenius in Florence in 1434 (*Vita*, p 87; 'Giovanni Tortelli', *ASI*, LXXVIII, 1920, pp. 171-2).

[2] C. Vasoli, 'Le "Dialecticae Disputationes" del Valla e la critica umanistica della logica Aristotelica', *Rivista Critica di Storia della Filosofia*, XII-XIII, 1957-8, where the Lombard background to Valla's philosophy is discussed.

of Epicureanism in a short treatise composed by Cosma Raimondi in 1431.[1] Influenced, no doubt, by this background, Valla published in 1431 a book with the provocative title *On Pleasure* (*De Voluptate*). In form it is a dialogue of the kind beloved by the Florentine humanists, an urbane discussion between literary gentlemen liberally sprinkled with classical quotations and allusions. In substance it is an attack, or a satire, on their current moral philosophy. The imaginary gathering is located at Rome. The speakers are mainly humanists of the curial and Florentine circles – from the Curia: Poggio, Cencio, Loschi and Valla's late uncle; from Florence: Bruni (supposed to be visiting as Florentine ambassador, which he did in real life in 1426) and Niccoli. There is one important outsider who plays the central role in the dialogue, Antonio Beccadelli, known as Panormita, a Sicilian humanist who had spent the last decade at various cities of central and northern Italy, including Rome and Florence, and since 1430 had been at the University of Pavia where he must have been well known to Valla. Panormita had achieved widespread notoriety by writing and publishing in 1425 one of the stranger productions of the early Renaissance, the *Hermaphroditus*. *Hermaphroditus* was a collection of accomplished Latin verses, dedicated, with what effect we do not know, to Cosimo de' Medici and including a good deal of ordinary humanist badinage.[2] Many of the verses however were obscene celebrations of sexual activity of various kinds. Panormita therefore had a reputation which made him a suitable mouthpiece for the expression of outrageous opinions, some of which he may have held.

In his preface[3] Valla says that he has been moved to compose

[1] G.Santini, 'Cosma Raimondi Umanista et Epicurea', *Studi Storici*, VIII, 1899. The treatise is also printed by E.Garin, *La Cultura Filosofica del Rinascimento Italiano* (Florence, 1961), p. 87.

[2] *Antonii Panormitae Hermaphroditus*, ed. F.C.Forbergius (Coburg, 1824). He also sent a copy to Bartolomeo Capra, Archbishop of Milan (*Lampax sive fax artium liberalium*, ed. J.Gruterus, II (Lucca, 1747), pp. 107-8), a remarkable indication of the tolerance which humanists expected and received in some ecclesiastical circles. The Archbishop later recommended him for the post of historiographer at Milan (Barozzi and Sabbadini, op. cit., p. 41).

[3] *De Voluptate* was revised several times. I follow the edition printed 'In aedibus Ascensianis', Paris, 1512, which has been thought to correspond with the first

this work because of the veneration which is often expressed for ancient philosophers, and which has been carried to the length of arguing that their virtues were such that they deserve to be in heaven rather than hell and ought to be admired and imitated by Christians. This is a betrayal of Christianity. 'What, I ask, is this but to avow that Christ came in vain into the world or indeed did not come at all.' The book therefore will be a Christian attack on the Stoics in which the help of Epicurus will be invoked. The dialogue then opens with Bruni declaring his preference for the Stoic philosophy as expressed by Seneca and also calling on help from Aristotle: a mild parody of the point of view which Bruni had in fact set out in his *Isagogicon*.[1] He argues that evils are commoner than good, vice than virtues, and that men must hold fast to the pursuit of virtue to combat the depravity of both nature and human nature. The main part of the book is a long reply to this by Panormita, defending the Epicurean point of view that the *summum bonum* is not virtue but *voluptas*, pleasure.[2] Most of his argument is a series of irreverent attacks on the ideals of Bruni and the Stoics. The enemy is the notion of the virtuous life (*honestas*) as an end in itself. It is absurd. If pleasure were not the purpose of life external goods and the sensual beauties and delights would be pointless. He delivers a long eulogistic account of the sensual pleasures, culminating in an attack on the practice of chastity or virginity: the vestal virgins must have been invented by old men who wanted to sanctify their impotence. The idea of giving one's life for one's country is equally absurd. The self-sacrificial heroes of republican Rome – so beloved by the Florentine classicists – do not deserve the admiration they get. The deaths in good causes of Cato, Scipio and Lucretia were not justifiable for the reasons which the Stoics give, that they were self-sufficient virtuous actions.

In a somewhat more serious vein Panormita makes his main

version of 1431 (M. de Panizza Bové, 'Le Tre Versioni del *De vero bono* del Valla', *Rinascimento*, VI, 1955). Valla's works have now been reprinted photographically from various editions in *Opera Omnia*, ed. E. Garin, Turin, 1962.

[1] *De Voluptate*, f. vi seq.
[2] f. xi v. seq.

point about morals.[1] Of course there are virtues and vices and it is no part of his purpose to deny it. But the aim of the virtues (*virtutes*) is not just virtuousness (*honestas*). To suppose that it is, is the great Stoic error. Virtues must have a utilitarian purpose: '*nullam honestatis, omnem utilitatis habuisse rationem, ad quam omnia referenda sunt.*'[2] Action therefore is, and should be, based on a calculation of pains and pleasures resulting from it. It is on this basis that the value of the actions of the classical heroes should be judged. Laws too are set up for the sake of *utilitas*, not *honestas*, and force us into desirable rather than undesirable actions for fear of the harm (*damnum*) which will result from disobedience. Horace should have written, *Oderunt peccare boni utilitatis* (not *virtutis*) *amore*. The pleasure and utility calculated may of course be of a high-minded sort. The contemplative life recommended by Aristotle in the *Ethics* (this is the occasion for a polite reference to Bruni's translation) is a superior form of pleasure and it is absurd to suppose that even Aristotle would have devoted so much effort to it if he had not expected some kind of reward. The sane philosophy of life is not the Stoic struggle against an oppressive multitude of external evils but the Epicurean acceptance of the dissolution of body and soul at death and concentration on the goods of this life. And indeed the whole purpose, not only of law but also of all civil life and the arts, is to maximise the utility and pleasure which are the purpose of life.

The Stoic and Epicurean viewpoints have now been stated. The later part of the book is occupied by an adjudication of the dispute from the lips of Niccolò Niccoli.[3] He begins by chiding both protagonists for their lack of Christian feeling. Panormita has put forward arguments which, as a Christian, he cannot possibly believe. But Bruni has been impious too. 'I grant to antiquity letters, the sciences and, what is greatly to be valued, the knowledge of eloquence. But as for morals, beware Leonardo lest you persuade yourself that the ancients were completely wise and that nothing can be added from our religion to their virtues.'[4] If a

[1] f. xl v. seq.
[2] f. xlvi v.
[3] f. lxvii seq.
[4] f. lxxviii.

choice must be made between the two ancient philosophies, how-ever, it must be said that the Epicurean is closer than the Stoic to Christianity. The veneration of the moral virtues for their own sakes is probably a relic of the history of ancient religion: virtues which had originally been means of serving gods came to be elevated into self-sufficient objects of life. Christianity has its own virtuous way of life but this is not to be regarded as an end in itself but as a means to celestial beatitude, the highest possible kind of pleasure. Therefore Epicurus, though mistaken about the nature of death, was nearer than the Stoics to the Christian truths in his estimation of virtue and pleasure.

How is one to regard the *De Voluptate*? Clearly it is not a serious piece of straightforward philosophy. It contains a large element of satire. But it is not merely a rhetorical exercise or a satirical fable like *Momus*. It stands in the same relation to serious thought as Voltaire's *Dictionnaire Philosophique* or some of Hume's *Essays*; it is criticism through mockery. The object of its mockery is the high-minded, rather pretentious moral philosophy of Bruni. Bruni's published philosophical writings are not men-tioned but he is clearly being portrayed as expressing a view genuinely based either on his *Isagogicon* or on some similar utter-ance and it is something recognisable as his own outlook which is being dealt with. Too little is known about the real-life opinions of Panormita and Niccoli for us to judge whether they are being seriously portrayed. In the book they are made to elaborate two serious or half-serious criticisms of Bruni's standpoint. The first point is that the Stoic choice of virtue as the end and purpose of life, roughly followed by Bruni, is paradoxical and that a moral system which makes moral action a means to some other end is more tenable. The second main point is that a philosophy which sees no end beyond moral activity is incompatible with Christian revelation. These are serious criticisms which accurately char-acterise the difficulties and limitations of the Florentine humanist position. The substance of the criticism made by Valla was in fact similar to that made by Alfonso of Cartagena in his critique of Bruni's methods of translation; Valla however draws the opposite deduction and argues not for a return to scholasticism but for an advance to utilitarianism. The adoption of a pagan philosophy of moral action in this life, even if the moral precepts themselves could be made to seem compatible with Christian teaching, was shown to be in reality no more Christian than a wholehearted hedonism. Moreover, by the assumption of standards related entirely to conduct in this world, it opened the way to utilitarianism and it was arguable that an honest utilitarianism was the logical outcome of their attitude.

The other works of Valla which are interesting in this connection were written in the next phase of his life, when his circumstances had again changed considerably. After further disappointments to his hope of a curial position, he went in 1435 to the court of King Alfonso v of Naples, who had recently come to Italy to enforce his claim to the throne in the face of papal opposition. The bitter struggle was to last another eight years before Eugenius iv finally accepted the inevitability of Alfonso's success. For those eight years Valla lived at the court and under the patronage of a king who was at war with the pope, in league with the enemies of the papacy at the Council of Basle and claiming portions of papal territory. This was the period in which Valla composed the book on the *Donation of Constantine* as a piece of propaganda against papal temporal power in Italy in defence of his master's policy. About the same time he composed two works of serious philosophical interest, *De Libero Arbitrio* and *Dialecticae Disputationes*.

De Libero Arbitrio is a criticism of the treatment of free will by Boethius in Book 5 of the *Consolation of Philosophy* and an attempt to offer an alternative approach. Boethius tackled the problem of reconciling human freedom with divine foreknowledge. His answer was that God operated in the sphere of eternity, so that all events were eternally present to him and his foreknowledge was not analogous with the foreknowledge of men in time, and did not conflict with the exercise of free will by human beings. Valla countered this by making a distinction between foreknowledge and necessity. Apollo, asked to foretell the future through an oracle, might prophesy catastrophe while disclaiming any responsibility for it because the control of events, as opposed to foreknowledge of them, was not his sphere but Jupiter's. The device of having two gods instead of one, said Valla, made it easier to point out the logical distinction between the two functions. The willing of future events rather than foreknowledge of them was the specially divine function and Boethius, in emphasising man's will and God's foreknowledge, was reversing the divine and human roles. The relationship between man and God is a mystery into which we cannot penetrate: Boethius should have taken to heart the words of St Paul (*Romans*, ix, 16): 'Thus it does not depend on man's will or effort, but on God's mercy,' instead of paying so much misplaced attention to the theories of philosophers.[1]

At the beginning of *De Libero Arbitrio* Valla claimed that he had answered the first four books of Boethius's *Consolation of Philosophy* in his *De Voluptate* and would now deal with the fifth and last. *De Voluptate* had in fact been mainly directed against Bruni rather than Boethius, who was seriously considered only towards the end;[2] it had, however, dealt with the fallacy of trying to use pagan philosophy for Christian purposes and in this sense might be regarded as a demolition of the approach associated with Boethius's name. The direction of attention to Boethius marks a new turn in Valla's own writings. He is not now satirising humanist philosophy but attacking scholasticism. It would not be a gross distortion to say that Boethius was the soul and origin of medieval philosophy. Writing in Latin, in the sixth century, he had tackled single-handed the task of adapting ancient philosophy to Christian purposes and handing it down in a form which was to be attractive to later centuries. The direction of scholasticism had very largely grown out of the inspiration provided by his translation of, and commentaries on, the works of Aristotle. The *Consolation of Philosophy* was not the most important of his works from the point of view of technical philosophy but it had been one of the central influential books of the Middle Ages, translated at one end by King Alfred and at the other by Chaucer and consistently admired in between. To claim that it was now answered was

[1] *Laurentii Vallae de Libero Arbitrio*, ed. M. Anfossi (Florence, 1934).
[2] *De Voluptate*, f. lxxx v.

to claim the overthrow of an essential part of the medieval attitude to the relation between philosophy and religion.

The *Dialecticae Disputationes* carried this line of attack much further in a lengthy onslaught on Aristotle himself and on the use of his writings by scholastic philosophers. It begins with a claim for freedom of speech in criticising Aristotelian philosophy: 'Philosophers always used to have freedom to say outright what they thought, not only against the leaders of other schools but against their own, and all the more so if they adhered to no school. How intolerable therefore are the modern Peripatetics who deny to a man of no school the freedom to dissent from Aristotle as if he were *sophos* (wise) rather than *philosophus* (a lover of wisdom) and as if no one had ever disagreed with him before.'[1] Valla then goes on to attempt to demolish a number of central Aristotelian concepts, sometimes in their original setting and sometimes in the form in which they had been used by Christian adaptors. He argues for instance that Aristotle's six transcendental categories are not really different categories but are all reducible to one: *res*.[2] He charges Boethius with a mistaken translation of Aristotle's *ousia* as 'substance' (*substantia*) when it should be 'essence' and points out that it is incorrect to use the same Latin word for *ousia* in all contexts because Aristotle uses it with different meanings.[3] He argues that Aristotle is wrong in making virtue consist in knowledge, when the will should be supreme, and that the Aristotelian conception of virtues as means between extremes is nonsensical because it makes everything depend on which particular moral characteristics the philosopher happens to designate as extremes.[4] He ridicules the Aristotelian distinction between act and potency: it is nonsense to say that a piece of wood is potentially a bow before it has been converted into one by a craftsman.[5] These are only a few simple examples of hundreds of destructive remarks which Valla made as he ploughed

[1] Valla, *Opera* (Basel, 1543), p. 644.
[2] *Dialecticae Disputationes*, Bk. 1, cap. 2.
[3] Bk. 1, caps. 5-6.
[4] Bk. 1, cap. 10.
[5] Bk. 1, cap. 16.

through the concepts of Aristotelian philosophy in a fairly long treatise.

The form of attack in the *Dialecticae Disputationes* was twofold, first, criticism of Aristotelian concepts from a standpoint of common sense, and secondly criticism of the Boethian adaptation of Aristotelian concepts from a standpoint of philology. Valla was using two weapons which he shared with other humanists and which were indeed the hallmarks of the Florentine approach just as much as his own: commonsense in philosophy and linguistic skill in translation. The difference between him and the Florentines was that he was prepared to go all the way in the criticism of scholasticism which these weapons made possible and to show how far-reaching the results might be if they were in radical hands. The implications of a serious scrutiny of such words as *ousia* and *hypostasis*, which were used for central philosophical and theological concepts, could be considerable. So were the implications of a radical reappraisal of Christian philosophy from a Pauline standpoint without the accretions of scholasticism. One fairly trivial example shows how easy it was to come into conflict with accepted doctrine. The first version of *Dialecticae Disputationes*, composed in 1439, contains a passage in which the procession of the Holy Spirit is discussed.[1] Valla argued that the natural interpretation of *'Cum autem venerit Paracletus quem ego mittam vobis a Patre, Spiritus veritatis qui a Patre procedit'* (*John*, xv, 26) was that the Spirit proceeds from God the Father only, that this was the view of the early Fathers, Latin as well as Greek, and that Augustine himself does not imply more than a temporal as opposed to an eternal procession from the Son. When Valla was writing this was a central question of debate between the Catholic and Orthodox theologians at the Council of Florence. The Eastern Church had always disputed the addition to the creed of the *Filioque* clause, stating procession from the Son as well as the Father, and the Western Church, partly because of its implications

[1] Printed by G. Zippel, 'Lorenzo Valla e le origini della storiografia umanistica a Venezia', *Rinascimento*, VII, 1956, p. 99. On Valla's attitude to religion see also G. Radetti, 'La Religione di Lorenzo Valla', *Medioevo e Rinascimento Studi in Onore di Bruno Nardi*, II.

1 A painting of an architectural scene in the ducal palace at Urbino by an unknown artist who seems to have been influenced by the principles set out in Leon Battista Alberti's work *De Re Aedificatoria* (*c.* 1470)

2 The Florentine Baptistry, mistakenly regarded by the early humanists as a Roman building adapted to Christian use. Its Romanesque decoration was an important source of inspiration for Brunelleschi and Donatello

3 Florence Cathedral begun to design of Arnolfo di Cambio in 1294. The dome was added in 1420–36

4 Ospedale degli Innocenti (orphans' home) built for the Florentine silk gild under Brunelleschi's direction in the early 1420s

5 The nave of S. Lorenzo in Florence looking towards the east

6 S. Francesco at Rimini, the Tempio Malatestiano designed by Leon Battista Alberti in the early 1450s. The exterior shows the use Alberti made of Roman forms like the triumphal arch

7 The apses which Brunelleschi added to the drum below the dome of Florence cathedral in 1438–44

8 The relief by Ghiberti (1401–2) for the competition to choose the sculptor for the east door of the Baptistry in Florence. The subject matter, the sacrifice of Isaac, and the actual shape were specified by the rules of the competition

9 A marble figure of Isaiah by Nanno di Banco which was designed to match the marble David of Donatello (plate 10)

10 Donatello's marble David was made originally in 1408–9 for the Porta della Mandorla. It was moved in 1416 to the Palazzo della Signoria, where it became a symbol of patriotic resistance to tyranny

11 Donatello's St George was made for the armourers' gild. The statue was originally adorned with a helmet and the right hand held a lance

12 Donatello's St Louis rests in a tabernacle whose design, based on elaborate classical motifs, may have been inspired by Brunelleschi

14 (*Above*) A relief made by Donatello about 1417 for the tabernacle on Or San Michele which held his St George (plate 11)

13 (*Left*) The bronze David of 1430–2 represents the climax of Donatello's work on the male figure in sculpture

15 The Feast of Herod, Donatello's bronze plaque for the Baptistry font at Sienna

16 Masaccio's Madonna and Child with St Anne, one of the artist's earliest surviving
paintings. The child is strikingly similar to an Etruscan bronze now in the Vatican,
from which it may have been copied

17 (*Right*) Masaccio's fresco of the Trinity was painted in 1425 for S. Maria Novella.
The chapel in the picture is a classical building painted in correct perspective

18 The Tribute Money (*above*): the central fresco of the cycle which Masaccio painted in the Brancacci chapel of the Carmine church in Florence

19 (*Left*) Adam and Eve are driven from the Garden of Eden by the angel in a scene from Masaccio's Brancacci frescoes

20 (*Right*) St Peter distributing the goods of the Christian community, Masaccio

21 Donatello's marble relief of the Ascension of Christ (*c.* 1428–30) now in the Victoria and Albert Museum

22 A bronze relief of the Irascible Son story made by Donatello for the high altar of S. Antonio in Padua (*c.* 1446–50)

23 The Isaac panel from Ghiberti's Porta del Paradiso (*c.* 1435) shows the same sort
of interest in perspective as does Donatello's work of this period

24 The Joseph panel of Ghiberti's Porta del Paradiso

25 The Flood, one of a series of frescoes in the Chiostro Verde in S. Maria Novella, painted by Ucello about 1440. It is a spectacular exercise in various forms of perspective drawing.

for papal authority, equally firmly asserted it. Valla wrote at the court of Alfonso v where criticisms of papal points of view were welcome. His argument was based on commonsense and scholarship but it was not one that he would have put forward lightly at Rome or Florence, and indeed a few years later, when he renewed his efforts to return to the Curia, he cut this passage out of the book. The revision did not save him from a reputation for heresy which was exploited after his return to the Curia by his old enemy Poggio. The enthusiasm with which he had taken up the anticlerical cause for Alfonso makes all the more remarkable his alacrity in renewing his efforts to return to the Curia after the reconciliation between Alfonso and Eugenius in 1442-3. The *Apology*, in which he did his best to excuse his past conduct, was certainly addressed to Eugenius and possibly written as early as 1443, although it was not until the next pontificate that he was received back into the Curia.[1] Valla certainly did not abandon his essential intellectual preferences,[2] but his change of course, from the *Dialecticae Disputationes* and the book on the *Donation of Constantine* to work on the *New Testament* and Thucydides, shows that he was responsive within fairly wide limits to the interests of his employers.

There is something absurd in the spectacle of the irreverent Poggio belabouring the irreverent Valla with charges of heresy, but part of the irony springs from the fact that Poggio was perfectly right. The influences of the Lombard interest in philosophy and the anti-papal climate of Alfonso's court, combined no doubt with his own disposition, had led Valla into realms where the Florentines did not tread and to the most serious confrontation

---

[1] The *Apologia* is printed in *Opera*. On the date see most recently G.Mercati, 'Intorno a Eugenio IV, L.Valla e fra L.Strassoldo', *Rivista di Storia della Chiesa in Italia*, v, 1951. Poggio's first invective came in 1451 and was followed by others and by answers from Valla.

[2] As late as 1457 he denounced Thomist metaphysics from a Roman pulpit in an address preserved as *Laurentii Vallae encomium Sancti Thomae Aquinatis* (ed. J. Vahlen, 'Lorenzo Valla über Thomas von Aquino', *Vierteljahrsschrift für Kultur und Literatur der Renaissance*, 1, 1886). See also H.H.Gray, 'Valla's Encomium of St Thomas Aquinas and the Humanist Conception of Christian Antiquity', *Essays in History and Literature Presented . . . to Stanley Pargellis*, ed. H.Bluhm (Chicago, 1965).

with philosophy in early humanism. Valla had the intellectual equipment of a religious radical of a certain kind: he was genuinely interested in philosophical and religious questions. Of all the fifteenth-century humanists he came closest to the intellectual temper of Erasmus, both in his superb classical scholarship and in his interest in the religious implications of philology. His *In Novum Testamentum Adnotationes* is the predecessor of Erasmus's Greek New Testament. His career in one sense demonstrates the tolerance of the Curial establishment, which allowed his classical scholarship to outweigh his doctrinal errors. His literary production during the years in Alfonso's service, however, showed the explosive potentialities of humanism in a situation where there was a positive external encouragement to religious radicalism. The circumstances and temptations of the Florentine-Curial school at the same period were precisely opposite. They had every reason to remain ambiguous about their philosophical and theological position. As men of letters par excellence they were strongly inclined to ignore the realms of scholastic philosophy and theology rather than to invade them. Since Florence and Rome were not strongholds of university scholasticism they were not driven into a confrontation. Their close involvement with the papal establishment would have made it impolitic to quarrel directly with the ideological basis of that structure. The result was that they could produce no more than a half-hearted moral philosophy, a stunted secularism which glorified some aspects of pagan philosophy but avoided following through its implications. This was a limitation in one direction; it had its advantages in others. It was in a sense more radical to ignore scholasticism than to confront it, and the pusillanimous attitude of the Florentine-Curial school of humanists in this sphere released their energies for more creative endeavours in others.

5
Social and Political Attitudes

The self-confident expression of republican and bourgeois attitudes in Florentine literature reached its height in the 1430s and 1440s. To this period belong Leon Battista Alberti's *Della Famiglia*, probably sketched in 1433-4 and revised and completed in the early 1440s, Matteo Palmieri's *Della Vita Civile*, probably composed about 1435-8, and the later books of Bruni's *History of the Florentine People*, describing the struggle with Giangaleazzo Visconti, composed between 1439 and 1444.[1] These books were much fuller and more elaborate than the brief utterances which foreshadowed them in the works of Bruni at the beginning of the century. In the light of later events, they seem to be expressions of a natural self-confidence which contrasts with the tortured analyses of Machiavelli and Guicciardini at the beginning of the sixteenth century, when the existence of bourgeois society and republican institutions was threatened and the problem of their preservation was uppermost: the menace of the alien monarchies and the revived papacy was a different matter from the challenge of Milan. Bruni, Alberti and Palmieri were writing at a time when the validity of this way of life was accepted more fully than ever before and not yet threatened with extinction, and it was for the first time given a full literary expression. They do not, however, express a common body of opinion. We must approach them separately, noticing their differences as much as their similarities.

[1] For the dates see Alberti, *Opere*, I, pp. 379-80; Palmieri, *Della Vita Civile*, ed. F. Battaglia (Bologna, 1944), p. xii; E. Santini, 'Leonardo Bruni e i suoi "Historiarum Florentini Populi Libri XII"', *Annali della R. Scuola Normale Superiore di Pisa*, XXII, 1910, p. 89.

They give us glimpses of attitudes, sometimes disparate, unco-ordinated and uncompleted, whose only unity is that they arise from the milieu of city humanism. They must be treated not as a body of doctrine but as indications of the way Florentine thought was moving, of striking novelties but also of limitations. The social and political utterances of these writers, to which the smaller works of Poggio must be added, fall roughly into two categories. On the one hand are the literary expressions of social attitudes to be found in the dialogues of Alberti and Poggio, on the other the deliberate political theory and history of Bruni, Palmieri and Poggio. They are entirely different genres and they give us insights of different kinds into the world of humanist thought. This chapter will start with the books written for enter-tainment, the chief of which is the masterpiece of early humanist prose, Alberti's *Della Famiglia*, and end with the works of political edification.

Alberti's relation with Florentine republicanism was ambigu-ous and contradictory. Though he was proud of his Florentine ancestry he showed himself bitterly conscious in many of his writings – it is a repeated theme in the *Della Famiglia* – of the dis-advantages which his family had suffered through the exile im-posed upon them by their fellow-citizens. In spite of his attach-ment to Florence and his enthusiastic admiration of its cultural achievements he never made it his own home: his residence there in the 1430s was entirely the result of the transference of the papal court in which he worked. Although he wrote by far the most powerful literary expression of bourgeois attitudes, he showed no inclination to join in Bruni's pious and sententious exaltation of the political virtues of the Florentines and their constitution. On the contrary he often expressed a contempt for their ordinary political ambitions which makes it easier to understand his eventual preference for life in the courts of princes. The anony-mous *Vita* reports that once, when he was asked to go to the seat of the Florentine government, the Palace of Justice, he first replied that he did not know where it was and then explained that he had forgotten that justice was supposed to reside there.[1] At one

[1] Muratori, xxv, col. 300.

point in the *Tranquillità dell' Animo* the principal speaker, Agnolo Pandolfini, is approached by two members of the *Signoria* with a request that he go to give his advice at the *Palazzo*, following the common Florentine custom of inviting distinguished citizens to speak their minds publicly and formally on serious political issues. He refused, explaining that it would be fruitless because he would have to say not what he believed but what was wanted by those who invited him.[1] *Theogenius* contains an eloquent passage in which the names of good citizens spurned and injured by their fellows is recalled,[2] and the *Della Famiglia* itself a passage in which the plain man's view of politics – a miserable, harassing way of life which is bound to procure you troubles and enemies and in which the only comfort is the expectation of profit and power – is put rather violently by one of the speakers, Giannozzo.[3] Giannozzo's words are reminiscent of the deathbed advice of Giovanni di Bicci de' Medici, no doubt also a hard-bitten man of affairs both financial and political, to his sons, to avoid meddling in politics and never go to the palace unless they are summoned.[4] They are met with a more conventional reply from another speaker, Leonardo, to the effect that public life is the only source of honour and glory: 'fame is born not in private leisure but in public experiences; it is on the public squares that glory is won.'

The *Della Famiglia* is built on this artful contrast between the plain man and the humanist, presenting two different, in part complementary and in part opposed, views of political and social life. The artifice arises no doubt originally from imitation of the rhetorical device of presenting two sides of a question independently before offering a resolution. But Alberti, the one humanist of the period who was clearly a literary artist of the highest power, rises above the limitations of the rhetorical inspiration. He was also, of course, enjoying the influence of Lucian's satirical fables, he was writing in Italian, and he was capable of literary characterisation. As a result the *Della Famiglia* portrays the

[1] Alberti, *Opere*, II, pp. 137-8.
[2] II, pp. 78-9.
[3] I, pp. 179-85.
[4] A.F.Gori, *La Toscana Illustrata*, I (Leghorn, 1755), pp. 189-90.

prejudices of the bourgeois and the literate attitude of the humanist not merely in rhetorical expression but also in lifelike personification, and satirises not only arguments but also types of people.
This is perhaps made most clear on some of the occasions when
Alberti's own character, which plays a minor role in the discussions, intrudes. At one point they are talking about the power
of love. Alberti himself says that its power must be enormous
when one thinks that such serious philosophers as Aristippus,
Metrodorus and Epicurus allowed themselves to be subdued by
it. 'When I think, Leonardo, of the majesty and fame of these
philosophers, and of others whom I omit for the sake of brevity,
when I think of their integrity and religiosity, and then see them
subdued and placed in such cruel positions by love . . .'[1] Alberti is
opposing his own conception of his own skittish character to the
sententious humanism represented in the dialogue by his relation
Leonardo. In this way the *Della Famiglia* gives a rounded and
lifelike picture of typical social attitudes within the scope of
bourgeois society, which Alberti was in a peculiarly favourable
position to observe intimately and, at the same time, characterise
with a certain amount of social and artistic detachment.

The *Della Famiglia* is set in Padua at the time of the death in
exile of Leon Battista's father in 1421. Relatives are present to pay
respects to the dying man. With the exception of a servant the
speakers are all members of the Alberti family. The main speakers
are two men with humanist pretensions – Adovardo, one of the
exiles of 1401, and a younger man, Leonardo – and a successful,
relatively unlettered man of business, Gianozzo. The dialogue is
in a real sense not only about the household in general (*famiglia*
has this wider meaning rather than 'family') but also about the
Alberti family in particular. The family's own history provided
occasions and examples for most of the aspects of social life on
which Alberti wished his characters to speak. It was a family of
spectacularly successful merchants. They had taken a great part in
the political life of the city, but their exile was the most harrowing
demonstration of the misfortunes incident to politics. They were
not only men of affairs but also notable for their pursuit and

[1] Alberti, *Opere*, I, p. 92.

patronage of the humanities. Alberti's composition was inspired in a general way by Xenophon's *Oeconomicus* but, whereas Xenophon's book really is mostly about the household, Alberti's ranges much further afield and at greater length. In the first book the ostensible subject, the upbringing of children, inspires a wide-ranging discussion of affections, virtues and vices. Book 2 is largely concerned with marriage but contains a great deal of political philosophy. Book 3, whose ostensible subject is *masserizia*, good husbandry, also contains a lot of political matter. Book 4, composed several years later in the aftermath of the bitter experience of the *Certame Coronario*, is about friendship. It has some connection with the more philosophical sections of the other books but not very much with the stricter theme of household management.

Book 3, which begins appropriately with the famous defence of the Italian language, is the one in which Giannozzo the plain merchant holds the floor most of the time. The ideas which he puts forward are clearly not the prejudices of any plain man but those of the bourgeois merchant. There is a classic expression of the honest hard-working merchant's feelings of disgust and contempt for the courtly way of life. Those who live in the houses of lords are mostly bad, 'they feed on others' bread, flee from working themselves and from honest effort'. Above all never lend a lord money. 'With a lord your promises are binding, your loans are gifts and your gifts are so much thrown away; he is a happy man who has the acquaintance of lords and did not lose much by it.'[1] On the other hand it is worth noticing that Giannozzo is proud of the fact that many of his relations were knights.[2] This is apparently a snobbish distinction separable from the seignorial world and compatible with city life, as it is also in Bruni's humanistic treatise *De Militia*.[3] Giannozzo presents straightforwardly the business man's advice for success in life. A man has three assets: his mind,[4] his body and time. He emphasises that good

[1] I, p. 252.
[2] I, p. 172.
[3] See below, p. 156.
[4] 'Quello mutamento d'animo col quale noi appetiamo e ci cruciamo tra noi' (Alberti, *Opere*, I, p. 168).

husbandry consists essentially in the conservation and use of these possessions: never waste an hour of time.[1] Leonardo the humanist remarks with a touch of bored amusement to the young listeners, 'be sure you remember these words, not sayings of philosophers but excellent and holy words like oracles of Apollo which you will not find in our books'[2] – while Giannozzo pours out his homespun wisdom. He recalls Gino Capponi telling his sons at the end of his life that all '*signori*' are the natural enemies of Florence ('Every lord, however small he is, who is near to you is your enemy unless he becomes your friend for his own benefit')[3] or the everyday letters of Datini the business man. It may be a deliberate sign of Alberti's declining sympathy with this world that in Book 4, composed after 1440, he introduces another Alberti, Piero, to tell us how well he had managed to get on with princes. He had made friends with Giangaleazzo Visconti by supplying information from his world-wide business correspondence, and with Ladislaus of Naples by coming to his aid at a crucial moment in a hunt.[4] (Giannozzo, true to character, thinks hunting a useless activity and says so.) Giangaleazzo and Ladislaus were of course the classic enemies of Florentine liberty. What Piero was doing was like telling an English patriot that Hitler and Stalin could be perfectly amiable if you handled them properly. This piece of dialogue was written at the time when Alberti was severing his connection with the Florentine world. Henceforth he lived more in the world of princes: the Este, the Malatesta, the popes.[5]

The first three books of the *Della Famiglia*, written in the 1430s, also contain elements of a humanist political philosophy. Alberti in particular allows his characters to develop two themes, first the familiar theme of the place of fortune in human affairs,

[1] 'Ma perdere un ora di tempo' (Alberti, *Opere*, I, p. 177).

[2] Alberti, *Opere*, I, p. 172.

[3] Muratori, XVIII, col. 1150.

[4] Alberti, *Opere*, I, pp. 270-9.

[5] Alberti's disenchantment with the Florentine world between the composition of Books 3 and 4 of the *Della Famiglia*, which can be connected in part with the *Certame Coronario* and his quarrels with his relatives, is indicated also in the anonymous *Vita* (Muratori, XXV, col. 298).

and secondly the goodness and naturalness of human society.

The concept of fortune is used by Alberti, as by other humanists, equally in discussing personal and political life. *Tranquillità dell' Animo* is mostly about the impact of fortune on the individual. *Theogenius*, a dialogue written about 1439-40 comparing the advantages of the externally successful life with those of the life of indigent contemplation, has something to say about the impact of fortune on both men and states. The counterpart to fortune is *virtù*, the armour of the individual or society against external events. The interaction of *fortuna* and *virtù* in the individual is developed at length in the *Tranquillità*. The *Della Famiglia* begins in the prologue with a movement from the idea of fortune as it affects the single family – some of the great families of antiquity had been adversely affected by fortune like the Alberti – to fortune as it affects states. The question posed by Leon Battista is whether the destinies of states are determined more by the external influences of fortune or by their internal *virtù*. The concept of *virtù* presents difficulties for the modern interpreter because it is a concept transferred in a semi-metaphorical manner from the sphere of individual behaviour to that of social behaviour, an example of the microcosm/macrocosm style of thought which came easily to Renaissance minds but is apt to seem to us an unjustifiable personification. It is perhaps impossible to define it more closely than by saying that it refers to the moral health of a society. Alberti apparently gives his definition of the *virtù* of a good state when he says that what seems in the light of history to matter in a state is 'just laws, virtuous princes, strong and constant deeds, love of one's country, faith, diligence and the chaste and praiseworthy observances of the citizens'.[1] Macedonia offered an example of this *virtù* up to the death of Alexander. Then private rather than public interests became uppermost in the actions of the rulers, and Macedonian success came to an end. Similarly the success of the Roman republic was unquenchable as long as the *virtù* of its citizens lasted. But when tyranny and the pursuit of individual advantage gained control, at the expense of the observation of good, established laws, the state began to

[1] Alberti, *Opere*, I, p. 4.

decline. Interior virtue Alberti concludes – it is not clear whether he applies this also to the evils which befell his own family – is more important than the blows of fortune. 'In civil affairs and in the lives of men we give more importance to reason than to fortune, to prudence than to chance.'[1]

The exposition of Stoic social philosophy comes from the lips of Leonardo, the accomplished humanist, towards the end of Book 2. Leonardo is at this point instructing the young Leon Battista in the pursuit of virtue. His argument is that a virtuous life requires constant exertion. This leads him to support the Stoic view of the world as a theatre for human effort against the idea that felicity consists in rest and inactivity. Leonardo repudiates 'the opinion of Epicurus who thinks the highest felicity in God is doing nothing'.[2] On the contrary the world was created for man to use. 'The Stoics said that man is established in the world as investigator and manipulator of things. Chrysippus judged that every thing was made to serve man.' As Protagoras said, man is 'the measure of things'.[3] This is developed into the view that a man should regard the world as a challenge to develop the potentialities that he has in him. He should express himself in 'magnificent and large things'.[4] Ambition is a virtue. Men should aim to rise 'to the highest level of perfection and fame'.[5] The ideal put forward by Leonardo is in fact an exaggeratedly competitive one. He urges Leon Battista to approach life as though it were a Venetian boat-race in which the first, second and third, and perhaps the fourth, places would deserve an honourable comment by the spectators but the rest of the competitors would have been better out of the race. So in life choose your weapons and aim for the highest place. 'So in the competition and conflict for honour and praise in mortal life I think it is best to choose a suitable craft and route for your abilities and make every effort to be the first.'[6] In this mortal race the acquisition of wealth, as long as it is free

[1] I, p. 9.
[2] I, p. 131.
[3] I, p. 132.
[4] I, p. 134.
[5] I, p. 137.
[6] I, pp. 138-9.

from avarice, is itself a laudable not a despicable aim, useful both to the household which acquires it and to the state in whose service it may be used. Like political success, wealth is more a result of the internal capacities of the man than of external fortune; the merchant is paid for his effort (*fatica*) not for his goods.[1] The most admirable professions are those in which the element of fortune, though never absent, is smallest. Alberti is including learned professions and fine arts as ways of earning a living (*guadagnare*), on the same level as commerce.[2]

Thanks to Alberti's precocious literary self-consciousness, the *Della Famiglia* gives us something like an introduction to city social attitudes. No doubt there are things in it, notably the preoccupation with personal ambition, which represent Alberti's own concerns; but the juxtaposition of the natural, and by now very well-established, bourgeois way of life and the humanist analysis of it in classical terms probably reflects accurately common Florentine attitudes in the period after the intellectual revolution of Salutati and Bruni. He brings out very well both the appropriateness of humanist concepts to urban society and the gap between them.

The only other writer who similarly describes contemporary attitudes is Poggio, some of whose Latin writings are the works closest in feeling to the *Della Famiglia*. Of course unlike Alberti he was not a wholehearted literary innovator. Poggio the professional rhetorician is remarkably different from Poggio the composer of dialogues in which he allows his natural talents a freer field. His ostensibly serious political utterances are mere imitations of Bruni and are interesting only as indications of Bruni's influence in his own circle. Among the writings that fall into this category are the following:

(i) His defence of the view that Scipio Africanus was superior to Caesar because he was more virtuous and contributed to the preservation of the Roman republic rather than to its destruction. This view, expressed by Poggio in 1435 in a routine piece of rhetorical composition for a favourite of Eugenius IV, was

[1] I, p. 141.
[2] I, p. 145.

challenged by Guarino who spoke up for Caesar, and then re-stated by Poggio at some length in a *Defensiuncula* addressed appropriately to a republican patrician, the Venetian Francesco Barbaro. It contains the familiar arguments developed many years earlier by Bruni.[1]

(ii) A curious exchange with Filippo Maria Visconti, the tyrant of Milan, in 1438. Poggio's contribution was a long letter putting the Florentine point of view about politics: again the argument popularised by Bruni that Florence was a republic and that the excellence of its culture depended on this political freedom.[2]

(iii) The long letter of consolation which he wrote to Cosimo during his exile in 1433-4, flatteringly comparing him with various unjustly treated Roman heroes.[3]

These are dull, derivative compositions.

In the Latin dialogues, however, he gave a free reign to a genuine interest in social attitudes based, not on philosophy or history, but on the story-teller's feeling for character and situation. Poggio was a good social impressionist. His dialogue *De Nobilitate* contains a brilliant survey of the social postures adopted by the nobility in various parts of Europe, including the earliest objective picture of English social mobility, presumably based on recollections of his years in the service of Cardinal Beaufort.

The English think it ignominious for noblemen to stay in cities; they live in the country cut off by woods and fields; they devote themselves to country pursuits, selling wool and cattle and they think it no shame to make money from agriculture. I have seen a man who has given up trade, bought an expensive estate and left the town to go there with his family turn his sons into noblemen and himself be accepted by the noble class. And many of inferior birth have been ennobled by some outstanding deed in battle for which the prince has rewarded them.[4]

This sort of realistic description however is not the main material

[1] Poggio, *Opera*, p. 357 seq (cf. Walser, *Poggius Florentinus*, p. 164 seq; Baron, *Crisis of the Early Italian Renaissance* (1955), I, pp. 54-5; II, pp. 391-4, 465-8).

[2] Poggio, *Opera*, p. 333; *Epistolae*, VIII, i.

[3] Poggio, *Epistolae*, v, xii.

[4] Poggio, *Opera*, p. 69.

of the dialogues. They are cast in the form of semi-philosophical discussions laced with humour between Poggio's humanist friends. What they do contain is a gallery of humanist attitudes to society.

The most interesting dialogues from this point of view are the *De Avaritia*, completed in 1428, and the *De Nobilitate* and *De Infelicitate Principum*, completed in 1440.[1] *De Avaritia* purports to record an after-dinner conversation in Rome between three papal secretaries, Cencio da Rusticci, Antonio Loschi and Bartolomeo da Montepulciano, and a Dominican official of the curia, Andrew of Constantinople. The discussion arises out of comments on some recent sermons by S.Bernardino in which he has attacked avarice. Loschi agrees to speak in defence of avarice. Andrew takes the other side and Bartolomeo sums up. Neither side is seriously in favour of avarice and there is no pretence that the argument is more than a game. The interest of the dialogue lies in the types of argument which the speakers choose to prove their point. Loschi's main argument is that the pursuit of money is an essential ingredient of urban civilisation which would quickly collapse if it depended on pious recluses.

Go through the whole city, the forum, the streets and churches; if you meet anyone who wants no more than he has, you have found a phoenix. Don't mention to me the boors amongst those hypocrites hanging about the market place who get their living without sweat or labour under the guise of religion, preaching to others the poverty and contempt for property which is their own rich fortune. Our cities will not be maintained by those idle and bewitched men who live in repose, but by men who are devoted to the upkeep of the human race. And if everyone of those neglected to produce more than he needed for his own use we should all, apart from anything else, have to till the soil. If everyone sows only what he needs for his own household, see what confusion will follow. People will be denied the use of the best virtues: mercy, charity, generosity, liberality. . . . All the splendour of cities will be removed, divine worship and its embellishments lost, no churches or arcades built, all the arts will come to an end. . . . What are cities, commonwealths, provinces, kingdoms, but public workshops of avarice?[2]

[1] All in Poggio, *Opera*.
[2] Poggio, *Opera*, pp. 12-3.

This is a blow at Poggio's favourite clowns, the mendicants; it is also a view of city civilisation as a result of moneymaking effort. Andrew's reply is equally characteristic of Poggio. His point, that the pursuit of money for its own sake is a corrupting vice, is backed up chiefly by allusions to the writings of Augustine and Chrysostom whom Poggio had been reading with great approval a few years earlier.

The dialogues on Nobility and on the Unhappiness of Princes are more one-sided. In both cases Niccolò Niccoli is the main speaker and he holds the floor most of the time with his opponents (Lorenzo de' Medici in the former dialogue, Carlo Marsuppini in the other) acting only as conventional foils for his extreme opinions. The two dialogues make essentially the same point, that the eminence conferred on individuals by social and political distinctions is a hollow sham and people are really distinguished only by the personal virtues which they cultivate privately. Niccoli attacks various views of nobility put forward by the other speakers, first Poggio's playful excuse for his collection of Roman sculpture that it confers a certain nobility on its possessor, then Lorenzo's argument that nobility involves personal distinction in action as well as thought. Poggio's survey of the different types of nobility found in various parts of Europe, which includes his picture of the English countryman, is put into Niccoli's mouth here. The conclusions which Niccoli draws from it are firstly that the accepted standard in some places is clearly absurd since it allows nobility to be acquired by inheritance which can confer no genuine personal distinction; and secondly that the geographical variations prove that conventional criteria cannot provide any single universal criterion. In their place he puts up the Stoic view that nobility is derived entirely from personal virtue, it is a 'splendour stemming from virtue which makes those who possess it illustrious from whatever condition of life they come'.[1] He rejects outright the notion that it requires any external glory, and insists that it can equally well be cultivated in obscurity. In the *De Infelicitate Principum* he propounds a similar view that happiness derives from the private exercise of virtue.

[1] P. 79.

This time he is attacking the illusion that popes and kings must be happy because of the power and splendour of their lives. Most of his speeches are devoted to expressing the utmost contempt for their way of life, devoted as it is entirely to self-gratification and useless aggrandisement. 'I condemn our bishops and all other lords and their false names who do everything for ostentation and as little as possible for true glory.' 'They consume their time and money in pleasures, in things deserving no praise, in war which is a plague to men.' 'Italy in our time has had no rest from war because of the lust of certain princes for other peoples' property.'[1] They have done nothing for the revival of letters in modern times and the culture of the ancient world would never have developed if men had not been able to live in freedom from them in the cities of Athens and Rome.[2] The cultivation of virtue is a private matter best pursued in private, avoiding worldly ambition.

In the last two dialogues Poggio was probably not only constructing an imaginary discussion but also faithfully representing the outrageous views of his old friend Niccoli who had died in 1437. Whether Poggio shared these views is of secondary importance. His literary instinct has enabled him to perceive an interesting attitude and to convey it effectively. Niccoli's attitude is remarkable because it is deliberately hostile both to the accepted standards of seignorial society and to the cult of the eminent, active citizen. He speaks in part, of course, as a scholar advocating the secluded life because it nourishes scholarship. But he is also expressing an extreme form of egalitarianism and individualism. In one of the dialogues Cosimo excuses himself by saying he really has too much to do with popes and princes to talk about them like this: Niccolò here is in a different position, 'freer than others in a free city, exposed to nobody's cupidity, always assuming the greatest licence in speech and not caring in what spirit his remarks are taken ...'[3] Niccoli is being regarded as an eccentric, but he is the kind of eccentric who can only exist in a free city. He is also of course an extremely influential eccentric,

[1] PP. 394-6.
[2] P. 408.
[3] P. 397.

the arbiter of classicism whose opinions were highly respected in his own circle, which was the hub of Florentine humanism.

The Stoic political philosophy, which was aired by the speakers in the *Della Famiglia*, was given its fullest expression by one of the less eminent members of the Florentine humanist circle, Matteo Palmieri, in his *Della Vita Civile* written about 1435-8. *Della Vita Civile* is remarkable not only because it is a full-scale treatise but also because it was written in Italian, and by an author who was not a professional literary man or a scholarly recluse but an upper-class Florentine playing an active part in the political life of his city.[1] Palmieri, who was born in 1406, inherited an apothecary's business from his father. His scholarly inclinations led him to seek a classical education in which Traversari and Marsuppini seem to have been among his teachers. In the 1430s he began to appear on the political scene. He was a member of the *balìa* which decreed the return of Cosimo in 1434 and thereafter was a frequent office-holder and sometimes employed as ambassador. Alfonso v, impressed by the oratorical skill which he displayed on an embassy to Naples in 1455, is supposed to have remarked 'think what the physicians (*Medici*) must be like at Florence if the apothecaries are like this'. In view of his later writings which included an extra-ordinary long philosophical poem the *Citta di Vita*, which earned him an accusation of heresy, Palmieri can hardly be regarded as a normal Florentine. His book does however demonstrate the complete acceptance of the humanist political philosophy by someone rooted and active in ordinary Florentine political life.

The *Vita Civile* is a dialogue in which the leading role is played by the same respected Florentine, Agnolo Pandolfini, who a few years later figured similarly as a paragon of wisdom in Alberti's *Tranquillità dell' Animo*. Palmieri's object, as he explains in the prologue, is to describe the best kind of life, that which is lived by a virtuous citizen in a good commonwealth, about which there is much excellent advice contained in Greek and Latin writers which ought to be made known to the Italian reader.[2] Pandolfini

---

[1] The records of Palmieri's life were collected by A.Messeri, 'Matteo Palmieri cittadino di Firenze del secolo XV', *ASI*, ser. 5, XIII, 1894.

[2] *Della Vita Civile*, ed. Battaglia, pp. 3-4.

says that for the good life you need both precepts derived from reading and action to put them into effect. You live well 'when you exercise with virtue the public offices for which you are required'.[1] The first part of the book is a discussion of upbringing and education based largely on Quintilian. Then he gets down to politics. Again the philosophical core of the argument here is entirely second-hand. Most of the concepts used can be found in Cicero's *De Officiis* and no doubt came from there and from one or two of Cicero's other works. Like Cicero, Palmieri analyses the moral life of the citizen through the four cardinal social virtues of prudence, fortitude, temperance and justice; he emphasises the importance of the supremacy of justice in political life; he believes with the stoics in the naturalness of social and political organisation governed by natural laws and in the propriety of man's exploitation of a world made by God for him; he resolves the conflict between the pursuit of virtue and utility by concluding that there is no conflict. Philosophically there is not a shred of originality in the book. Perhaps its doctrines were not necessarily less truly held or helpful because they had been received rather than created; once again one must remember that the political experience of Cicero was easy to relate to Florentine circumstances. Still, it remained a body of thought taken over from an external tradition.

There are moments, however, when one can see Palmieri beginning to bring the ancient wisdom into relation with the live questions of Florentine politics. The question of justice in political behaviour leads him on to the just war and thence to political expansion. The imperialism of republican Rome, he says, was never arrogant, it aimed at a relationship of friendship rather than subjection. Florentine expansion has sometimes and ought always to follow this example.[2] The relationship of Florence with its conquered neighbours, Arezzo, Pisa, Volterra and the like, was an intermittent but burning question in the fifteenth century and the War of Lucca was in the recent past when Palmieri was writing. Another familiar classical theme was the danger of

[1] *Vita Civile*, p. 11.
[2] *Vita Civile*, pp. 107-8.

internal strife within the state leading to tyranny – Macedonia and Rome fell in this way. So in Florence, says Palmieri, civil discord arising from factional interests has always been the greatest danger, and the cause of tyranny when that has occurred.[1] This leads him on to the problem of the just arrangement of political life to avoid discord; offices in the state must be allotted in proportion to virtue as well as to wealth and good family, and efforts must be made to distribute the burdens of taxation equitably.[2] These are echoes of ancient writers, but the questions they touch were the liveliest in Florentine politics at a time when elections were being managed to ensure the safety of the Medicean party and when taxation for war was a cause of repeated popular dissatisfaction in the city. Again when Palmieri is talking about the useful things which a state should provide for its citizens he singles out, with obvious reference to Florence's use of the Porto Pisano and the efforts to preserve the state galley fleets, 'maritime ports or at least navigable rivers . . . (no city was ever truly noble which lacked a nearby port)' and the supply of shipping.[3] His next subject was the question of *condottieri*. Which are preferable, mercenaries 'engaged at a price' or native citizens? Obviously the latter. Palmieri deludes his readers, or himself, when he says that the Florentine conquests of the past were made by citizen armies; but the problem of dealing with expensive, unreliable, indispensable mercenaries was one of the cruxes of city-state policy.

The counterpart to Palmieri, the citizen-scholar, and the source of his opinions was Bruni, the scholar from Arezzo who was accepted by Florence as an intellectual ornament and as an influential man of affairs. Bruni's thoughts, as we have seen, were formed by his unique position: a combination of an active political career, with high scholarship, respected even by people like Filelfo who were hostile to the Florentine school. By the time he wrote his mature works the fortunes of the oligarchy had become a matter of daily concern to him. Palmieri was a disciple taking over Bruni's themes and vulgarising them, not very

[1] *Vita Civile*, pp. 110-13.
[2] *Vita Civile*, pp. 113-17.
[3] *Vita Civile*, pp. 155-6.

imaginatively. Bruni himself never wrote such a systematic treat-ise of political philosophy but he was at the real point of inter-section between classicism and contemporary politics where they came nearest to fusion.

The instinct to reach for classical parallels in his everyday political thinking is shown for instance in a short piece which he wrote in 1431 as an apologia for the conduct of Florentine policy in the disastrous and humiliating War of Lucca.[1] This is not a piece of Latin rhetoric but plain Italian prose; the literary motiva-tion is at its lowest level in Bruni's works. He is a worried Floren-tine trying to make a reasonably honest case for an unattractive policy. He starts by saying that he wants to make it clear at the outset that he was personally opposed to the war: 'before the Florentine people decided on it I did not like the Lucca Enter-prise and I always discouraged it, not because it seemed to me unjust or wicked but because wars lead to such evils and devasta-tions of the country and other very harmful things that when my nature confronts them it withdraws and regards them with horror. But once it had been decided it was my duty and that of every citizen to accept what the city had decreed.' Then he goes on to show that Florence had received intolerable provocations from Lucca: Lucca had helped her enemies Giangaliazzo and Ladislas and then, after accepting Florentine help against Braccio, deserted her ally when Filippo Maria attacked. Eventually so much resent-ment was aroused among the Florentine people that the demand for war became irresistible and the *Signoria*, which had tried to curb popular excitement, had to yield to it. Bruni, probably quite naturally, takes the position of one explaining to an outsider how a republican regime works. His point is that the *Signoria* could not check the wishes of the sovereign people beyond a certain point. Also it was impossible for such a policy of aggression to be adopted, as some critics of Florence had suggested, insidiously and deceptively, because the deliberations of a republic could not be secret. Reflecting on these events Bruni drew a parallel from the history of the Roman republic. 'We know that in the first war

[1] *Difesa di Leonardo Bruni Aretino contro i riprensori del Popolo di Firenze nella impresa di Lucca*, ed. P.Guerra (Lucca, 1864).

between Carthage and Rome the Senate disliked the enterprise and had already replied that it did not want to meddle in the Messana affair but nevertheless the Roman people was determined to make the attack and did so and the Senate had to yield to the will of the people.' In this way the affinity of experience made a natural link between contemporary politics and classical writing about politics.

Much of Bruni's considerable output of writing about politics is pure rhetoric. A good example of this is the speech which he made as Chancellor, on the occasion of delivering the baton to Niccolò da Tolentino as commander of the Florentine army, in 1433.[1] The theme was that a military commander's services to a city were greater than all others. 'The greatest philosopher yields to the greatest captain; Plato is not to be compared with Alexander nor Aristotle with Caesar.' It is very unlikely that this was Bruni's private opinion. When there is a lot of rhetoric like this, and in Bruni's case there is, one is of course led to ask whether he had any real opinions at all. Was it all a matter of writing suitable pièces d'occasion? As far as the results are concerned the answer to this question in a sense does not matter very much. Bruni propagated certain recognisable attitudes to politics which were taken over by other people; when we see the effect of Bruni on Palmieri, or more remotely on Machiavelli, it is clear that his creation of a body of new doctrine is not an illusion however it was done. The answer to the question matters more if one wants to know about the mechanism by which the new attitudes were arrived at and the relation between literature and life. It would be difficult to discover the real political thoughts of, for instance, Filelfo, Valla or Alberti, because they were evidently not much interested in politics for its own sake. In Bruni's case however there is so much painstaking adaptation of classical political thought to the contemporary situation that he was clearly concerned to draw real political inspiration from the classics.

This can be illustrated from three examples. The first is another piece of occasional rhetoric, an oration which he composed in 1426 for the funeral of Nanni Strozzi who had the unusual distinction of being both a member of the great Florentine family and a *condottiere*

[1] *Traversari/Mehus*, II, cols. 17-19.

in the service of the city.[1] Bruni used the occasion for a panegyric first of the city of Florence and then of the dead man. The panegyric of the city is like a version of the *Laudatio* of 1400 brought up to date. It has similar expressions of enthusiasm for the republican constitution, Roman origins, commercial success, defence of liberty in war and cultivation of humane studies. This is all high-flown rhetoric. Its unreality is shown, for instance, when Bruni boasts of the incomparable wealth which Florence was willing to pour out in the war against Milan; 'this very long Milanese war waged with incredible expenditure in which we have spent more than three and a half million florins and yet now at the end of the war men are more ready in payment of taxes than they were at the beginning as if money sprouted every day spontaneously by some divine force.' In the context of the acute political disputes about the distribution of the burden of taxation which were to issue in the *catasto* of 1427 this reads ironically. Nevertheless the ideal, republicanism linked with high culture, is genuine; in 1426, as in 1400, Florence was engaged in a life and death struggle with a Milanese tyrant and the funeral oration shows the continuity of Bruni's vision of the city commonwealth cultivating commerce and the arts under the aegis of its free constitution. The ideal is seen from a different angle in a work composed about ten years later whose form exempts it from the usual limitations of humanist style: a pair of biographies of Dante and Petrarch.[2] These lives, especially Dante's, were of course already the subjects of a well-developed mythology. Bruni set out in conscious reaction against the traditions, particularly against Boccaccio's poetic view of Dante's life, to retell the biographies with an emphasis on other things. Beatrice and Laura were relegated to the background. Petrarch was presented, as he had always appeared to the humanists, primarily as a sort of literary Columbus, the discoverer of Latin antiquity and style. Dante, more remarkably, was reworked into a model of the active civil life, a man who fought for his city and played a part in its politics without diminishing

---

[1] 'Oratio in funere Nanni Strozae Equitis Florentini', S. Baluze, *Miscellanea*, IV (Lucca, 1694).

[2] Bruni, *Schriften*, p. 50 seq.

his studies. So far as the traditions allowed, his life was rewritten on the model of Cicero's. Significantly, Bruni's interest in Dante's political life did not extend to his political writings. *De Monarchia*, which nowadays figures in histories of political thought a chapter or two before Bruni himself, was dismissed as a book 'written in an unpolished fashion and without grace of expression'. Evidently that medieval collection of fable and philosophy meant as little to Bruni as it does to us, which shows how completely he had severed the links with the medieval tradition of political thinking. Bruni's account of Dante is in its own way as bizarre as Dante's view of the Roman Empire but it serves to demonstrate how completely he had taken over the Aristotelian-Ciceronian ideal of the citizen scholar, philosophy and politics illuminating each other in an active this-worldly life.

The third of these smaller political works by Bruni is the one in which the connection between politics and humanism is closest. Probably in 1421 Bruni wrote a small treatise on military service, *De Militia*, which he dedicated to Rinaldo degli Albizzi.[1] The point of the book is to show, mainly by using classical examples, that it is possible to have a military class of citizens who will perform the function of defending the city but will also be genuine citizens playing a proper part in peaceful social life. Bruni was reacting of course against the bitter Florentine experience of expensive and unreliable mercenary troops in much the same way as another chancellor of the city, Machiavelli, was to react a century later. He adduced a variety of evidence from antiquity in support of his idea, drawn mostly from Aristotle's *Politics* and Cicero's *De Officiis* and stretching from Plato's auxiliaries to the heroes of the Roman republic. The crux of his argument, however, was the equivalence between the knightly class of modern times and the equestrian order of Republican Rome. The Roman *equites* were a class of men who fought in the republic's wars but also had a proper civil role in peacetime; there was no reason why the modern knight should not do the same, alternating civil life and military service for the city. The conception was not entirely

---

[1] Edited by C.C.Bayley in *War and Society in Renaissance Florence* (Toronto, 1961). On the date see Baron, *Crisis of the Early Italian Renaissance* (1966), p. 553.

without foundation because there were a few citizens who were in the technical sense knights. In practice Florence, like other cities, fought its wars almost entirely with mercenary troops and was entirely dependent for military expertise on the seignorial world of the *condottieri*, Braccio, Sforza and their like, who lived by selling their services. The insulting words which Hawkwood was supposed to have spoken to a Florentine politician, 'go and make cloth and let me manage the army', made the point.[1] By a curious transposition Bruni was trying to adapt the seignorial institution of knighthood, which had only a marginal connection with city life, to the Roman republican idea of an equestrian order. The idea of a citizen's duty to defend his country and, connected with that, the baseness of pure mercenary service is, however, an important outcome of Bruni's conception of the free republic. It is the beginning of a political ideal which is to have a long history, stretching through Machiavelli and beyond. Its origin is inseparable from the meeting of city state politics and classical history.

Bruni's more theoretical works are the closest approximation to genuine political philosophy which we shall find. The most striking thing about them is the contrast between the boldness of their acceptance of the Aristotelian-Ciceronian tradition, without regard for scholastic political philosophy, and the poverty of original thinking displayed in them. If they are unmistakably the foundation of the tradition which was to lead to Machiavelli's *Prince* it is equally clear that they have little of its original realistic analysis. With all their immaturity and awkwardness, however, Bruni's works reveal clearly enough the vision of an independent secular republic which, in the minds of the humanist circle, had entirely supplanted any other view of politics and which provided a rough but compelling framework for their attitude to society.

An equally novel and more satisfying compartment of humanist literature was the new mode of contemporary history of which Bruni was also the chief practitioner. The word contemporary must be stressed. The first book of Bruni's *History of the Florentine People* had been a revolutionary essay in ancient history. As he

[1] G.Cavalcanti, *Istorie Florentine* (Florence, 1838-9), I, p. 448.

plodded through the long history of the city Bruni came eventually to periods where political events were akin to those of his own experience and eventually to the crises of his own lifetime. In the course of the book therefore the view of history became a view of contemporary politics. It was as novel in a different sphere as the antiquarian research which distinguished the early chapters because it imposed upon contemporary events a view of them as part of a continuous process of city politics, governed by the principles of those politics. This is a different view of events from that of the medieval chronicler, even the city chronicler like Villani. The chronicler's account is episodic, a record of memorabilia rather than a continuous narrative of the fortunes of a political society. Bruni's aims at following the literary precepts laid down by Cicero[1] and illustrated by Livy: his history is strictly related to the time sequence of the years but within this framework it is a flowing narrative, it pays attention both to the dramatic arrangement of events and to political explanations and is broken by elaborate speeches which allow the author to convey the issues of a situation while exploiting the delights of rhetorical composition.

This new history was essentially a classicist's innovation, not an expression of the advanced self-awareness of the ordinary Florentine, remarkable as that might be. This appears quickly enough if one compares Bruni's historical writings with those of his non-classicist contemporaries. The last sections of Bruni's *History* were written in the last years of his life, some forty years after the latest event which he describes, the death of Giangaleazzo Visconti in 1402. By this time there was already a body of Florentine historical writing about the duel with Giangaleazzo which can be used for contrast with Bruni's approach. An old-fashioned, near-contemporary account is contained in the chronicle attributed to a member of the Minerbetti family. Minerbetti's approach to history, as he explains at the beginning of the book is a matter of making 'a record of those things I hear happen in various places and by whom they are done or brought about ... not ... everything I hear about but those which occur at Florence

---

[1] *De Oratore*, II, xv; *Orator*, xx.

or elsewhere which seem to me to deserve to be written down.'[1]
In his account of the years 1400-1402 the duel with Giangaleazzo
does dominate and the death of the tyrant is marked by a digress-
ion on his villainous early life, but quite unconnected events, notably a rising against King Sigismund in Hungary, are interjected
into the primarily Italian history where the author thinks they are
sufficiently memorable. The account of the year 1401 begins with
three chapters on the state of affairs at Bologna; Milan and Florence are competing for the friendship of its new lord Giovanni
Bentivoglio. Then comes a feeler from Rupert the new King of
Germany to Florence, then the Hungarian episode, then a pro-
Milanese conspiracy unearthed at Pistoia in August, an agreement
between Giangaleazzo and the lords of Mantua and Ferrara in
September, then back to the descent of Rupert into Italy in the
autumn. The aim is to construct a chronological sequence of
episodes. There is little attempt to connect them rationally or
artistically in an account of Milanese or Florentine policy. A quite
different approach, which is important in fifteenth-century
Florentine historiography, is exemplified by the memoirs of a
patrician called Buonaccorso Pitti who himself played a prominent
part in Florentine diplomacy at this time. Pitti was twice sent to
Germany in 1401 by the commune to make arrangements with
King Rupert for an attack on Giangaleazzo and also met him at
Venice after his defeat at Brescia in an attempt to persuade him to
carry on the war. He gives invaluable details of the haggling over
payments for Rupert's expedition which throw a flood of light on
the nature of relationships between Italian cities and German
princes. But, apart from a sombre reflection on the poor management of affairs which, in his view, would probably have led to
disaster if Giangaleazzo had not mercifully died, there is no
attempt to put his embassies in historical perspective.[2]
    A third and in some ways more interesting account is con-

---

[1] *Cronica Volgare di Anonimo Fiorentino dall anno 1385 al 1409 già attribuita a Piero di
Giovanni Minerbetti*, ed. E.Bellondi (*RIS*, xxvii, ii), p. 4. The account of 1400-02 is
on pp. 260-73. The fullest modern account of these events is in D.M.Bueno de
Mesquita, *Giangaleazzo Visconti*, chs. 17-21. Cf. above, pp. 45-6.

[2] *Cronica di Buonaccorso Pitti*, ed. A.Bacchi della Lega (Bologna, 1905), pp. 114-34.

tained in the history of these years written by the silk merchant Gregorio Dati. Dati's book has some of the qualities of reported experience but it also has the aim of providing an embracing narrative and is, in addition, an explicit attempt to analyse the Florentine position. Dati has a rare passion for explanation. He explains the willingness of Pisa and Lucca to follow Milan, from envy of Florence's commercial success, based in turn on an infertile geographical situation which had driven her citizens to seek their fortunes in the world as merchants. When he comes to the final crisis of 1402 he explains that the Florentines had calculated that Giangaleazzo's resources were overtaxed and that he could not keep up his current rate of military expenditure for much longer.[1] They were also, he says, comforted by the prediction of a holy hermit in the *contado* of Arezzo that Giangaleazzo would die that year and they had political hopes of an alliance with Pope Boniface IX to oust the Milanese from Bologna. The mixture of highly rational and irrational calculation is a convincing picture of the state of public opinion in Florence in the summer of 1402. If one is looking for a realistic and self-conscious picture of the Florentine commercial mind analysing events one can hardly do better than read these pages.[2]

Bruni's account is very different in style from all the others. Its distinguishing characteristic is its artistry. He devoted the last book of his *History* to this crisis. His narrative is unified, it is not interrupted by diversions to other topics or by abstract consideration of Florence's position; he allows the theme of the duel between a tyranny and a republic to emerge out of the course of events as he recounts them. The early paragraphs describe the scene on the borders of the *contado* in 1400-01 with the menace of Giangaleazzo's threat as his control tightens over the neighbouring cities. Then the new hope offered by the election of Rupert in Germany is presented together with the new evidence of Giangaleazzo's intervention in Bologna. The certainty that war is coming in Tuscany persuades the Florentines to pay for

[1] Borne out by the modern analysis by Bueno de Mesquita (op. cit., pp. 292-7).

[2] L' *'Istoria di Firenze' di Gregorio Dati*, ed. L. Pratesi (Norcia, 1902), pp. 56-76. Cf. the analysis in Baron, *Crisis* (1955), I, pp. 140-60.

Rupert's descent into Italy. Most of the next section is then devoted to the fiasco of Rupert's expedition and the failure to keep him in Italy. At this point, which is in a sense the climax of the story, Bruni ingeniously inserts a debate at Venice in which the envoys of Milan and Florence state the justifications for their cities' policies. The speeches are no doubt largely imaginary, though the terms in which the policies are stated – defence of Italy against the foreign invader on the Milanese side, defence of liberty against the tyrannical aggressor on the Florentine side – are drawn from the authentic language of the propaganda of these years as we know it from the exchange between Loschi and Salutati. The device of the speech enables Bruni to state the issues as he saw them without breaking the narrative. He then moves on to the final struggle at Bologna and the death of Giangaleazzo.[1] In Bruni's hands the historical material has been worked into a narrative which is probably less revealing than any of the other three accounts about the state of mind of Florentines at the time, except for the humanists, but gains, not as source material but as literature, by its artistic view of events.

The latest period which Bruni described as a historian was the decade between 1430 and 1440 which he treated briefly in his book on his own times, *Rerum Suo Tempore Gestarum Commentarius*. His intention in this book was explicitly not to write a full history but to give a general picture but since the difference was mainly a matter of abbreviation, cutting down the detail, it did not make a vital difference to his way of regarding political history.[2] The last episode which he describes is the invasion of Tuscany by the *condottiere* Piccinino in 1440 leading to his defeat at Anghiari. There are several contemporary or near-contemporary accounts of this episode in Italian. The course of events, in the simplest outline, was as follows. Piccinino came into Tuscany from the North early in 1440. He was acting for Florence's enemy Filippo Maria Visconti and the expedition came partly in the hope

---

[1] Leonardo Bruni Aretino, *Historiarum Florentini Populi Libri XII*, ed. E. Santini (*RIS*, xix, iii), Bk. 12, pp. 279-88.

[2] L. Bruni, *Rerum Suo Tempore Gestarum Commentarius*, ed. C. de Pierro (*RIS*, xix, iii, Bologna, 1926). On the purpose see editor's preface, pp. 407-8.

of using support within Florence for Rinaldo degli Albizzi and others who had been exiled by Cosimo. Piccinino's army came into the Mugello and advanced very near to the outskirts of Florence. Then it was diverted south-eastwards and further away from Florence into the Casentino, chiefly because of the attraction of cooperating with a local lord, the Count of Poppi, who was an enemy of Florence. Florence sent a fairly small force into that area which Piccinino was unable to destroy. Finally he attacked it on 29th June when it was entrenched in a favourable hilltop position at Anghiari. Piccinino was repulsed with heavy losses and by this victory Florence recovered control of Tuscany with greatly increased prestige.

One of the contemporary accounts was written by Neri Capponi, a member of the great Florentine family who was himself a hero of these events. At the beginning of 1440 he was Florentine ambassador to Venice and to Francesco Sforza; later in the year he was one of the commissaries representing the republic with the army which won the battle of Anghiari. His account therefore has the great merit of being written with an intimate knowledge of Florentine policy. It is also a fluent and intelligent narrative. Its drawback is that Capponi, like Pitti earlier, describes events for the most part as he had seen them. The events of the earlier part of the year are described from the point of view of the diplomatists in Lombardy. He gives a fascinating account of the difficulty of persuading Venice or Sforza to do anything to help Florence but says comparatively little about Florentine policy at home. The events of the summer are seen from the point of view of the army; there is a full account of the manoeuvres involving the armies of Piccinino and Florence and the towns from Bibbiena to Perugia. Capponi was writing memoirs, valuable because they are by an acute and well-informed observer but still memoirs.[1] The other lengthy account of the period is contained in Giovanni Cavalcanti's *Storie Fiorentine*. Little is known about the author of this work except that he was a member of a Florentine family and wrote it in the debtors' prison 'to give vent to my passions'.[2] It is

[1] *Commentari di Neri di Gino Capponi* (Muratori, xviii), cols. 1191-7.
[2] Cavalcanti, *Istorie Fiorentine*, i, p. 2.

an account of politics seen by a citizen of no eminence who was acute and sceptical and a student of gossip. He is an excellent counterpart to Capponi. He describes events as seen from Florence. Within the framework provided by the movements of Piccinino's army his narrative is a rambling inconsequential affair. Its value is in the amount of intimate detail which it contains, picturesque descriptions of the refugees fleeing into Florence from the Mugello and of the fate of an unfortunate lady mistaken for a spy, rumours of the debates in Piccinino's camp which led him to move into the Casentino rather than try to raise rebellion in Pistoia. Cavalcanti is the spicy reporter giving the ordinary man's picture of events.[1] A third, different in character from both these accounts was written a little later by Domenico Buoninsegni. This is a plain statement of events: the movements of Piccinino's army, the sending of the Florentine army into the Casentino, the battle, the changes of sides and lordship by the towns of the Casentino which followed.[2]

Bruni's version is entirely without picturesque detail but, within the limits imposed by its brevity, it gives a rational account of the progress of a campaign with reasons as well as happenings. The initial appearance of Piccinino to the North of the city led to trouble within because of fear of increased taxation and the influx of refugees. Therefore a committee of ten was appointed to conduct the war. Piccinino's movement into the Casentino was a mistake; he underestimated the plight of Florence and was too much affected by the Count of Poppi's invitation. The defeat of Piccinino at Anghiari is explained by two factors, the lie of the land and the weariness of his army after a march in intense heat. If the victory had been followed up, Bruni thought, Florence could have put a decisive end to the war but the commanders were divided and therefore the full advantage was lost.[3] Bruni grasps the campaign as a whole and at each point weighs the possibilities. His narrative has much less value as a historical source than Cavalcanti's or Capponi's and would probably have had still less

[1] Cavalcanti, II, pp. 62-152.
[2] D.Buoninsegni, *Storie della Citta di Firenze* (Florence, 1637), pp. 71-4.
[3] *Rerum suo tempore gestarum commentarium*, pp. 456-8.

value if had been of equal length. It is remarkable not for the information it gives but for the way it sees contemporary history. Cavalcanti said that Bruni glorified Florentine history excessively by his analogies with Rome: 'the great orator messer Leonardo d'Arezzo who has made common, inferior things magnificent and splendid with his ornate style and eloquence – I say common and inferior not in themselves but with respect to the superb deeds of the Greeks and Romans to which he has equated the deeds of our Florence.'[1] There is also of course an element of stuffiness; Bruni had been one of the Ten who directed the war and he takes the establishment view of events. At the same time there is a large artistic gain. Bruni is giving literary expression to politics conceived as a process of calculated statecraft. Neither the writer of memoirs nor the annalist could do this. It demands a continuous and at the same time deliberately selective narrative. It does not make the practice of politics any more rational but it is a new way of looking at them and for this reason the imitation of classical history involved an intellectual change.

The writer who came nearest to bridging the gap between humanist and vernacular history was Poggio. Late in life Poggio rather surprisingly composed two substantial pieces of contemporary history. The first of these is contained in the second and third books of the *De Varietate Fortunae* which he published in 1448. These books carry on the study of the role of fortune in human affairs from the ancient world into modern times. Book 2 contains a string of examples of the working of fortune on the destiny of rulers from Richard 11 of England to Pope Martin v. Book 3 is entirely devoted to the history of the papacy under Eugenius iv. Having lived through this pontificate at the heart of the Curia Poggio was as well qualified to write about it as Bruni was to write the history of Florence during his chancellorship. Like Bruni his approach was that of the humanist writer of Latin. But there was a difference. Poggio was not devoted to the papacy or to any other political institution in the way that Bruni was devoted to Florence and he was incapable of Bruni's high-

[1] Cavalcanti, ii, p. 215, quoted by C. Varese, *Storia e Politica nella prosa del Quattrocento* (Turin, 1961), p. 106.

minded seriousness. In the *De Varietate Fortunae* he makes one of his speakers, Loschi, defend the study of modern history against the charge of triviality, not on the ground that the deeds of modern times were as grand as those of antiquity, but by pointing out that many of the battles of the ancients would probably have seemed pretty laughable affairs if one had witnessed them before they had been dignified by literary artistry.[1] What Poggio did have was an interest in character and situation. He approached the pontificate of Eugenius IV without reverence for the man or the office but with an interest in the interplay of personalities which caused the train of disasters. 'Some people trace the cause of so many evils to the pope himself as a man eager for wars, others blame his advisers, believing that he was himself in favour of peace but persuaded into war. I saw many virtues in him, either true or as some suppose feigned. But whether it is to be attributed to the vice of the men or of the times, certainly the Roman church did not suffer such ill fortune in any earlier pontificate.'[2] He traced the political history of Eugenius's pontificate mostly in relation to Italy, starting with the pope's attack on the nephews of Martin V, which he attributed to the interested advice of some of the cardinals and which he regarded as the initial cause of the trouble. He paid a great deal of attention to the characters of the main actors in the story, including a long and damning account of Cardinal Vitelleschi who was in charge of papal armies in the papal state.

Poggio's other piece of contemporary history is contained in the *History of Florence* which he composed when he was chancellor after 1453. The *History of Florence* is really a history of the city in Poggio's lifetime; half of it is about the period since 1410 and in some later parts where his memory was active his talents as a contemporary historian are clear. His account of the events of 1440 for instance manages to provide a coherent narrative. He allows his hatred of Vitelleschi to obtrude but he also gives a vivid picture of the anxiety of the Florentines in the face of Piccinino and of their difficulties in deciding whether to press for Sforza to

[1] *De Varietate Fortunae*, pp. 77-8.
[2] *De Varietate Fortunae*, p. 88.

come south or try to handle the threat themselves.[1] Poggio's history is in tone, though not of course in the breadth and thoroughness of its treatment, the nearest in this period to Machiavelli.

The use of classical allusions and models and indeed the acceptance of a version of Stoic political philosophy drawn from Cicero is common to all these writers. The use which they make of the classics varies from straightforward copying, through various forms of assimilation, according to the degree of literary ingenuity which they possessed. The obstacles to the formation of a highly developed political philosophy were at this stage insuperable because of the dominance of a rhetorical tradition which determined that ancient political philosophy should be used for literary purposes. Poggio's defence of the superiority of Scipio Africanus to Julius Caesar, which grew into a defence of the republican against the monarchical polity and in a sense no doubt expressed a real preference for republicanism, originated in a piece of composition undertaken as he explained 'to exercise my skill'.[2] On the other hand Palmieri, an active and serious politician, took over Cicero's political thought en bloc without relating it very much to real political preoccupations. Even in Bruni the degree of asimilation of ancient political thought is much less than it had been in Marsilius of Padua or than it was to be in Machiavelli, both of whom were using it seriously to grapple with real practical and theoretical problems. Even in the realm of history, where there was a considerable amount of vernacular writing, springing directly out of the experience of individual Florentines, the separation between the writings of such men as Dati and Capponi and the highly artificial history of Bruni prevented this period from producing a Guicciardini or a Clarendon. There is therefore a large degree of unreality in all the political writing of this school. It was caused partly by the suddenness and completeness of the acceptance of an ancient mode of political thought and history, partly, perhaps, by the relative simplicity of the problems facing Florentine society, which were much less challenging in a

[1] *Poggii Historia Florentina* (Venice, 1715), pp. 338-47 (Books vii-viii).
[2] 'exercendi ingenii causa' (Poggio, *Opera*, p. 365).

philosophical sense than those faced by Marsilius or Machiavelli.

For masterpieces of humanist political and historical writing we must wait until the days of Machiavelli and Guicciardini when the classical and native worlds are more completely fused. The essential revolution in intellectual concepts, however, is the work of this age, not the age of Machiavelli, and the immaturity of humanist thought should not conceal the immense innovations of classicism. Two connected revolutions have been made. First, the introduction of the idea of the secular city state as the natural political organism, self-sufficient and requiring no metaphysical justification beyond the utility and advantage of its citizens. Second the grasping of politics as a continuous process of the interplay of policies instead of a series of discreet episodes. The second is a change of perspective, akin to that which Bruni had introduced into the historical imagination by his account of the ancient world in terms of cultural change, and also to that simultaneously made by visual artists in their new perception of realistic human beings in a unified space.

6
The Architecture of Humanism

The vision of the ideal city, peopled by virtuous men living the good life, which the early Florentines bequeathed to Machiavelli and through him to the idealists of modern times, was accompanied by an aesthetic vision of a material city of suitable splendour to house the political virtues. The conceptions of the ideal secular state and the ideal secular city, the system of social relationships and the material setting, often connected in modern utopianism, were born at the same time. Bruni's *Laudatio Florentinae Urbis*, whose main purpose is to proclaim the political virtues of the Florentines, includes a panegyric of their city, the splendour of its *palazzo*, its bridges, churches, private houses and suburban villas.[1] Palmieri has a passage on the setting of civil life which embraces the 'magnificence of spacious edifices', the dignity of the magistracies, the solemnity of divine worship and the splendour of living of the private citizens. City walls, 'sacred temples', private dwellings 'by which the dignity of man is appropriately embellished', squares, bridges, ceremonial processions and religious observance, which 'makes the city more magnificent when it is celebrated marvellously and solemnly', should all combine to form a proper stage for the exhibition of the civic virtues.[2]

The first Renaissance treatise on architecture was Alberti's *De*

[1] Klette, *Beiträge*, II, pp. 88-9. Baron, *Crisis of the Early Italian Renaissance* (1955), I, pp. 169-71, has stressed Bruni's related conception of the city as a series of concentric circles.

[2] Palmieri, *Vita Civile*, pp. 164-5.

Re Aedificatoria, probably composed mainly between 1444 and 1450.[1] Although a treatise on architecture in the fullest sense, concerned with the technical planning and construction of individual buildings, this book is dominated by the idea of a city within which the buildings are to perform utilitarian and aesthetic functions related to a social framework. Alberti begins a classification of buildings by saying that he must first enumerate the classes of citizens for whose needs and pleasures they are to be erected. He divides the important inhabitants of a city, in platonic fashion, into three classes distinguished respectively by wisdom, which makes proper arbiters of religion and law, by experience in the execution of business, and by wealth. The main types of buildings are those belonging to the state, to the chief citizens and to the populace. He then proceeds to consider the general layout of a city, its geographical site, its walls, roads and streets, bridges and drains.[2] Coming down to individual buildings he again divides them according to social function, starting with the ruler's palace and then going on the public buildings, temples, schools, hospitals and senatorial palaces before dealing with private houses. 'The state (*res publica*) includes sacred things, through which we worship God and which are supervised by the bishops, and secular things by which the social relations (*societas*) and well-being of men are preserved, which are cared for by senators and judges within the city and by military commanders outside.'[3] He makes it plain that he has in mind something far removed from the unplanned, higgledy-piggledy building of a medieval town. He speaks with disapproval of the medieval Italian custom of filling towns indiscriminately with towers and refers, with a surprise suggesting disapproval, to the vanished piety which had

[1] The dating is investigated by C.Grayson, 'The Composition of L.B.Alberti's "Decem libri de re aedificatoria"', *Münchenes Jahrbuch der Bildenden Kunst*, ser. 3, XI, 1960; Idem, 'Die Entetehung von Alberti's Decem libri De Re Aedificatoria', *Kunstchronik*, XIII, 1960. References below are to the Latin text in L.B.Alberti, *L'Architettura (De Re Aedificatoria)*, ed. G.Orlandi and P. Portoghesi (Milan, 1966). The eighteenth-century translation by J.Leoni, *Ten Books on Architecture*, has been conveniently republished, ed. J.Rykwert, London, 1955.

[2] *De Re Aedificatoria*, IV, i, (I, p. 265 seq.).

[3] *De Re Aedificatoria*, V, vi, (I, p. 357).

given modern Rome, according to him, 2,500 churches, more than half of which were ruined.[1] In a properly planned city the public buildings would be spread about to lend an air of magnificence and the streets and squares arranged for convenience and beauty.[2] Alberti expressed for the first time the vision of geometrically ordered splendour and convenience which has since been the inspiration of urban idealists and often the curse of city-dwellers. Before he died it was given pictorial expression in a famous painting in the ducal palace at Urbino in which a circular temple is set in a spacious square flanked by noble Renaissance palaces. The painter is unknown but the design follows the precepts of Alberti.[3] (Plate 1.)

Before the days of Pope Nicholas's abortive schemes for the reconstruction of Rome in the middle of the century town planning of this wholehearted kind played little or no part in actual building schemes for big cities. Brunelleschi is reported, by his posthumous biographer, to have produced a plan for the rebuilding of the Florentine church of S.Spirito, in the 1430s, in which the axis of the building would have been reversed so that its facade looked towards the Arno and could be approached from a square leading down to the river;[4] but there is no evidence that such a grandiose scheme was seriously considered. Evidently, however, Bruni and Palmieri already regarded a city's buildings, both the existing ones which they admired in Florence and those which they could imagine in an ideal commonwealth, as important adjuncts of its social life, giving expression to its dignity and aspirations.

The humanists' ideal was, at least in a modified form, grasped by their fellow-citizens. The idea of deliberate improvement and embellishment of a city by communal action on a small scale was not new in Italian cities or in communes elsewhere in Europe. But the first half of the fifteenth century witnessed a series of

[1] *De Re Aedificatoria*, VII, v, (II, p. 699).

[2] *De Re Aedificatoria*, VII, i, (II, pp. 529-33).

[3] K.M.Clark, 'Architectural Backgrounds in XVth Century Italian Painting', *The Arts*, I-II, 1946-7.

[4] Antonio Manetti, *Vita di Filippo di Ser Brunellesco*, ed. E.Toesca (Florence, 1927), p. 79.

efforts to embellish the city of Florence which were regarded both by natives and by foreigners as constituting a remarkable communal achievement. Most of these enterprises took the form of church buildings rather than civic buildings in the ordinary sense. They were, none the less, communal efforts planned and financed for the most part by lay citizens, not by the religious corporations. Florentine laymen like others regarded the splendour of the churches which they served as a matter of pride and a suitable field for competition. In 1432 for instance the *Operai* of the church of San Lorenzo obtained permission from Pope Eugenius for the canons of the church to wear a particular kind of tippet. S. Lorenzo was an important church serving a section of the city. Among its supporters were the Medici, who lived only a few yards away, and it is fair to conclude that Cosimo's influence probably had something to do with the new privilege. The permission to wear the tippet put the canons of S.Lorenzo onto the same ceremonial level as the canons of the cathedral. It was therefore taken as an affront by the wool gild, the *Lana*, which was responsible for the cathedral. They made representations to the pope to amend the privilege to ensure that 'an obvious and great difference should be apparent between the two chapters both inside and outside the church' and got the commune to write asking him to withdraw it: 'Although the church of S.Lorenzo is notable and collegiate and has a large flock of parishioners and is very dear to us and our people, nevertheless its dignity is not to be compared with that of the cathedral church.' Cosimo, whose family fortunes were increasingly linked with S.Lorenzo, in a sense got his own back eight years later, in 1440, when the funeral of his brother Lorenzo was celebrated in the same church with unheard-of ecclesiastical honour in the presence of nine cardinals and the pope's standard.[1] This rather trivial incident illustrates the degree of importance attached to the external marks of status in churches and the degree of control exercised by laymen. The building enterprises of fifteenth-century Florence were designed

[1] D.Moreni, *Continuazione delle Memorie Istoriche dell' Ambrosiana Imperial Basilica di S.Lorenzo di Firenze* (by P.N.Cianfogni) (Florence, 1816-17), I, pp. 36, 42; II, pp. 398-403; Gaye, *Carteggio inedito d'artisti*, I, p. 128.

at least as much to glorify the patrons and their city as to promote religion.

The most striking building plans of the first half of the fifteenth century were the following:

(i) The cloth-merchants' gild, the *Calimala*, undertook the addition of sculptured bronze doors to the northern and eastern entrances to the Baptistry between 1403 and 1452.[1]

(ii) The commune in 1406 ordered the ' major gilds to provide sculptures for the niches in Or San Michele within ten years. Or San Michele is a square hall standing in the heart of Florence on a street leading from the cathedral square to the square before the Palazzo della Signoria. In the course of the fourteenth century it had become a shrine, graced within by a tabernacle by Orcagna and supposed to be decorated outside by a series of fourteen statues of saints, set in niches on the walls by the *Parte Guelfa* and 13 of the more important gilds. Most of the niches were still empty but they were filled in the next twenty years.[2]

(iii) The most famous effort was the completion of the cathedral. The cathedral had been rising in fits and starts under the patronage of the commune and the *Lana* since 1294. In the first two decades of the fifteenth century the apses with their chapels at the east end and the drum above the central crossing were completed. They then proceeded in the next three decades to crown the building with a great cupola and a lantern.[3]

(iv) In 1421 the silk gild began the construction of a foundling hospital, the Ospedale degli Innocenti, which was to continue through the greater part of the century but made rapid progress in the early years.[4]

(v) About 1420 the *Parte Guelfa* began to rebuild its palace.[5]

[1] W. and E. Paatz, *Die Kirchen von Florenz* (Frankfurt, 1940-54), II, 197-9.

[2] Paatz, IV, 491-5.

[3] Paatz, III, pp. 332-3; H. Saalman, 'Santa Maria del Fiore: 1294-1418', *Art Bulletin*, XLVI, 1964.

[4] C. von Fabriczy, *Filippo Brunelleschi sein Leben und seine Werke* (Stuttgart, 1892), pp. 245-59; G. Morozzi, 'Ricerche sull'aspetto originale dello spedale degli Innocenti di Firenze', *Commentari*, XV, 1964.

[5] Fabriczy, *Brunelleschi*, 291-8; M. Salmi, 'Il Palazzo della Parte Guelfa di Firenze e Filippo Brunelleschi', *Rinascimento*, II, 1951.

(vi) The rebuilding of S.Lorenzo began in 1418 apparently with a plan by the chapter and the parishioners to put up a large new church to rival the great mendicant churches of S.Croce and S. Maria Novella which had been built in the fourteenth century. In the course of the 1420s the wealthiest of the parishioners, the Medici, took the lead. They completed the Old Sacristy out of their own resources by 1429 and combined with seven other families to start the rebuilding of the east end. Then the work lapsed for lack of money until it was resumed in 1442 when Cosimo took over the major part of financial responsibility.[1]

(vii) At S.Croce, the Franciscan church and convent, a reconstruction of the second cloistered courtyard which included the building of the Pazzi chapel was begun in the 1420s.[2]

(viii) The rebuilding of the church of the Camaldolese convent of S.Maria degli Angeli was begun in 1434 with money left by Pippo Scolari and entrusted to the *Calimala*. The money ran out a few years later.[3]

(ix) The church of S.Spirito, the Augustinian convent on the south side of the Arno, was rebuilt through the enthusiasm of its parishioners who began work on the foundations about 1435-6. In 1439 they persuaded the commune to allot them the proceeds of a salt tax. Most of the work was done in the 1440s and after.[4]

(x) In 1435 Cosimo de' Medici persuaded Pope Eugenius to replace the Silvestrine monks occupying the convent of S.Marco with Observant Dominican friars. Cosimo then in 1437-42 paid for a complete rebuilding of the convent including a library to house a fine manuscript collection. This was probably his largest effort of patronage.[5]

These building efforts were the cause of considerable pride and admiration. The commune pointed out proudly to Pope Eugenius

[1] Paatz, II, pp. 465-6.
[2] Paatz, I, pp. 536-42; H.Saalman, 'Michelozzo Studies', *Burlington Magazine*, XLVIII, 1966.
[3] Paatz, III, 107.
[4] Paatz, V, 118-19.
[5] Paatz, III, 9-10; Morçay, *St Antonin*, pp. 65-77.

the 'expenditure and care devoted by our people to that magnificent construction [the cathedral] which was not halted or neglected even amidst the din of wars.'[1] Visitors concurred. When Ciriaco d'Ancona visited the city in the early 1430s his description of it started by expressing his wonder at the walls, the dome of the cathedral, the bronze doors of the Baptistry, the old Palazzo and the bridges.[2] By the middle of the century there was much more to wonder at. These architectural enterprises are the background to the extraordinary blossoming of the visual arts of architecture, painting and sculpture which took place in Florence in the same period. They are important for painting and sculpture for two reasons: firstly because the architecture included a great deal of sculptural decoration which provided the opportunity for Donatello's innovations and secondly because they gave employment to the presiding genius of the visual arts, Filippo Brunelleschi, who, if he had not been so constantly entrusted with the planning of new buildings, would probably not have made the innovations in style and technique which profoundly affected the other arts as well. In the first place, however, the extensive patronage of building made possible the development of a new style of architecture inspired by the humanists. The humanists and their disciples were acutely conscious of the difference between the gothic architecture which had become normal in fourteenth-century Italy and the style of classical architecture which they could see in the remains of Roman buildings. The main impulse to the creation of a new style was given by the desire to imitate and recreate the glories of the classical past. Like the new fashion in political thought it was derived from the literary enthusiasm for the classics transferred into a non-literary sphere. Classical models were inevitably transmuted, in architecture much more than in political thought, by association with modern needs; architects studied temples and even called their buildings temples but they were in fact building churches. Nevertheless the influence of classical imitation was extremely strong.

We do not know how much of this influence came from

[1] Gaye, *Carteggio Inedito*, I, 129.
[2] G.Colucci, *Delle Antichità Picene* (Fermo, 1742), xv, p. xci.

classical writings about architecture. Vitruvius's *De Architectura*, written at the end of the first century BC was the obvious source of information about classical building. It had been known in the Middle Ages, it was used by Boccaccio in fourteenth-century Florence and it was an important source and model for Alberti's treatise. A manuscript of it was among those copied by Poggio in his expeditions from Constance.[1] Perhaps the best evidence for the use of his work in Florentine artistic circles is provided by the extensive plagiarism in Lorenzo Ghiberti's *Commentarii*, but Ghiberti was writing towards the middle of the century. The best direct evidence of early humanist interest in architecture is a passage in Guarino's denunciation of Niccolò Niccoli written in 1413:

Who could refrain from bursting into laughter when this man to demonstrate his understanding of the laws of architecture, stretching out his arms, points out ancient buildings, surveys the walls, diligently explains the ruins and half-fallen vaults of ruined towns, how many steps there were in ruined theatres, how many columns on the floors lie prostrate or stand upright, how many feet wide the foundation is, how high the tops of the obelisks rise.[2]

This sounds like a reader of Vitruvius correlating his teaching with existing remains in and around Florence.

The indirect influence of classical humanism was certainly immense, not only in inspiring a general veneration for antique forms but also, as in the case of political thought, investing the peculiar circumstances of Florence with a confused classical aura. The existence of Roman remains was one piece of evidence which the Florentines adduced to support their theory of the Roman origin of the city. In the *Laudatio* Bruni spoke of the 'traces of antiquity' to be seen everywhere in the city. In his invective against Loschi, Salutati listed a number of supposed Roman remains: a capitol, a forum, an amphitheatre, a 'place called the

---

[1] E.Panofsky, *Renaissance and Renaissances* (Stockholm, 1960), I, p. 178.

[2] *Epistolario di Guarino*, I, pp. 39-40. On the whole subject see E.H.Gombrich, 'From the Revival of Letters to the Reform of the arts', *Essays in the History of Art presented to Rudolf Wittkower*, ed. D.Fraser, H.Hibbard and M.J.Lewine (London, 1967).

Baths', a former temple of Mars, the remains of an arch and an aqueduct, and so on.[1] In sober truth Florence was not very rich in Roman remains. It did, however, contain several admirable buildings constructed during the twelfth century, before the northern-European gothic had invaded Italy, in a romanesque style in which many motifs of classical architecture, including classical capitals and round arches, were imitated. One of these buildings, the Baptistry (Plate 2) which stands opposite the west door of the cathedral in the centre of the city and to which the new bronze doors were being added at this period, was singled out for special approbation as a monument of classical architecture converted to Christian use illustrating the Roman origins of the city. In the *Paradiso degli Alberti*, Luigi Marsigli was reported as saying that it was originally a temple of Mars, later dedicated by the Christians to St John the Baptist, and as praising its classical architecture.

One sees this temple of singular beauty and in the most ancient form of building according to the Roman manner, which, properly regarded, will be judged by everyone not only in Italy but in the whole of Christendom to be a most notable and singular work. Look at the columns in the interior which are all uniform with architraves of finest marble bearing with the greatest art and ingenuity the great weight of the vault which can be seen from below making the pavement more spacious and graceful. Look at the pilasters with the walls supporting the vault above with the galleries splendidly made between one vault and the other. Look properly within and without and you will judge it an architecture useful, delightful, permanent, resolved and perfect for every glorious and happy century.[2]

The author of this historically misguided passage, Giovanni Gherardi da Prato, was not only a literary man but also played a part in the most prominent architectural enterprise of the time in Florence, the construction of the cathedral dome, about the time

---

[1] Salutati, *Invectiva*, pp. 26-8. Bruni has a shorter list at the beginning of his *History of the Florentine People*: an aqueduct, a theatre and the temple of Mars converted into the Baptistry (p. 6).

[2] *Paradiso degli Alberti*, III, 232-3.

when this was written.[1] The features which he described are among those which inspired Brunelleschi.

The realisation of the humanist ideal in architecture required something more than the theoretical desire to create buildings in a classical style. The architecture of humanism, unlike its written works, was produced by a marriage with technical and aesthetic skills which probably owed little to the humanist tradition. These skills were partly the product of the long Florentine experience of building the cathedral and the other great churches of the fourteenth century, partly the product of the mathematical and mechanical inventiveness of the founder of Renaissance architecture. The creator of the new style was Filippo Brunelleschi who was born in 1377.[2] He was trained as a goldsmith and several notable examples of sculpture from his hand survive: prophets for the silver altar in Pistoia cathedral, an entry in the competition to choose the sculptor for the bronze doors of the Baptistry in 1401, the wooden crucifix in the Gondi chapel in S.Maria Novella, and the polychrome majolica reliefs for his own Pazzi chapel. It was common for artists to practise as architects. Brunelleschi and Ghiberti were consulted about work on the cathedral as early as 1404. But little is known of his early work. For many of his contemporaries Brunelleschi was chiefly famous not for his stylistic innovations but for his technical achievement in building the stupendous dome which crowns the cathedral. This work occupied him intermittently from 1417 to 1434. In the second decade of the fifteenth century the builders completed the octagonal drum above the central crossing of the church and were faced with the daunting task of making the dome itself (Plate 3). This was a technical rather than an aesthetic problem. The general shape of the dome was probably determined by earlier plans and by the shape of the building below but they had no experience of

[1] H.Saalman, 'Giovanni Gherardo da Prato's designs concerning the Cupola of Sta Maria del Fiore in Florence', *Journal of the Society of Architectural Historians*, XVIII, 1959.
[2] The materials for his biography are in C. von Fabriczy, *Filippo Brunelleschi*; Idem, 'Brunelleschiana', *Jahrbuch der Königlich-preussischen Kunstsammlungen*, XXVIII, Beiheft, 1907.

building a dome on this scale.[1] Brunelleschi was first consulted in 1417. In 1418 a competition was held and he submitted a model. The relationship between his entry in the competition and scheme finally adopted is not clear but in 1420 a final model was made jointly by him and Ghiberti and the two of them with another man were appointed *provveditori* for the building of the real thing.[2] The building of the dome was regarded as such an achievement that it quickly gave rise to legends about Brunelleschi's genius and his rivalry with Ghiberti from which it is difficult to disentangle his real contribution. It is clear, however, that his services included innovations in the methods of construction and the form of the brickwork and the invention of new kinds of scaffolding and machines for raising the materials.[3]

The story of the building of the dome underlines an aspect of Brunelleschi's equipment. He was a daring technical innovator with a knowledge of mathematics and mechanics. His daring was sometimes ahead of his capacities. In 1421 the Signoria, describing him as '*vir perspicassimi intellectus et industriae et inventionis admirabilis*', granted him a patent for a machine for pulling cargoes along the river Arno.[4] It is not known that anything came of this. In 1430, during the war with Lucca, Brunelleschi, who also had experience of building fortifications, persuaded his fellow citizens to support an ambitious scheme to divert the river Serchio to flood the enemy camp. In fact it seems to have flooded the Florentines.[5] His ingenuity bore fruit, however, not only in the solution of engineering problems of the cathedral dome but also

[1] The connection of the dome as it was built with earlier plans and its relation to medieval systems of proportion is shown by a sketch made in the 1420s during the course of the building, recently examined by H.Saalman, 'Giovanni Gherardo da Prato's Designs concerning the Cupola of Sta Maria del Fiore in Florence', and W. Braunfels, 'Drei Bemerkungen zur Geschichte und Konstruktion der Florentiner Domkuppel', *Mitteilungen des kunsthistorischen Institutes in Florenz*, XI, 1965.

[2] This stage is examined by P.Sanpaolesi, 'Il concorso del 1418-20 per la Cupola di S.Maria del Fiore', *Rivista d'Arte*, xv, 1936.

[3] Drawings of some of them have survived: G.Scaglia, 'Drawings of Brunelleschi's Mechanical Invention for the construction of the Cupola', *Marsyas*, x, 1961.

[4] G.Gaye, *Carteggio inedito d'Artisti*, I, pp. 547-8.

[5] Gaye, pp. 125-7; *Commentari di Neri di Gino Capponi* (Muratori, XVIII), pp. 1169-70.

in the invention of a method of perspective drawing which must have required some knowledge of geometry. His posthumous biographer described Brunelleschi as *'arismeticho et geometra'* and tells us that his intellect was admired by the physician and astronomer Paolo Toscanelli.[1] There is no direct evidence of his mathematical studies but the fact that he was born into the literate bourgeoisie of Florence – his father was a successful notary – makes it likely that he was decently educated and knew some mathematics.[2] Brunelleschi's career would have been impossible except in a social framework which allowed a man to be both educated and a practising craftsman.

Brunelleschi's biographer, Antonio Manetti, writing half a century later, described two panels which had been painted by him with an accuracy which created an illusion of exact representation of architectural scenes, both of well-known buildings in Florence.[3] One was a painting of the Palazzo della Signoria as seen from a position at the corner of the piazza so that one corner of the palazzo would be nearest to the observer and two faces would be seen in dramatically receding perspective. This panel was cut off at the roof of the building so that it could be actually held up at the correct distance from an observer to cover precisely his vision of the real palazzo and to be completed by the real sky above it. The second was more ingenious. It was a painting of the Baptistry made from a point just inside the door of the cathedral, facing it across the square. The part of the picture which represented the sky was burnished and, 'he had a hole in the panel on which there was this painting situated in the part of the Baptistry where the eye struck, directly opposite any one who looked from that place inside the central door of the cathedral where he would have been placed if he had portrayed it.' According to Manetti the observer was then supposed to hold up the back of the painted panel to his eye, looking through the hole, and to hold a mirror at arm's length in which he would see the painting reflected, por-

[1] Manetti, *Vita*, p. 23.

[2] P. Sanpaolesi, 'Ipotesi sulle conoscenze matematiche statiche e meccaniche del Brunelleschi', *Belle Arti*, 1951.

[3] Manetti, *Vita*, p. 10 seq.

traying the Baptistry exactly as he would see it in nature from the same spot.

The panels are lost but Manetti's description of the second one suggests that it was made by careful mathematical calculation. The arm's length, the distance from the panel to the mirror, was the *braccio*, a common Florentine unit of measurement. The panel itself was half a *braccio* square. The distance from Brunelleschi's viewpoint in the doorway to the nearest part of the Baptistry, the width of the portion of the piazza which he would have had to take in to frame the frontal view of the Baptistry, and height of the Baptistry itself (excluding the lantern) are all about 60 *braccia*. So presumably he had chosen a subject for his panel which could conveniently be reduced to a uniform scale within a square. The device of the hole in the panel shows that he had grasped the importance of the observer's viewpoint in relation to the construction of a realistic scene in the picture. It seems likely that he had made a plan of the square and an elevation of the Baptistry to scale (his biographer tells us elsewhere that he made scale drawings of ancient buildings at Rome) in order to construct an accurate section through a visual pyramid.[1] It is more difficult to gauge precisely what knowledge of mathematics and optics lay behind Brunelleschi's epoch-making realisation that it is possible to make a convincing representation of space on a flat plane by the measured convergence of all the objects in the scene on a single vanishing point. It is certain, however, that his mathematical and technical skill had made possible an artistic and psychological revolution of the first order.

The precise role of mathematics in Brunelleschi's architecture has not been and perhaps never can be identified. Apart from one rather unhelpful remark by his biographer (to the effect that he made a ground-plan of S. Spirito on the basis of which he explained to his clients how it would look when built, and then constructed a wooden model for them)[2] we have no evidence

[1] There are valuable accounts of the development of perspective in E. Panofsky, 'Die Perspektive als symbolische Form', *Vorträge der Bibliothek Warburg*, 1924-5; J. White, *The Birth and Rebirth of Pictorial Space* (London, 1957), ch. 8; R. Krautheimer, *Lorenzo Ghiberti*, ch. 16.

[2] Manetti, *Vita*, p. 78.

about his methods of design. Hypotheses about them can be deduced from the measurements of his buildings as they stand now. Some students of these measurements have thought that they suggest the use of a priori systems of proportion such as Alberti recommended later in his book on architecture.[1] On the face of it this seems likely. No serious reader of Vitruvius could be ignorant of the notion that there are ideal proportions to which an architect should conform. Brunelleschi could have learnt of suitable proportions for rooms, columns and entablatures from Vitruvius. If his circle of friends included Toscanelli he might have learnt about the Pythagorean harmonies which were referred to in Alberti's later book. It is difficult to prove the existence of these influences. It has been suggested that the ground plan of the Pazzi chapel and the relations between the heights of various internal members of S.Spirito reveal the use of the 'golden section'.[2] But the golden section is a simple geometrical relationship which could easily be produced casually in a plan composed of squares and circles and the predominance of these geometrical shapes in Brunelleschi's architecture is perhaps more important than any abstract preference for particular numerical proportions. It is almost as difficult to point to the role played by perspective drawing in his designs. It seems likely that he originally developed perspective for architectural purposes. It gave him the power not only to draw existing buildings realistically but also to predict the appearance of planned buildings precisely. This may have contributed to the sense of harmonious, unified planning conveyed by some of his buildings, notably the complicated interior of S. Spirito.[3] Similarly, his engineering skill presumably gave him a surer command over the shape of his buildings than his pre-

[1] On systems of proportion in Alberti and after see R. Wittkower, *Architectural Principles in the Age of Humanism* (London, 1962), part iv.

[2] D.Nyberg, 'Brunelleschi's Use of Proportion in the Pazzi Chapel', *Marsyas*, VII, 1957 (but cf. G.Laschi, P.Roselli and P.A.Rossi, 'Indagini sulla cappella dei Pazzi', *Commentari*, XIII, 1962, pp. 34-5). R.Zeitler, 'Über den Innenraum von Santo Spirito zu Florenz', *Acta Universitatis Upsalensis*, 1959.

[3] Cf. the remarks about the nave of S.Lorenzo by R.Wittkower, 'Brunelleschi and "Proportion in Perspective"', *Journal of the Warburg and Courtauld Institutes*, XVI, 1953.

decessors had had. This technical equipment must have been important for an innovator who was faced with the task of converting a new set of architectural shapes into real buildings of brick and stone. The technical innovations both in perspective and in mechanics probably owed a great deal to the medieval knowledge of optics and mathematics and little to humanism – though again the interest in geometry with which Niccoli was scornfully credited by Guarino in 1413 raises the possibility that his combination of humanist and aesthetic interests embraced this field too and that perhaps he helped to inspire Brunelleschi. In any case technique was put to work in the construction of buildings whose style was intended to be a fulfilment of a humanist ideal.

The passage about the Baptistry in the *Paradiso degli Alberti* indicates that in the 1420s Florentine humanists could not distinguish between genuine Roman remains and the relatively recent creations of the twelfth-century Romanesque. The confusion was similar to their failure to distinguish between Roman script and the hands of early medieval manuscripts[1] and it had a similar result. In the early classical buildings of Brunelleschi the imitation of classical models seems to have had less influence than the imitation of the three chief Florentine Romanesque monuments, the Baptistry itself (Plate 2) and the churches of SS. Apostoli (Plate 4) and S.Miniato. The historical confusion resulting from the telescoping of the evolution from ancient Rome to modern Florence therefore had important aesthetic consequences. The first unequivocal example of the new classical style was the loggia which Brunelleschi built under the patronage of the Silk gild for the orphanage, the Ospedale degli Innocenti, in 1419-24 (Plate 5). The loggia consists of an arcade of round arches resting on corinthian capitals. Each column is joined to the main wall of the building with similar round arches springing from consoles and the space between the arcade and the wall is covered by a series of cupolas. The use of round arches, corinthian capitals and an architrave makes this, in a sense, a classical building, but where the sources of the style can plausibly be identified it generally appears that they are to be found in Romanesque. The general

[1] See above, p. 21.

shape of the structure – round, profiled arches, capitals, round columns, a series of cupolas – strongly recalls the arcade and side aisle on either side of the nave of the church of SS. Apostoli. The use of an architrave to enclose the arcade, running along the top and turned down at the side, is a device found in the Baptistry and S. Miniato, not in classical architecture, and the pilaster with a corinthian capital, to the side of the arcade, may also come from the Baptistry. The closest model for the capitals seems to be found in Fiesole cathedral.[1] The proportioning of the slender forms to produce the exquisite lightness of the arcade is Brunelleschi's work; the inspiration for the forms themselves is a mixture of the desire to be classical and the belief that this could be done by imitating the older churches of Tuscany.

In 1429, with the help of Giovanni di Bicci's money, Brunelleschi had largely completed a substantial new building, the Old Sacristy at San Lorenzo, which is a radical departure in ecclesiastical architecture (Plate 6). Its main room is a cube surmounted by a pendentive dome, whose lower curve rounds off the upper corners of the cube. This form is repeated on a smaller scale in the altar room which opens out of one of the main walls. The use of a pendentive dome is a departure from pointed gothic vaulting, a return to classical roundness. But whether it was developed out of romanesque domes such as those of the baptistries in Florence, Pistoia or Pisa, or directly inspired by classical or byzantine models in Venice, Ravenna or Rome, is uncertain. In reconstructing Brunelleschi's intentions in the Old Sacristy one must take account of the tradition that he objected to the bronze doors which were later added by Donatello on either side of the opening into the chancel and probably also to the heavy porticoes built around them.[2] In the remaining decoration the chief features are

[1] H. Folnesics, *Brunelleschi* (Vienna, 1915), pp. 13-23; H. Saalman, 'Filippo Brunelleschi: Capital Studies', *Art Bulletin*, XL, 1958, p. 115. The most useful analyses of Brunelleschi's buildings are still those in Folnesics, op. cit., and in C. von Stegmann and H. von Geymüller, *Die Architektur der Renaissance in Toscana*, I (Munich, 1885). Modern studies include P. Sanpaolesi, *Brunelleschi* (Milan, 1962) and E. Luporini, *Brunelleschi* (Milan, 1964).

[2] The evidence is discussed by H. W. Janson, *The Sculpture of Donatello* (Princeton, 1957), II, pp. 136-40.

the roundels of low relief sculpture in the upper part of the building (also done by Donatello but probably with Brunelleschi's concurrence), fluted pilasters with corinthian capitals at the corners of the lower part of the building, an entablature running round the walls to divide the lower half of the cube from the dome, and an arched entablature framing the entrance from the main room into the chancel. The entablatures are more elaborate than anything to be found on the Innocenti loggia. The horizontal one has a prototype in the Baptistry. The arched entablature may owe more to observation of genuine Roman relics.

About the time when Brunelleschi was completing the construction of the Old Sacristy in 1429 the opportunity was offered to him of designing another building with a similar plan. The Pazzi chapel also consists of a large rectangular room surmounted by a cupola with a smaller rectangular space for the altar opening off it (Plate 7). We may suppose that Brunelleschi had learnt some lessons in the Old Sacristy for the second attempt produced in general a more satisfying building. The dome, the main arch into the altar space, the pilasters and the entablature are similar. The shape of the building was changed by adding a barrel-vaulted space on either side of the main square under the cupola. In addition to this crucial change in the dimensions of the main room there are significant differences in decoration. The roundels contain coloured reliefs by Brunelleschi himself instead of Donatello's dark stucco. The barrel vaults are decorated with flat coffering. The entablature above the pilasters is less obtrusive. The pilasters themselves are more numerous and shorter, rising from a low step instead of from the floor. In comparison with the Old Sacristy, the effect of the changes was to produce a lighter, more elegant building, more reminiscent in spirit of the Innocenti loggia.

The Old Sacristy had been begun as part of a more ambitious plan to rebuild the whole of the church of S. Lorenzo. For financial reasons this made slow progress. The rebuilding of the east end, adjacent to the sacristy, was carried some way in the 1420s but this was followed by a long gap before work was resumed in 1442 and the building of the nave can have made little progress before Brunelleschi died in 1446. In spite of these interruptions

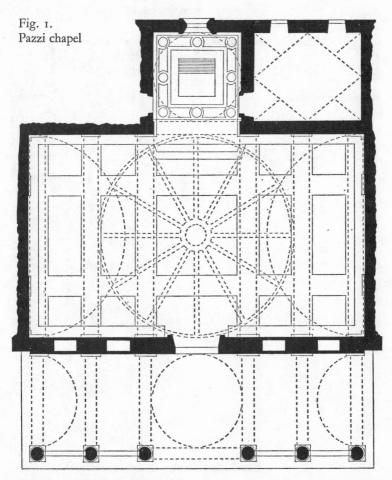

Fig. 1.
Pazzi chapel

the probability is that S. Lorenzo, in its general plan if not in some of its details, represents Brunelleschi's first attempt to apply his new architecture to a whole church (Plate 8). The pointed arches and rib vaulting of gothic have been replaced by a design inspired by SS. Apostoli or some other romanesque basilica. There are two arcades of corinthian columns supporting round arches with entablatures similar to that used in the sacristy. Between the capitals and the arches Brunelleschi has introduced square cushions to give

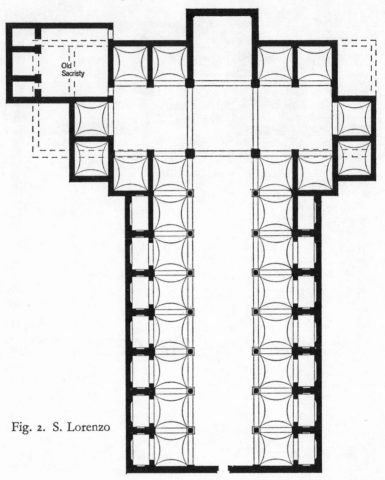

Fig. 2. S. Lorenzo

extra height: a new device which was to be copied by later Renaissance architects. Above the arcade is a clerestory with tall, round topped windows and a flat, coffered roof. The aisles are rows of cupolas between the arcades and the outer walls, like those in the Innocenti loggia. Each column is matched by a pilaster on the wall and between the pilasters are round arches opening into shallow side chapels.

By 1430 a new style of architecture had not only been imagined but created. The rapid influence of Brunelleschi's ideas is shown by the enthusiastic imitation of his new style in the sculpture and painting of his contemporaries, Donatello, Michelozzo and Masaccio, where gothic forms disappeared to be replaced by motifs similar to those used in his architecture. The tabernacle in which Donatello's statue of St Louis was placed on the outer wall of Or San Michele, probably designed about 1422-5, is a delightful classical confection whose main features were probably inspired, like much of Brunelleschi's architecture, by prototypes in the Baptistry.[1] (Plate 25.) This tabernacle was made for the *Parte Guelfa* and it is an interesting illustration of Brunelleschi's wide influence that about the same time, when he was also involved in the projects at the cathedral, San Lorenzo and the Ospedale degli Innocenti, he designed a new palace for that important political association.[2] The *Parte Guelfa* palace, with its round arched windows on the upper storey, is the first of the Renaissance palaces. The most remarkable application of Brunelleschian ideas outside architecture is the chapel in Masaccio's fresco of the Trinity in S.Maria Novella, painted in 1425 (Plate 31). The iconographical significance of this fresco, both of the Trinity itself and of the room in which it is contained, is obscure. About the physical structure of the room which Masaccio painted, however, there can be no doubt that it was a direct and complete adoption of Brunelleschi's innovations, taking over both the style of classical architecture and the technical invention of perspective drawing. The room is made up of classical architectural motifs: its most prominent features are the arch opening into it and resting on classical columns and the arched coffered roof which has been shown to depend on Brunelleschi's ideas not on direct imitation of classical models. The room is designed with so careful a use of perspective drawing that it is possible to reconstruct its ground plan and Masaccio must have worked from an imaginary plan, building up the flat picture to scale by geometry in the manner used by Brunelleschi in making his panels.[3]

[1] Janson, II, p. 52.

[2] M. Salmi, 'Il Palazzo della Parte Guelfa di Firenze e Filippo Brunelleschi'.

[3] E.Panofsky, *Renaissance and Renaissances*, I, p. 167; H.W.Janson, 'Groundplan and Elevation in Masaccio's Trinity Frescoes', *Essays ... presented to Rudolf Wittkower*.

The features which stand out in the buildings which Brunelleschi designed in the 1420s are the round-arched arcade, the round cupola and the flat wall decorated with pilasters and entablature. Not only the individual motifs but also the general style of the architecture, with its preference for simple, clear, square and circular spaces and flat walls, owes much to the inspiration of the Baptistry and SS. Apostoli. However classical in intention it is very much a Florentine style, a Renaissance of Florentine Romanesque with a new sureness and elegance. In the years after 1433 Brunelleschi seems to have designed buildings of a somewhat different type under a new inspiration. This interpretation of his development can be put forward only hypothetically and with reservations because the history of his buildings is in many respects obscure. It presents difficulties which are not paralleled in the literary history of the period or in the history of painting and sculpture, chiefly resulting from the fact that in the fifteenth century large buildings took a long time to put up. Many of the major works of contemporary painters and sculptors were completed rapidly and can be dated confidently within a few years and this makes it possible to construct a history of their artistic development. Several of Brunelleschi's major works, however, although they were first planned long before his death, were finished long after by other hands. This is true of the Pazzi chapel, the churches of S. Lorenzo and S. Spirito and the lantern of the cathedral dome. It means that in these cases, even if the progress of building is not badly documented, there is extreme difficulty in deciding how much of the final work is really the execution of Brunelleschi's intentions and also how much his intentions changed between his first conception of the work and his death. This uncertainty makes it possible either to interpret his oeuvre with emphasis on the unity of style, on the grounds that the construction of most of the major works overlaps,[1] or to postulate a sharp break in style.[2] On the whole the second interpretation seems the more convincing. Most of the works which were

[1] The interpretation developed by Luporini.

[2] The interpretation put forward by L.H.Heydenreich, 'Spätwerke Brunelleschis', *Jahrbuch der preussischen Kunstsammlungen*, LII, 1931.

certainly conceived in 1434 or later, the church of S.Maria degli Angeli, the apses at the base of the cathedral dome, and the lantern, express an interest in concentric, polygonal forms and in the alternation of spaces and masses which is foreign to the smooth surfaces and simple plans of the 1420s. The distinction between S.Lorenzo and S.Spirito is smaller. Both were churches for large congregations, in which Brunelleschi would have found it difficult to avoid a conventional general plan, but S. Spirito has features which link it fairly clearly with the post-1434 style. The simplest and most obvious explanation for this change is that Brunelleschi's later style followed a large injection of direct influence from genuine Roman architecture, from which its characteristics could be derived. There is no direct evidence to support this hypothesis, except the appearance of the buildings themselves but it is fairly easy to see how it may have happened because the change coincides with a period when Brunelleschi is likely to have been subjected to a strong new Roman influence, arising out of the connections between Florence and the papal Curia.

The Roman court of the post-Schism period was the centre of a new interest in the ruins of ancient Rome which is the beginning of serious classical archeology. The central figure in the early stage of this development was perhaps Poggio; at any rate it is best known to us from his writings. After his return to the Curia in 1423 Poggio seized the opportunities offered by residence at Rome to improve his acquaintance with the classical remains of the city itself and the surrounding country. In June 1427 we find him writing to Niccoli about a visit to Ostia with Cosimo de' Medici and mentioning an inscription on the road there, 'on a tomb made of a single marble slab on which the fasces are also engraved.'[1] In September 1428 he wrote to Niccoli about a visit to Ferentino with Bartolomeo da Montepulciano, another papal secretary, which had yielded more inscriptions which he sent to Niccoli for help with the abbreviations. 'It was hard work for me to read those letters, both those which are in the tower, because they are difficult to see and largely destroyed by age, and those on

[1] Poggio, *Epistolae*, I, p. 209.

the rock. I sweated for many hours and I sweated in the midday sun. But *labor omnia vincit.*[1] In 1429 he was in Monte Cassino with Cardinal Branda Castiglione, again on the lookout for Roman remains and in the summer of 1430 he sent Niccoli a lengthy account of remains at Grottaferrata and Tusculum where he thought he had discovered Cicero's house.[2] Poggio gave his archeological interests a more systematic literary expression in two important works. In 1429 he compiled a volume of inscriptions from Rome which is the beginning of the serious study of this kind of evidence, developed over the centuries into the modern *Corpus Inscriptionum Latinarum.*[3] Some years later he wrote the dialogue *De Varietate Fortunae*, which purports to record a conversation between him and Antonio Loschi, also a papal secretary at the time, on a tour of Rome in 1427. They surveyed the city from the Tarpeian Rock, and moved by the vastness of the ruins spread before them, discoursed on the mutability of fortune demonstrated by the fall of Rome. These reflections led them to a lengthy enumeration of the ruined buildings actually visible in Rome.[4]

Poggio was not alone in his archeological interests. In 1421 Ciriaco d'Ancona, an eccentric business man with a taste for antiquities, was employed by Gabriel Condulmer, Cardinal Legate in the March of Ancona, on the restoration of the fortifications of Ancona. The study of the arch of Trajan at Ancona gave him a new inspiration to the study of classical remains which he was to pursue with a restless passion through many parts of Italy and the eastern Mediterranean for the next thirty years. Ciriaco, an autodidact, who unlike the proper humanists had to teach himself Latin as well as Greek, was no philosopher or synthesiser; but, as in the case of Niccoli, his literary weakness was compensated by a fanatical antiquarianism. Unlike Niccoli, he was a traveller. His unrivalled energy in visiting and recording

[1] Poggio, *Epistolae*, I, p. 219.

[2] Poggio, *Epistolae*, I, pp. 283-4; 324-6.

[3] Poggio's compilation is printed in *Corpus Inscriptionum Latinarum*, VI, i, pp. xxviii-xl. Cf. G.B. de Rossi. *Inscriptiones Christianae Urbis Romae*, II (Rome, 1888), p. 339.

[4] *De Varietate Fortunae*, pp. 5-25.

remains, not only in Italy but also along the routes of the Venetian galleys in Greece, Asia Minor and Egypt, won him the respect of Bruni and the Florentine circle. He had closer contacts with Rome. On his first visit to Rome to see the ruins in 1423 he was entertained by his old employer Cardinal Condulmer and by Martin v's nephew Antonio Colonna, Prince of Salerno. In 1431 Condulmer became Pope Eugenius iv. Ciriaco's acquaintance with the eastern Mediterranean made him an enthusiastic proponent of reunion of the churches and joint action against the Moslems. At the court of Eugenius iv he appears to have been valued both as an archeologist – he visited Roman remains in the company of Cardinal Giordano Orsini – and as an expert on the Eastern Question, which acquired a new importance in papal policy at the time of the councils of Ferrara and Florence. If not the most discriminating, Ciriaco was by far the most widely experienced archeologist of his age. He had seen the temple of Hadrian at Cyzicus and wrote the first Renaissance description of the Parthenon: *in summa civitatis arce ingens et mirabile Palladis Diuae marmoreum templum, diuum quippe opus Phidiae*. His connection with the Roman court may have encouraged archeological interests there and is in any case evidence that they were respected.[1] Naturally the archeological interests of members of the Curia centred on nearby Roman remains rather than distant Greek ones. In spite of the troubled state of Rome and the pope's long absence Condulmer's pontificate saw a new official concern for the preservation and restoration of the city's buildings. The pope paid for work of restoration not only at the Lateran, St Peter's and other churches but also at the Pantheon and other classical buildings.[2] Sometime in his pontificate Eugenius wrote an undated letter to the civil authorities of Rome in words expressing a dear sentiment of the humanists, and no doubt composed by one of them, forbidding the theft of stone from the

[1] The main source for Ciriaco's life is Francesco Scalamonte's posthumous account printed in G.Colucci, *Delle Antichità Picene*. Modern reconstructions by G.B. de Rossi, *Inscriptiones Christianae Urbis Romae*, ii, p. 156 seq.; E.W.Bodnar, *Cyriacus of Ancone and Athens* (Brussels, 1960).

[2] E.Müntz, *Les Arts à la Cour des Papes pendant le XVe et le XVIe siècle*, i (Bibliothèque des Ecoles Francaises de Rome et d'Athenes, 1878).

Colosseum, 'for to demolish the monuments of the City is to diminish the excellence of the City and of the whole world.'[1] Before the end of the pontificate the veneration for those monuments received a fuller expression in a learned survey compiled by a papal secretary: Flavio Biondo's book with the optimistic title *Roma Instaurata* (*Rome Restored*) dedicated to Eugenius in recognition of his concern for its subject.

One member of the papal court who joined enthusiastically in the fashion for Roman archeology was Leon Battista Alberti and in the decade following the death of Eugenius in 1447 Alberti produced two works in which the aesthetic consequences of that enthusiasm are very clearly visible. Sometime in the early 1450s he designed for Sigismondo Malatesta the exterior of the church of S.Francesco at Rimini, the Tempio Malatestiano (Plate 9). The Tempio Malatestiano, like Brunelleschi's early buildings, is an adaptation of classical motifs to the building of a church but the two styles do not have much more in common than this. Alberti's models were genuine Roman buildings. The doorway in the western facade is framed by an arch resting on heavy square pillars. To either side of the doorway are half-columns standing out from the pillars. We do not know precisely what Alberti intended to put on the unfinished upper storey of the facade but the ensemble that was built is clearly inspired by the design of an imperial triumphal arch. The northern and southern sides of the building are flanked by arcades of round arches, again resting on heavy square pillars, reminiscent of the arches of the Colosseum, which convey the impression of a series of cavernous niches. The result is a building which, although it is only a shell enclosing a structure of a different kind, appears to have all the massiveness of the Roman architecture which inspired it.[2] About the same time Alberti was writing the *De Re Aedificatoria*. This is a large and detailed work which abounds in classical allusions and was no doubt inspired by a variety of influences. Two of them stand out particularly. The first is Vitruvius's treatise, which Alberti by no means followed slavishly but which probably gave him the idea of

[1] R. Lanciani, *Storia degli Scavi di Roma*, I (Rome, 1902), p. 51.
[2] Wittkower, *Architectural Principles*, pp. 37-41.

writing a work on architecture, dealing with its general principles, the techniques of building and the planning of different
kinds of buildings. The second is his direct acquaintance with the
remains of Roman architecture. Alberti's knowledge of classical
architecture was in a sense as one-sided as Brunelleschi's had
been; he had presumably never seen a Greek building and therefore the Greek conception of a column as an independent member
not part of a wall or its decoration, was unknown to him.[1] He had,
however, devoted a great deal of study to the remains of Roman
imperial architecture which was for him the style of the ancients
which he wished to revive. He saw the history of architecture as
beginning in Asia and Greece but brought to perfection in Italy[2],
and he said that the lack of good accounts of the subject had compelled him to proceed by investigating every ancient building of
any merit which he could find, 'examining, measuring and drawing them,'[3] so that he knew from his measurements, for instance,
that the Romans did not always follow the canonical rules for the
dimensions of columns.[4] In some cases he refers to specific
ancient models, praising for example the wall niches and the use
of coffering in the Pantheon and the coffering in the Basilica of
Constantine.[5] In other cases unspecified models such as the
ruined Basilica Aemilia or the arches of Constantine and Septi-
mius Severus can be discerned behind his remarks.[6]

The earliest surviving building at Florence which bears very
clear marks of a Roman model is the choir of SS.Annunziata.
This was completed in the years 1470-7 under the direction of
Alberti himself but it is likely that the essentials of the plan were
not altered by him and that they date from the original design
made by Michelozzo in 1444, when the rebuilding was first
planned.[7] The choir is a round building with semi-circular apses

[1] Wittkower, p. 34.
[2] De Re Aedificatoria, B. 6, cap. 3.
[3] De Re Aedificatoria, B. 6, cap. 1.
[4] De Re Aedificatoria, B. 7, cap. 6.
[5] De Re Aedificatoria, B. 7, cap. 10-11.
[6] L.B.Alberti, Zehn Bücher über die Baukunst, ed. M.Theuer (Vienna, Leipzig, 1912), pp. 625, 635.
[7] L.H.Heydenreich, 'Die Tribuna der SS.Annunziata in Florenz', Mitteilungen

opening concentrically off the main space. It appears to be a direct copy of the nymphaeum in the Orti Liciniani which was then believed to be a temple of Minerva Medica and the choice of this plan fits excellently with Alberti's historically confused belief, expressed in De Re Aedificatoria,[1] that Christian churches should ideally follow a concentric plan common in Roman temples. The use of the plan by Michelozzo in 1444 suggests that this line of thought was already influential in Florence before Alberti wrote. The adoption of a rather mechanical imitation, presumably at the behest of a patron, conforms with the general impression of Michelozzo's artistic personality which his works convey. After earlier apprenticeship to Ghiberti and partnership with Donatello, Michelozzo, like Brunelleschi, moved over to a primarily architectural career and in a long life (1396-1472) designed a large number of buildings. He differed strikingly from Brunelleschi in his eclectic inventiveness and willingness to juxtapose motifs drawn from different styles sometimes incongruously.[2] As a sculptor his most substantial independent work is the tomb for Bartolomeo da Montepulciano, Poggio's friend at the court of Martin v, of which pieces are now to be seen in Montepulciano cathedral and the Victoria and Albert Museum. It happens to be the first contemporary work of art mentioned in humanist literature: Leonardo Bruni saw part of it being transported to Montepulciano in a cart about 1430 and was inspired to write a letter to Poggio which is unfortunately a peroration about the vanity of sepulchral monuments instead of a description of what he had seen.[3] It had been commissioned by Bartolomeo in 1427, two years before he died, so it may well conform closely to his wishes[4] and parts of it are just what one might expect a rather

des Kunsthistorischen Instituts in Florenz, III, 1930; W.Lotz, 'Michelozzos Umbau der SS.Annunziata in Florenz', ibid., v, 1937-40; Paatz, I, pp. 65-8; S.Lang, 'The Programme of the SS.Annunziata in Florence', Journal of the Warburg and Courtauld Institutes, XVII, 1954.

[1] De Re Aedificatoria, Bk. 7, caps. 4 and 10.
[2] See the remarks by H. Saalman, 'The Palazzo Comunale in Montepulciano', Zeitschrift für Kunstgeschichte, XXVIII, 1965, pp. 6-9.
[3] Bruni, Epistolae, II, pp. 45-8.
[4] J.Pope-Hennessy, Italian Renaissance Sculpture (London, 1958), pp. 290-291.

pedantic humanist to prefer. The unidentified toga-clad figure in an oratorical pose and the relief of Bartolomeo taking leave of his family (Plate 48) are realistic imitations of Roman sculpture in which the desire to be slavishly classical is more apparent than the independent inventive power of the sculptor. It is possible that the design of the choir of the Annunziata follows a similar wish expressed by Cosimo de' Medici, who seems to have been the patron behind the early stages of the rebuilding of that church.

Brunelleschi is said to have criticised the Annunziata choir, 'for several reasons, chiefly because it was built at the end of the church in such a way that there was not a convenient link with the nave.'[1] The connection with the nave is certainly an awkwardness which Brunelleschi would scarcely have tolerated. Some ten years earlier Brunelleschi had himself designed an independent church, without this disadvantage, which has a good deal of similarity with the choir and may even have helped to give Michelozzo the idea. S.Maria degli Angeli, designed in 1434, is the strongest argument for the hypothesis that Brunelleschi came under a powerful Roman influence in the early 1430s. The strongest argument against the theory is a famous passage in Antonio Manetti's biography which describes a joint visit to Rome by Brunelleschi and Donatello. Manetti says that they went to see sculpture but Brunelleschi became interested in the buildings and their 'musical proportions'. They devoted a great deal of time to drawing and measuring them and Brunelleschi got to know the various kinds of capitals and entablatures and the orders of the columns so that he could later use them appropriately in his own buildings.[2] In the biography this episode comes immediately after the competition for the bronze door of the Baptistry, in the early years of the fifteenth century, and most modern writers have accepted this chronology. There is no evidence of a visit to Rome in the early 1430s. There was a tradition, first written down more than a century and a half later, that Brunelleschi went to Rome to work for Eugenius on the recommendation of Cosimo, who wrote, 'I send to you a man whose powers are so great that he

[1] Heydenreich,' Tribuna der SS Annunziata', p. 277.
[2] Manetti, *Vita*, pp. 18-23.

could build a vault over the world.'[1] This attractive story is, alas, far too late to be accepted as good evidence. On the other hand Donatello certainly did spend a year at Rome in 1432-3[2] and there is a gap in the generally rather well-preserved evidence for the presence of Brunelleschi in the cathedral building accounts from December 1432 to July 1434. Brunelleschi reappears about the time when the papal court fled from Rome to Florence and his reappearance was closely followed by a letter sent out on his behalf from the papal chancery[3] and the dedication to him of the Italian version of Alberti's *Della Pittura*. The dedication makes it certain that Brunelleschi was in contact with Alberti at this period; it is probable that, like other Florentine artists, he was influenced by the connection, and possible that the friendship grew in a visit to Rome partly devoted to the study of Roman architecture. Though there may have been important earlier trips, in Brunelleschi's stylistic evolution the crucial Roman journey makes more sense in 1433 than in 1402.

The first and most important building in Brunelleschi's later style was never completed. Little of it now remains and its character can only be reconstructed from early plans and drawings. Brunelleschi was commissioned to reconstruct the church of the Camaldolese convent of S.Maria degli Angeli where Ambrogio Traversari had been a monk before he became general of the order. He produced a revolutionary design, a concentric polygonal church in which the main space was divided by eight massive pillars with wide apses between them, one of them forming the entrance, the others seven chapels (Plate 10). The upper part of the building can only be reconstructed hypothetically with the aid of a drawing, perhaps of the model, made in the middle of the fifteenth century. But the plan must have been crowned with a cupola rising from the inner columns and it is only the shape of the outer walls of the apses and their relation to the cupola which is really obscure.[4] Brunelleschi had designed the first concentric

[1] F.Bocchi, *Le Bellezze della Città di Firenze* (Florence, 1591), p. 248.

[2] V.Martinelli, 'Donatello e Michelozzo a Roma', *Commentari*, VIII, 1957.

[3] Heydenreich, *Spätwerke*, p. 8; Fabriczy, *Brunelleschiana*, p. 81.

[4] P.Sanpaolesi, *Brunelleschi*, pp. 86-90.

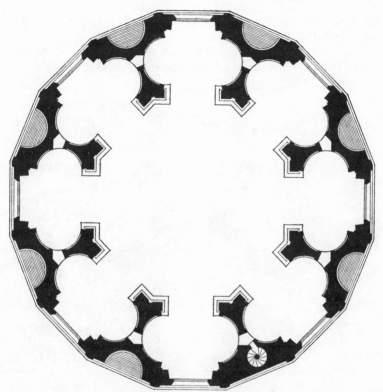

Fig. 3. S. Maria degli Angeli

Renaissance church, the first expression of that preference for church plans based on the circle which was eventually to lead to the designs of Bramante and beyond.

S. Maria degli Angeli was followed by two additions to the cathedral dome: the semicircular apses at the base of the drum and the lantern crowning the dome. The apses have a particular historical interest as the only pieces of Brunelleschi's later work both completed in his lifetime and surviving intact as clear evidence of his intentions (Plate 11). They were begun in 1438 and finished in 1444. Internally the apses are half-cupolas. It is their external shape which is most interesting. The face of each is cut by four large semicircular niches. Between each pair of niches are

197

two half-columns supporting an entablature which runs round the top. The result is a strongly undulating wall surface.

The lantern was probably designed in 1436 (Plate 12). It was not completed until long after Brunelleschi's death. It is probable

Fig. 4. Cathedral Lantern

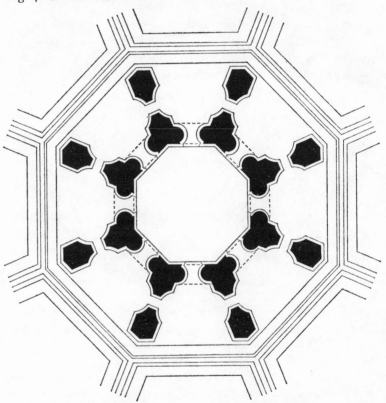

however that the wooden model which also survives is Brunelleschi's own work and enables his intentions to be compared with the final result.[1] The lantern is analogous in design with the romanesque structure which caps the roof of the Baptistry, and also with the ornamentation sometimes used at the head

[1] P.Sanpaolesi, 'La Lanterna di S.Maria del Fiore e il suo modello ligneo', *Bollettino d'Arte*, XLI, 1956; cf. Heydenreich, *Spätwerke*, pp. 21-8.

of a bishop's staff, such as the elaborate classicised example carried by Donatello's St Louis, to which it has a surprisingly close resemblance. In this case a simple idea has become a fairly complex piece of architecture. The conical roof rises from eight pillars, each decorated with pilasters and half columns, supporting narrow round arches. From each of the main pillars is thrown out a buttress consisting of a scroll resting on a round arch. Apart from the fact that Brunelleschi seems here to have invented the scroll, which plays so large a part in later Renaissance architecture, the interest of the design is its general similarity with the plan of S. Maria degli Angeli. Too much cannot be made of this because, of course, a lantern could hardly be anything but concentric. Still, the combination of a central space within the main pillars and an outer space circumscribed by the buttresses, is rather like the combination of the main room and apses in S. Maria degli Angeli, with the decoration turned inside out.

Brunelleschi's last building, the church of S. Spirito, is much more difficult to evaluate because of its complicated building history (Plate 13). Brunelleschi's association with the building began in 1434 when he provided the first design but little more than the foundations had been built when he died in 1446. S. Spirito was Brunelleschi's second attempt at designing a church in the form of a basilica. As in S. Lorenzo he retained the conventional cross plan with a long nave. As at S. Lorenzo the nave is bounded by arcades of corinthian columns carrying round arches with a clerestory and a flat, coffered roof above and the aisles are formed by a series of cupolas. Here the resemblance ends and significant differences begin. Brunelleschi was later said to have regarded his model for S. Spirito as 'a church designed according to his intentions.'[1] He was certainly not hampered, as he had been at S. Lorenzo, by the need to arrange the transepts to contain a certain number of chapels. The plan of S. Spirito is much more uniform and coherent. Unlike S. Lorenzo, it departs radically from the Florentine gothic tradition by making the east end and the transepts exactly equivalent in breadth and design to a section of the nave. If the nave had been cut off at the third column of the

[1] Manetti, *Vita*, p. 80.

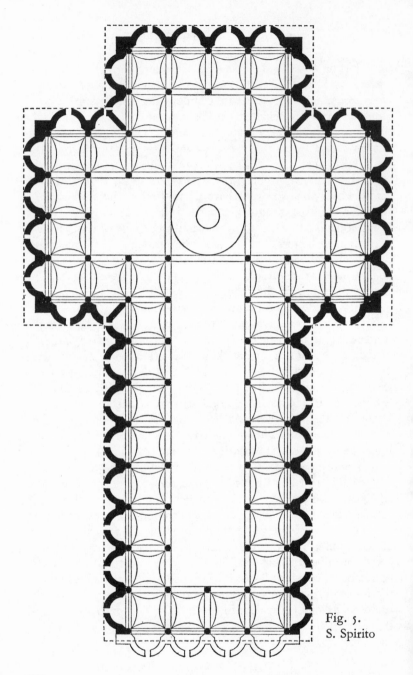

Fig. 5.
S. Spirito

arcade the result would have been a concentric church and, as it is, the diagonal views from different directions across the high altar, through a forest of columns, slightly reminiscent of Moorish architecture, are similar. The general plan, therefore, went a long way towards abandoning the east-west axis of the gothic church for a centralised plan, emphasised by the lighting from the dome over the crossing. The other main difference from S. Lorenzo is the structure of the walls. At S.Lorenzo the columns of the arcade were matched by pilasters separating quadrilateral side chapels, lipped with columns which tend to cut them off from the aisles. At S.Spirito the columns are matched by half-columns separating semi-circular side chapels which are more obviously part of the same space as the aisles and the nave. The result is that the walls have a quite novel, undulating form, which is matched symmetrically, not only on each side of the nave, but also right around the transepts and the east end. This again emphasises the equality of all four arms of the church. Brunelleschi's plan may have envisaged that the undulation of the outer walls would be visible also outside: the present flat sides are an addition. He may also have intended that the undulating wall should be carried round the west end of the church, which was flattened by his successors, and it has even been conjectured that he intended the nave to have a barrel-vault instead of its present flat roof.[1] If these speculations do in fact represent his plans correctly, and if they had been put into effect, the impression of roundness and concentricity would have been still stronger; even without them it is strong.

This then was the first Renaissance architecture, an evolving style, originally inspired by the humanist desire to recapture the classical past, paid for by laymen who accepted the validity of this ideal, deeply affected by the interpretation of the Florentine past and then, increasingly, by the contemplation of genuine Roman architecture. Like the humanist political thought it is a curious mixture of contemporary Florence and ancient Rome in inspiration. If the interpretation adopted here is correct, its evolution, like that of literary humanism was deeply affected by the relationship between Florence and contemporary Rome.

[1] Sanpaolesi, *Brunelleschi*, pp. 77-80.

7
Realist Art

The best known achievement of early fifteenth-century Florence is its realist art. The sculpture of Donatello and the painting of Masaccio, in the decade from 1420 to 1430, portrayed human beings and the natural space in which they lived more nearly as they appeared to the common-sense observer, with more regard for their human emotions and less for their symbolic significance, or for the patterns of abstract form which could be created out of them, than ever before. One of the reasons for the rapid success of pictorial realism at this time was the long period of preparation for it, which had created a tradition of craftsmanship in which the new impulse of the fifteenth century could work quickly and effectively. The art of the fifteenth century built on the work of artists a century and more before. The sculpture of Nicola and Giovanni Pisano, who worked in Tuscany between 1258 and 1314, had initiated the trend towards the realistic representation of the human body with the obvious help of models from Roman sarcophagi. The frescoes of Giotto, who died in 1337, made a sudden leap towards realism, both in the portrayal of human emotions and in the representation of space, and opened up new possibilities for artists just as Masaccio was to do a century later. Florentines of the later fourteenth century were aware of Giotto's innovations in painting. Filippo Villani, writing in about 1400 on the edge of the Salutati circle, already regarded modern Florentine painting as a Renaissance of the arts, starting with Cimabue, after centuries of decadence, plainly visible in the many barbaric paintings of the earlier medieval period which adorned the churches. He thought that Giotto was as good as, or better than, the ancients because his figures represented nature so faithfully that they seemed 'to speak, to weep, to rejoice'. Villani's evaluation of Giotto as a painter is in fact rather like Salutati's, or his own, estimation of Petrarch as an orator. They were geniuses who had recovered the lost arts of antiquity.[1] The artists of the later fourteenth century, however, did not develop or even maintain the advances made in this direction by Giotto. They were interested in other things. For them ecclesiastical and symbolical values play a larger part, human and natural values a smaller part, than in the art of Giotto. Attempts have been made to explain this general phenomenon as a result of the psychological shock administered by the Black Death of 1349 or as a result of the increased social power of the lesser bourgeoisie and the mendicant orders.[2] Whatever the reason, the painting of Orcagna and his successors marks a regression as far as realism is concerned. In the painting of Spinello Aretino (c. 1350-1410), Lorenzo Monaco (c. 1370-1425) and Bicci di Lorenzo (1373-1452) there is more feeling for Giottesque realism. But there is also an increased interest in rich pattern-making derived from Sienese art and the courts of the North. The new naturalistic realism was not heralded by Masaccio's immediate predecessors or contemporaries in the main stream of Florentine painting, and has a closer connection with the work of the Pisani and Giotto a century or so before.

We are concerned here not with the general history of Florentine art at this period but with a particular revolution in artistic expression which was chiefly the work of two artists, Donatello and Masaccio, and which appears to be closely connected with the intellectual innovations of the literary humanists. Before going further their lives must be briefly sketched. Donatello was probably born in 1386. He comes into the light of history for the first time in 1404 when he was working for his older contemporary Lorenzo Ghiberti on the sculpture for the north door of the Baptistry. In the next twenty years he is known to have worked on

[1] *Filippi Villani Liber de Civitatis Florentiae Famosis Civibus*, ed. G.C.Galletti (Florence; 1847), pp. 35-6.

[2] M.Meiss, *Painting in Florence and Siena after the Black Death* (Princeton, 1951); F.Antal, *Florentine Painting and its Social Background*, pp. 187-213.

a number of sculptural commissions for the church of Or San Michele and the cathedral. Between 1425 and 1438 he worked intermittently in partnership with Michelozzo on various commissions in and out of Florence, including the tomb of John XXIII in the Baptistry, the tomb of Cardinal Rainaldo Brancacci at Naples (on which he worked at Pisa in 1426-7), a tabernacle of the sacrament for a papal chapel at St Peter's (on which he worked at Rome in 1432-3) and an outdoor pulpit for the cathedral at Prato very near Florence. In the same period he did other big commissions on his own account such as work for the bronze font in the Baptistry at Siena and a marble cantoria for the cathedral at Florence. In the late thirties and early forties he was heavily engaged on work for Cosimo de' Medici's sacristy at San Lorenzo. After this he seems to have spent most of the years 1444 to 1453 at Padua where he did much work for the shrine of St Antony inside the cathedral and the equestrian statue of the *condottiere* Gattamelata outside it. Donatello was an artist of endless energy and inventive power and these qualities continued to develop uninterrupted until his death in 1466. His treatment of age when he was old was as powerful as his treatment of youth when he was young. What concerns us here, however, is his youth and middle age, the period roughly from 1408 to 1437, when he was about fifty, during which he made striking contributions to the development of realism, first in work on the large communal projects at Florence and then in a variety of particular commissions for patrons in and out of the city.[1]

Masaccio's biography, in contrast to Donatello's, is Shakespearean in its elusiveness.[2] He was born in 1401. There is a

[1] J.Pope-Hennessy, *Italian Renaissance Sculpture* (London, 1958), pp. 269-70. There is a great deal of biographical information in H.W.Janson, *The Sculpture of Donatello* (Princeton, 1957) to which this chapter is indebted for the dating of individual works and much else. Important recent amendments are contained in V.Martinelli, 'Donatello e Michelozzo a Roma', *Commentari*, VIII-IX, 1957-8, and M.Lisner, 'Zum Frühwerk Donatellos', *Münchener Jahrbuch der Bildenden Kunst*, 1962.

[2] Modern accounts in M.Salmi, *Masaccio* (2nd ed., Milan, 1948), U.Procacci, *Tutta la Pittura di Masaccio* (4th ed., Milan, 1961). There is a general attempt to reconstruct the chronology in U.Procacci, 'Sulla cronologia delle opere di Masaccio e di Masolino tra il 1425 e il 1428', *Rivista d'Arte*, XXVIII, 1953.

probable early work dated 1422,[1] the year in which he entered a gild, so that his independent output would seem to begin at about this time. He probably died in Rome in 1428. His brief life between these two dates is almost entirely a field for conjecture. One of his main works, the fresco of the Trinity in Santa Maria Novella, was probably done in 1425.[2] It is certain that he spent much of 1426 in Pisa working on another, the polyptych for the Carmine church.[3] Beyond this there is hardly any certainty about the dates or order of composition of his works. His third major work, the cycle of frescoes in the Carmine church in Florence, was done in collaboration with Masolino, a successful older painter who came from the same part of the Tuscan countryside, but there is no direct evidence of the date or the distribution of work except the fact that the frescoes were unfinished at Masaccio's death; the rest is conjecture based on analysis of styles. Though the greater part of Masaccio's working life was probably spent in Florence, it is also probable that he collaborated with Masolino on two other major enterprises which would have entailed lengthy periods in Rome: the frescoes in S.Clemente and an altarpiece for the Colonna chapel in S.Maria Maggiore.[4] The man survives in his astonishing works; it is vain to hope to reconstruct his biography.

The origins of Renaissance art are to be found in sculpture rather than in painting and it is characteristic of the most revolutionary painter of the period, Masaccio, that sculptural influences are prominent in his work. There are good artistic reasons for this. Renaissance art set a much higher value than earlier art on realism in the portrayal of the human body, on the imitation of classical forms and on the realistic representation of space. These are all aspects of art in which sculpture has a large part to play. The natural place for the development of the realistic nude or

[1] L.Berti, 'Masaccio 1422', *Commentari*, XII, 1961.

[2] E.Borsook, *The Mural Paintings of Tuscany* (London, 1960), p. 143.

[3] Documents in G.Poggi, 'La Tavola di Masaccio pel Carmine di Pisa', *Rivista d'Arte*, 1903, pp. 188-9.

[4] K.Clark, 'An early Quattrocento Triptych from Santa Maria Maggiore', *Burlington Magazine*, XCIII, 1951.

draped human figure was in figure sculpture. Sculptural relics of classical art in the shape of sarcophagi, statues, busts and engraved gems were much commoner and more accessible to the artists of the Renaissance than antique paintings, though these did exist and may have had some influence. The representation of space on a flat plane is more naturally a painter's than a sculptor's province, but the new space was an environment for the human figure and the painter's search for it was inspired partly by the dramatic and bodily realism which he desired to take over from sculpture and for which he had therefore to find a suitable setting. For all these reasons Renaissance painting was invaded by a solid realism partly derived from the touchable substantiality of sculpture.

There was also a factor of patronage which encouraged the rapid development of sculpture in the early decades of the fifteenth century. It happened that these years saw a series of ambitious, expensive and prolonged sculptural enterprises which were patronised by the commune and the gilds of the city to adorn the architectural monuments of Or San Michele, the Baptistry and the cathedral, and which provided an unusual wealth of opportunities for sculptors to collaborate and compete at public expense.[1]

(i) The first of these enterprises was the elaborate sculptural ornamentation surrounding the North door of the cathedral, called after the almond-framed relief of the Assumption of the Virgin in the arch above it, the Porta della Mandorla. This was begun in 1391 and carried on intermittently until 1423 under the auspices, like the rest of the fabric of the cathedral, of the wool gild, the *Lana*.[2]

(ii) In 1400 the cloth merchants' gild, the *Calimala*, held a competition to select an artist for a pair of bronze doors for the northern entrance to the Baptistry. The work on them lasted from 1403 to 1424.

(iii) In 1406 the commune set in motion the process of filling the niches on Or San Michele with sculptured figures of saints.

---

[1] Cf. the list of architectural enterprises above, pp. 172-3.

[2] C.Seymour, 'The Younger Masters of the first campaign of the Porta della Mandorla', *Art Bulletin*, XLI, 1959.

(iv) About the same time the sculptural decoration of the western facade of the cathedral was undertaken. Statues of the four evangelists seated to be placed in niches, two on either side of the main west door, were completed in 1408-15. A further row of three standing prophets higher up on the facade was begun in 1415.[1]

(v) Finally a series of eight standing figures of prophets for niches in the east and north faces of the Campanile at third-storey level was begun in 1414 and most of them finished in 1422.[2]

The earlier phases of these projects contain some hints of the future. The lower reliefs around the Porta della Mandorla include a figure of Hercules, remarkable not only because he is a pagan hero in a Christian setting or because he is set in a pattern of leaf decoration which must be derived from some antique model, but also because the unidentified artist has paid serious attention, in a manner clearly influenced by classical sculpture, to the male nude (Plate 14). This muscular figure is enthusiastically modelled on the ancient gods and betrays a new interest in the real anatomy of the human figure. A few years later in 1401 Brunelleschi and Lorenzo Ghiberti took part in the competition to choose a sculptor for the bronze doors of the Baptistry, an event which has often been taken as the inception of Renaissance sculpture[3] (Plates 15, 16). The problem presented to the competitors was to portray the sacrifice of Isaac in a bronze relief within a quatrefoil. The solutions entered by Brunelleschi and Ghiberti both in different ways show the influence of antiquity and of a heightened interest in the human form. Ghiberti, who was never to be whole-heartedly classical and was much influenced by the sculpture of Northern Europe, nevertheless has an Isaac whose kneeling, sideways-looking torso was derived from some ancient Niobid statue and a pair of waiting servants drawn from figures on a sarcophagus; but they are compressed gracefully within the gothic outline. Brunelleschi has less elegance, less accommodation to the outline, perhaps less direct quotation from ancient art, though one of his

[1] C. Seymour, *Sculpture in Italy 1400-1500* (London, 1966), pp. 54-8.
[2] Seymour, pp. 67-70.
[3] The episode is fully analysed by Krautheimer, *Ghiberti*, chs. 3-4.

servants is the classical thornpicker; but he has a striking vivacity and dramatic force: the knife is really on the point of slitting Isaac's straining neck. This dramatic realism looks forward to another perhaps more fundamental aspect of art in the generation to come. A further stage in the investigation of the male nude is found in the wooden crucifix in Santa Croce made by Donatello about 1412 (Plate 17). The legend that Brunelleschi criticised it as a Christ for being like the body of a peasant may well be groundless, but it brings out the truth that Donatello had carved it with comparatively little conventional interest in formal grace and an original concern for anatomical truth.

The main series of statues which was to bring the human figure into real life starts with two works which were made in 1408-9 for the tops of the buttresses on either side of the Porta della Mandorla (though they were quickly found to be unsuitable and removed). One of these was a David by Donatello. The other was an Isaiah by Nanni di Banco,[1] a young artist of Donatello's generation who was employed independently on the same projects as Donatello in the period 1400 to 1420 and who made significant advances in the adaptation of classical models before he died early in 1421. For two *Old Testament* characters, often portrayed in medieval sculpture, they have fresh, realistic faces and poses which are a partial emancipation from the more stylised figures of the previous century. Isaiah has the face and figure of an interesting senator rather than a prophet and his stance, though formally contrived to match David's on the other buttress, shows the beginnings of the attempt to convey in stone the distribution of the body's weight and the anatomy beneath the toga (Plate 18). David has been transformed from a bearded, harp-playing patriarch into the boy of the Goliath story (Plate 19). A few years later in 1416 he was removed from the cathedral to the Palazzo della Signoria, with a new inscription, 'To those fighting bravely for the fatherland even against the most terrible foes the Gods give help,' to symbolise the defence of Florence against the tyrants.

David and Isaiah were followed shortly after by another pair of

[1] J.Lanyi, 'Il profeta Isaia di Nanni di Banco', *Rivista d'Arte*, XVIII, 1936.

statues of a somewhat more traditional kind by the same sculptors: Nanni's St Luke and Donatello's St John the Evangelist, both seated and enveloped in ample folds of drapery, were two of the four evangelists for the facade of the cathedral. Another marked step forward came in 1410-15 with another pair of works, again designed by these two artists to be placed on the same building, this time Or San Michele: Nanni di Banco's Quattro Santi Coronati (Plate 20), the group of four legendary late-Roman martyrs who were patron saints of the Stone-masons, and Donatello's St Mark (Plate 21). Both these figures are advances in the use of ancient models. The four figures in Nanni's group are perhaps more obviously togaed Romans imitated from classical figures than any previous sculptures. Partly for that reason they have a new, if rather stiff, realism. The grouping appears to be directly imitated from Roman funeral monuments. Donatello's St Mark, in significant contrast, is a figure in which the classical influence is less obvious but the capacity to represent bodily weight and the anatomy beneath the drapery, learnt from Roman sculpture, has been amalgamated with the gothic vision of the evangelist. Donatello did not borrow as blatantly as his rivals.

Nanni di Banco's contribution to this line of development ended here. He died in 1422 and his last work, the exquisite Assumption which gives the Porta della Mandorla its name, was a creation of seductive, sinuous beauty which had little to do with the new realism. Donatello went on from one conquest to another, breaking through into an entirely new world of expression through the human form. His striking triumphs in this field in the next twenty years included the St George for the Armourers' niche at Or San Michele (1415-17), the so-called 'beardless Prophet' for the Campanile (1416-18), St Louis for the *Parte Guelfa* niche at Or San Michele (1423-5) and *Zuccone* for the Campanile (1423-5). St George is a representation of the saint as a young man in armour – the statue has lost the helmet which originally adorned his head and the lance which he held at the ready in his left hand – in an attitude of preparedness for action (Plate 22). The head is the youthful appolline head of the marble David. The attitude is a development from the stance of St Mark with the weight realistically concentrated on one foot. The armour, so fully represented, presumably in deference to the Armourers' gild, is a hindrance to modern appreciation but what is clear is the dramatic realism with which Donatello has infused the work, the impressive combination of serene confidence in the face with the alert posture of the body. The 'beardless prophet' returns again to the problem of the representation of aged humanity in draperies (Plate 23). The body is not particularly interesting. The face, balding, beardless to reveal the features, bony and deeply lined, is a study of a grim personality which has been developed from classical portraiture into a deeper psychology. *Zuccone* (the identity of the prophet he was intended to represent is lost and the traditional name means only 'old man') carries this line of development further (Plate 24). The figure, with the right shoulder freed from the enormous mass of the toga, is still nearer to the type of the Roman orator. The face is still more striking in its representation of powerful age: gaunt and unattractive with a high-domed, balding head and a wide mouth, apparently on the point of utterance, supporting the legend that Donatello, while he was working on the statue, kept saying 'speak, speak'. In contrast, the St Louis made for the *Parte Guelfa* is a technical tour-de-force of a very different kind (Plate 25). The figure is clothed in elaborate loose robes so that the naked body appears only at the toes and the neck. The whole structure is made up of separately cast pieces of bronze. Yet, with the exception perhaps of the right glove raised in benediction, Donatello achieved the illusion of a real body within the shell, through an extraordinarily sensitive concern with the relation between body and drapery. The clothes cover a real body and their style is thus quite different from the vague swirls characteristic of the drapery of Gothic figure sculpture.

About seven years after these statues were made Donatello created the most remarkable representation of the human body to be seen in the fifteenth century, the bronze David. Between the Campanile statues and the bronze David he had executed some small bronze figures of naked angels for the font in the Baptistry at Siena. Their smooth, rounded, youthful forms, in lively attitudes, show the influence of classical models (Plate 26). They were an advance in representing the nude in the round with an impression of free movement and they foreshadowed what was to come. The bronze David is the culmination of Donatello's early interest in the youthful male form (Plate 27). The statue is supposed to represent David but, since it was not designed for a church – we do not in fact know for what or whom it was made and have no record of it before 1469 when it stood in Lorenzo de' Medici's palace – Donatello was able to go much further away from the traditional iconography and feeling of religious sculpture. This is a pure celebration of the beauty of the male nude. The face is not the face of the humble slayer of Goliath but of a proud and rather cruelly beautiful boy. The extravagant hat is probably a fashionable decoration. The pose of the hips, the arms and the legs is a pose of swaggering sensuality. No doubt Donatello's homosexuality helps to explain it. Regarded historically it is the complete breakthrough in figure sculpture: the human body represented for the sake of its own naturalistic beauty, related only by a kind of parody or inversion to its ostensible religious subject.

While Donatello was realising the potentialities of the human body another movement, in which he also played a part, though not such a decisive one, was exploring the possibilities of the realistic representation of space. The revolution carried through in this aspect of art is one of the most remarkable changes of the early fifteenth century. It was not unheralded: the frescoes of Giotto painted a century earlier are clear precursors, and early fourteenth-century Florentine painting as a whole had made considerable strides in this direction. But the solution of strict perspective drawing, *costruzione legittima*, came as a culmination which gave sudden clarity where there had been uncertainty before and, in one respect, created the conditions for several centuries of European art. This is a rare case of technique matching a psychological need and opening up a world of possibilities.

The first step in this development, as we have seen, was taken by Brunelleschi and the recollection of it is preserved in Manetti's story about his two panels.[1] What the observer saw, looking

[1] Above, p. 179.

through the hole in Brunelleschi's panel, must in fact have looked very like a real reflection in a mirror. Thus the medieval painter's ideal, 'to discover things unseen that are hidden beneath the shadow of things natural,' as it was expressed by the writer of a painter's handbook at Florence in the late fourteenth century,[1] was replaced by the ideal of an exact representation of the field of vision. Or at least the new ideal came to be regarded as attainable and played a large part in artists' purposes. The precise character of the revolution is important. It was based on a simple mathematical principle, that light comes to the eye of the beholder in a direct line from the object he sees, so that there is a visual cone with the apex in the eye and a section through the cone at any point will be struck by rays with the same relative distance between them. Painting a picture is representing a section through the visual cone, which is the same as holding up a frame and painting exactly what you see through it. The method is particularly appropriate for painting architectural scenes, especially those including buildings with marked quadrilateral features, like the Baptistry or of course Brunelleschi's own early classical buildings. Hence the tendency towards a space clearly defined by architecture which is a common feature in Italian painting. Brunelleschi's perspective is not the only way of representing space realistically. It ignores the movement of the eyes and the fact that there are two of them. But this simplicity was one of its attractions; it gave an immediate, satisfying, measurable command over space.

We do not know how far Brunelleschi rationalised his system, which was probably evolved about 1420,[2] into mathematical formulae useful to painters. This step however was decisively taken by Leon Battista Alberti and published in his *Della Pittura* in 1435-6. Alberti, like Brunelleschi, was interested in mathematics and he may have had a more advanced training in it. At

[1] G.C.Argan, 'The Architecture of Brunelleschi and the Origins of Perspective Theory in the fifteenth century', *Journal of the Warburg and Courtauld Institutes*, IX, 1946, p. 97; Cennini, *Il Libro dell'Arte*, ed. D.V.Thompson (New Haven, 1932), p. 2.

[2] There is no definite evidence for this generally accepted date. It is based on the position of the story of the panels in Manetti's life and on the dates of the earliest paintings apparently embodying Brunelleschi's doctrines.

one stage in his youthful studies in the 1420s he is supposed to have taken up the subject as a recreation and later in life he published a number of mathematical problems. Before the *Della Pittura* he had published a *Descriptio Urbis Romae* in which he attempted to provide the materials for a plan of the remains of ancient Rome '*ex mathematicis instrumentis*', by using a simple device to take bearings on distant points.[1] He also manufactured a contraption, of which we unfortunately have only a vague description, for presenting pictures to give an illusion of reality, which may have been something like Brunelleschi's panel and mirror.[2] The first book of the *Pittura* is devoted to a description of surfaces and light, leading up to a method of perspective drawing. Alberti starts with a quadrangle (ABCD), the frame of the

Fig. 6.

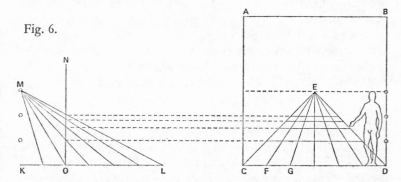

picture, 'the open window through which I see what I want to paint'. Then he determines the size of the human figures in the foreground and takes a third of their height, a notional *braccio*, as the unit of measurement into which the base line is divided. He chooses a vanishing point (E) not higher than the head level of the foreground figures, to correspond with the eye level of an actual observer of the scene, and joins the point to the divisions on the base line, thus obtaining the 'orthogonals' (EC, EF, EG, etc.), showing diminution of size towards the background. To determine the points along the orthogonals at which objects at

[1] Published in *Opera Inedita*, ed. Mancini (Florence, 1890).
[2] *Vita* (Muratori, xxv), col. 299.

various distances should properly be placed a second set of lines must be made. This is done by drawing another base line (KL), divided like the base line of the picture, and a line (MK) perpendicular to it, the height of the vanishing point from the base line but to one side, and joining up the point to the divisions. Another perpendicular line (NO) is drawn to cut across this second set of lines. The points of intersection along this line, joined up with the orthogonals in the first quadrilateral, will give the proper distances in the picture between lines which are the same relative distances apart in reality. As the line NO is shifted to right or left it will give a more rapid recession for a close observer and more gradual recession for a distant observer. With these two sets of lines the painter can determine the proper position within the picture of an object anywhere on the real ground-plan of the scene to be painted and he can adjust his picture at will to give the illusion of close or distant observation. With some adaptation any point at a known position above or below the real ground-plan can also be sited accurately.

Alberti's method does not involve measurement. It is not intended for the precise representation of architecture but for the rough approximation to real space that the painter wants. Fourteenth-century artists had used simple mathematical devices of this kind but they used them for parts of their pictures, not the whole, so that the results look to the post-Albertian eye like half-hearted efforts at perspective, which indeed they are. They never developed a system which would give the illusion of a single, coherent space throughout a picture. Alberti did just that. Given the presupposition of a simple, straight-line space with a single vanishing point, Alberti provided a method for representing spatial relationships accurately as they would be seen by an observer at a certain point. The resources out of which he developed his system were the traditional practices of painters and medieval mathematics and optics. This knowledge was widely available but only Alberti made the psychological leap necessary to conceive of a unified space.[1] The innovation has profound

[1] Alberti's achievement has been made clearer by S.Y.Edgerton, 'Alberti's Perspective: A New Discovery and a New Valuation', *Art Bulletin*, XLVIII, 1966, on which this account and the drawing on p. 213 are based.

implications for art. If a picture is spatially realistic there is a stronger inclination to make it temporally and emotionally realistic too. Hence artists would be more inclined to paint a single realistic moment rather than, in medieval fashion, a sequence of points in a story.

The earliest surviving work of art which has sometimes been thought to show the influence of Brunelleschi's teaching is the small marble relief which Donatello made about 1415-17 to be placed on the wall of Or San Michele below his statue of St George (Plate 28). It depicts St George on horseback slaying the dragon with a cave in a rocky hillside on one hand, the princess standing before a vaguely classical building on the other, and a view of distant trees. The suggestion of perspective is given by the receding square slabs on the floor of the building. But in fact there is no more than a groping towards Brunelleschian exactness. What is really remarkable in the work is that Donatello seems here to have invented the technique of *rilievo schiacciato*, low relief, which, without making the figures and objects stand out from the flat plane (as for instance in Ghiberti's contemporary North Door) manages to convey the impression of roundness and distance by a subtle use of shadows created by very low relief. Donatello was making his relief approximate as nearly as possible to a painting, tackling with a sculptor's materials the painter's problem of creating an illusion of depth on a flat plane. The *schiacciato* technique, combined with some rudimentary perspective and a space bounded on the sides by the hill and receding columns, does make some advance in the solution of this problem, and the fact that Donatello should have turned aside to this from his main work on figure sculpture seems to reveal a remarkable interest in the representation of space. A decade later, about 1425, Donatello made a further experiment in the same vein in a bronze panel in low relief which he made for the font in the Baptistry at Siena, depicting the scene of John the Baptist's head being brought before Herod (Plate 29). From the point of view of accurate spatial realism, this is a considerable advance on the St George panel and seems to have been designed deliberately to show off a mastery of the perspective representation of a complicated architectural setting. The scene in which the main action takes place is bounded at the rear by a wall in which there are a series of windows. Through the windows another room can be seen in which there are further figures and, through windows at the rear of that, two further enclosed spaces in one of which there are still more figures. The architecture is done not only with a great deal of sculptural skill but also with a use of controlled perspective. The front compartment contains Donatello's first essay in the creation of a dramatic story picture showing a moment of high emotion conveyed by the gestures and faces of realistic figures. At one side of the table is the head, presented to Herod who draws back with his hands raised while two children scuttle away from the horrifying object. The other side is dominated by the malign figure of Salome in swirling robes with a group of partly interested and partly horrified onlookers. One might see the work as an achievement of realistic drama in realistic space if it were not that the head appears twice: it is also in the room at the back, apparently being brought into the front room. The panel seems to have been created at a moment when realism has made a large technical advance but has not yet captivated the psychology of the artist to the extent that he feels bound to show one moment of time only in a unified picture.

The same transitional combination of a single real space with a sequence of events is found in the greatest work of Donatello's younger contemporary, Masaccio. About the same time as Donatello was contributing to the Siena font Masaccio was painting the pictures which made the most impressive contribution to the development of spatial realism. Masaccio, who cannot have begun to paint before 1415, was the heir to the early advances made by Brunelleschi and by Donatello. The earliest traditions, too late to have much value as independent evidence say that, 'he was much loved by Filippo di Ser Brunellescho and he taught him many things. And when Filippo heard of his death he was greatly upset and used often to say to members of his household "we have had a great loss".'[1] It is certain that Masaccio was in contact with Donatello when they were both working at

[1] *Il Codice Magliabecchiano cl. XVII 17*, ed. C.Frey (Berlin, 1892), p. 82.

Pisa in 1426. But the paintings themselves are much better evidence of the contacts between the group. Masaccio's achievement was to place real human figures, partly inspired by Donatello's sculpture, in a real space, partly inspired by Brunelleschi's perspective drawing.

Masaccio's earlier surviving works from the early 1420s are in some respects conventional altar pieces representing the Virgin and Child with various attendants. Already, however, his developing skill in painting figures in the round makes some of them seem like real persons breaking through cardboard scenery. In the Madonna with St Anne in the Uffizi, although some of the environment is conventionally flat and some is not by Masaccio, the Virgin herself has a powerful unconventional face and holds a strikingly round-bodied child, probably a direct copy of a piece of antique sculpture (Plate 30). The development of this approach in a larger and freer field can be seen in Masaccio's three major surviving works dating from the years 1425-8: the fresco of the Trinity in Santa Maria Novella, the polyptych for the altar of the Carmine church at Pisa, and the contributions to the frescoes in the Carmine church at Florence.

The Trinity fresco is a puzzling work of art (Plate 31). It owes more, and more obviously, to Brunelleschi than any other painting of the period, for its prominent architectural motifs and its perspective would have been unthinkable without his work and probably impossible without close collaboration between the two artists. But the psychological implications are difficult to unravel. The fresco represents a small chapel, the iconographical significance of which is not clear,[1] but which is certainly completely classical and untraditional in style. Within this ostentatiously avant-garde and realistic setting Masaccio has placed, not real people, but a vision of Christ crucified, the Holy Spirit and a majestic God, flanked by the Virgin and St John. The figures are executed with a good deal of rounded realism though there is some difference between the Trinity and the other two figures.

[1] U. Schlegel, 'Observations on Masaccio's Trinity Fresco in Santa Maria Novella', *Art Bulletin*, XLV, 1963; O. von Simson, 'Über die Bedeutung von Masaccio's Trinitätsfresko in S. Maria Novella', *Jahrbuch der Berliner Museen*, VIII, 1966.

The resources of spatial realism have been applied with a daring which seems to leap far ahead of the year 1425, for Masaccio is not merely following the formula of creating a space which will look like a real space but has also lifted the scene well above the level of the observer and placed the vanishing point appropriately to create an impression of height and to emphasise the awesomeness of the figure of God. He has also, however, placed the entirely naturalistic and probably portrait figures of the donors outside the chapel but within the same space. The result is an extraordinary mixture of realism, symbolism and illusionism more reminiscent of a much later period in the history of painting. Painted in 1425 it shows Masaccio's revolutionary temperament but not the direction of his other substantial achievements which were probably later.

The Pisa polyptych on which he was working in 1426 was a complicated set of panels, now dispersed. The enthroned Madonna which was the centre-piece is now in London, the Crucifixion, which probably stood above it, is in Naples, and four separate figures of saints and three panels for the predella with story pictures (the Adoration of the Magi, the martyrdoms of St Peter and St John the Baptist and stories of St Julian and St Nicholas) are in Berlin. In the Madonna the realism of the Uffizi Madonna has been carried further (Plate 32). She has entirely shed the appearance of a patterned figure on a panel and become a real woman seated in real space. The illusion is created partly by her throne, a strange piece of furniture apparently made up of fragments of Brunelleschian architecture but drawn with perspective to make a realistic space around the seated figure. Still more it is conveyed by the use of light and shade. The mother and child are sitting in a real light which comes clearly and consistently from the left side of the painting and is used to define the outlines of figures and clothes. The Crucifixion displays other powers (Plate 34). It has no background. It presents a less realistic but highly dramatic scene. The tortured Christ on the cross is made powerful by the bright light falling on stretched muscles. It perhaps owes something to Donatello's wooden crucifix. At his feet the Magdalen is seen from the back, enveloped in a dramatic red cloak. She has fallen to her knees and her hands are thrown up in ultimate despair. The powerful representation of emotion is another aspect of Masaccio which appears here for the first time. Perhaps the clearest advances in realism are in some of the predella pictures. The Adoration scene is especially remarkable because here Masaccio advanced for the first time from the representation of space with the aid of an architectural setting, to an open space made real by the modelling of figures and the use of light (Plate 33). The Magi and their attendants are very simply represented as people on a ground, sharply defined by the bright light, with horses behind them. It has often been pointed out that this everyday scene, including two entirely unadorned cloaked figures, happens to contrast particularly strongly with another famous Adoration done at Florence about a year later by the fashionable painter Gentile da Fabriano. This is a riot of glittering detail with no attempt whatever at a spatial framework, a painting designed entirely to entertain by picturesque profusion. Masaccio's, in contrast, is a scene of restrained simplicity in which nearly everything is sacrificed to the realistic effects of light and shade.

The walls of the Brancacci chapel in the Carmine church at Florence were decorated by Masaccio, Masolino and later Filippino Lippi with a series of scenes depicting incidents drawn from the Bible and the *Legenda Aurea*, with a concentration on the life of St Peter. The scenes which are generally thought to be by Masaccio are the Expulsion of Adam and Eve, the Tribute Money, St Peter curing the sick with his shadow, St Peter baptising the Neophytes, St Peter distributing the Goods of the Community and the Death of Ananias. Masaccio is also thought to have had a hand in the paintings of St Peter raising the son of Theophilus, St Peter Enthroned and the Raising of Tabitha and the Curing of the Cripple. In these frescoes the capacity for the portrayal of human emotions and the physical world was developed and exercised on a much grander scale.

There are two elements in the realism of the Brancacci frescoes and it is the combination of the two which makes them impressive. One is the portrayal of realistic space. The other is the portrayal of human emotion, not by symbolical gesture but by direct representation of body and face, carrying forward the developments already made in Donatello's sculpture. In the Tribute fresco the sense of serenity and gravity is created by the extremely satisfying pattern of senatorial stances in the circle of heavily draped figures around Christ in contrast to the vulgar demanding figure of the collector (Plate 35). Like the visitors in the Pisa Adoration, but even more clearly, the apostles stand in a large luminous landscape. The impression of space is assisted by a building to one side, this time in more developed perspective than the rudimentary stable of the other painting. But space is primarily created by the distant hilly background, the placing of the figures on a realistic ground and the light and shadow falling on them. It is a space of air and light. Masaccio has learnt Brunelleschi's lesson and then thrown away the architectural support which he had provided, to create a space purely by the use of light. It is all the more surprising that, like Donatello's Feast of Herod relief, the Tribute portrays not one moment in time but three, the collector demanding the money, Peter finding it in the fish's mouth and Peter handing it to the collector. But apart from that limitation the space is completely realised.

The Brancacci frescoes are populated by two sorts of people, ordinary mortals and the apostles. In the ordinary people the psychological investigation of the human face is carried further and Masaccio exercised his skill in depicting a variety of interesting, moving and even amusing faces. He also probably included portraits of living Florentines. The most powerful use of bodily naturalism is in the fresco of the Expulsion, remarkable for the delicate realism of the nudes, defined by light, but also for the anguish conveyed by Eve's face and the stances of the two figures (Plate 36). The other frescoes record the meeting of erring and suffering humanity with the superior race of apostles. The Tribute is psychologically less interesting than the other frescoes. The only ordinary man in it is the collector. The apostles here, as in the other scenes, are robed figures whose demeanour owes much to Roman statuary and to the recent statues of the cathedral and Or San Michele. Masaccio has in a sense introduced a humanist iconography by making them essentially a group of orators with faces of varying individual interest but tending to be rather generalised compared with the non-apostles. The other frescoes give rein to the interest and skill in portraying everyday emotion. The nude man in the Baptism of the Neophytes was singled out for admiration by later critics as 'the man who shivers' (Plate 37). But still more impressive than this tour-de-force are the faces of the individuals in the frescoes of Peter curing the Sick and Distributing the Goods (Plates 38, 39). Here for the first time is a transcription of the emotions of ordinary undignified humanity which involved a leap from symbolical representation to naturalism as striking as the conquest of space.

About the same time as Masaccio was executing the Brancacci frescoes Donatello made a sculptured plaque in which he carried further the technique of low relief initiated in the St. George panel. This plaque depicts the Ascension of Christ who is at the same time handing the keys to St Peter above a circle of apostles (Plate 40). There are some good reasons for supposing that the Ascension was originally designed to be part of the decorative scheme of the Brancacci chapel.[1] Even if this attractive theory is not correct the Ascension shows Donatello pursuing some of the same ideals as the Masaccio of the Tribute Money. Not only is there a similarity in the pattern of the two works: the grouping of the apostles around Christ. There is the same attempt to create the illusion of substantial robed figures and spatial landscape. Considering that one is paint and the other marble the similarity is rather a striking indication of the common, supporting aims of the two artists.

Moving forward again a few more years into the 1430s we come to the point when ideas of pictorial realism were crystallised by Alberti and acquired a more definite status among artists. The years 1432-5 when Donatello visited Rome and the Curia then moved to Florence are also the years in which Alberti's *Statua* and *Della Pittura* were published. There must at this period have been considerable contact between Alberti and Donatello and Brunelleschi and possibly other artists as well. Donatello's bronze David

[1] J.Pope-Hennessy, *Catalogue of Italian Sculpture in the Victoria and Albert Museum* (London, 1964), I, pp. 70-73.

corresponds to the canons of proportion laid down in *Statua*. There seems to be a similar relationship between *Della Pittura* and Donatello's relief of the Feast of Herod, now at Lille, produced about the same period (Plate 41). The subject of this relief is the same as that of the bronze on the Siena font and it also has an elaborate architectural setting. This time however Donatello seems to have taken pains to conform to the rules laid down in Book 1 of *Della Pittura*. The foreground edge is very obviously divided into units equal to a third of the height of the foreground figures, as *Della Pittura* recommends, and the parallel lines of the stone floor very obviously recede towards a vanishing point at about the right level. The architecture is if anything more complicated as if to display an advanced technical grasp of perspective but the time sequence has gone and this time only a single dramatic moment is depicted. For some years after this Donatello displayed a rather ostentatious passion for perspective drawing. It appears in the circular relief plaques which he made for the dome of the Old Sacristy at San Lorenzo about 1437, some of which seem to have quite unnecessarily elaborate architectural settings (Plate 42), and in the reliefs for the High Altar of S. Antonio in Padua (late 1440s) where, for instance, the 'Irascible Son' story is set in an enormous arena of rather bewildering complexity (Plate 43). These architectural settings are not especially attractive; they seem to be the products of delight in the new-found mastery of space.

How was the artistic revolution related to the intellectual world of humanism? That there was a connection between them can be established in the most decisive way, as we have seen, by the reflection in artists' practice of the doctrines expressed in Alberti's Latin *De Statua* and his *Della Pittura*, written in Latin and translated into Italian by 1435-6.[1] How far was Alberti

[1] *Della Pittura*, ed. L.Malle (Florence, 1950); translation, *On Painting*, by J.R. Spencer (London, 1956). On textual problems, C.Grayson, 'Studi su Leon Battista Alberti', *Rinascimento*, IV, 1953; Idem, 'L.B.Alberti's "Costruzione Legittima"', *Italian Studies*, XIX, 1964. *De Statua* in *Leone Battista Alberti's Kleinere kunsttheoretische Schriften*, ed. H.Janitschek (Vienna, 1877). Grayson has concluded that the Latin version of *Pittura* preceded the Italian version made *c.* 1435-6 and that *Statua* may be earlier than either ('Studi su L.B.Alberti', p. 61; *Dizionario Biographico degli Italiani*, I, p. 705).

reflecting the artists' achievements; how far was he setting forth an independent humanist ideal which the artists accepted? The dedicatory letter with which the Italian version of the *Della Pittura* starts is addressed to Brunelleschi and names as the foremost exponents of modern art Donatello, Ghiberti, Luca della Robbia and Masaccio.

I used to wonder and regret that so many excellent and divine arts and sciences which we know from remains and accounts of them abounded in those most virtuous ancient times were today almost entirely lost. Painters, sculptors, architects, musicians, geometers, rhetoricians, astrologers and similar noble and marvellous intellects are rarely to be found and rarely estimable nowadays. So much so that I thought that Nature, mistress of all things, grown old and dry, no longer gave birth to the giants and geniuses which she produced so copiously in her younger and more glorious days. But since I have returned from the long exile in which we Alberti have grown old to our supremely beautiful city I recognised first in you Filippo (Brunelleschi) and our very good friend Donato the sculptor and in those others Nencio (Ghiberti) and Luca and Masaccio a genius for every admirable thing equal to those who were famous in these arts in ancient times.

Thus the humanist marvel of the Curia declared his friendship and admiration for the practising artists and the *Pittura* turns out to be in fact both a composition in the best humanist manner and a set of precepts related to the actual practice of the artists.

Della Pittura seems to have three main themes which do not quite correspond to the divisions between the three books. The first book as we have seen is mainly a practical account of perspective drawing with mathematical and optical preliminaries. It, or Alberti's conversation, probably encouraged artists to put its ideas into practice, but it is probable that it was also based partially on the experiments of Brunelleschi and Masaccio. Most of the second book is about the composition of a picture, according to the requirements of pictorial realism. Alberti advocated the use of colour solely for realistic representation and never for symbolism. Gold, which abounded in the religious painting of the time, was to be avoided. Even black and white should be used sparingly because they did not exist purely in nature. Figures should be based on the observation of nature, 'keeping in mind in what way nature, marvellous artificer of things, has composed planes in beautiful bodies.' In a striking anticipation of the practice of artists for centuries to come Alberti stressed the need for anatomical knowledge – the painter must start with the bones, then add the flesh and the clothes. Figures should represent realistically the motions of the body appropriate to the actions and emotions which the painter was trying to convey: runners throwing their hands and feet, dead bodies seen to weigh heavily on those who carry them, the weight of the living body appearing to rest where it actually would rest. The composition of a painting as a whole must include a variety of figures, expressing distinct emotions and contributing to the 'story' (*istoria*) which the picture represents. 'In an *istoria* I like to see someone who admonishes and points out to us what is happening there; or beckons with his hand to see; or menaces with an angry face and with flashing eyes so that no-one should come near; or shows some danger or marvellous thing there or invites us to weep or laugh together with them. Thus whatever the painted persons do among themselves or with the beholder, all is pointed towards ornamenting or teaching the *istoria*.'

The third theme is the most humanist. It is the nature and standing of the artist and his art. The second book opens with a eulogy of painting as a noble activity, supporting religion, bringing glory to its exponents, making them indeed seem almost godlike. This consideration of the artist is continued in the third book where Alberti discusses the intellectual equipment of the artist. He must know geometry. He must associate with poets and orators who will give him indispensable assistance in choosing subjects and arranging his compositions; Phidias for instance confessed that it was from Homer that he learnt how to portray Zeus with proper majesty. Painting is a liberal art like poetry and rhetoric, proper for educated men, not an activity for unlettered artisans.

De Statua which is a simpler and shorter work with a single theme is concerned with the representation of the human body in sculpture. The purpose of sculpture is again the representation of nature. Sculptors aim that, 'the works which they undertake, as far as it is in their power, shall appear to the observer to resemble closely the real bodies of nature.' But apart from portraits, of which Alberti approves, the aim is to represent an idealised nature. There is a proper relationship between the sizes of the different parts of the body which the sculptor should observe. The later parts of *Statua* set out precisely the proportions which he should follow.

The crowded dramatic scenes, full of expressive figures, which Alberti regarded as the painters' proper ambition recall most strongly Donatello's Paduan reliefs of a decade later but most of Alberti's critical standards were foreshadowed in the works of art produced by Donatello and Masaccio in the 1420s. It would therefore be possible to regard Alberti's doctrines as a commentary on modern art rather than an independent body of theory drawn from humanist sources and it is reasonable to suppose that Alberti was at least influenced by the works of art which he had seen. With the exception of the debt to the medieval optical tradition, however, the material of the *Della Pittura* is entirely humanist. Although the subjects of the major works of contemporary art were Christian the subjects which Alberti mentions are exclusively classical. When, for instance, he condemns the use of gold he does not refer to the haloes of saints; he says, 'even if one should paint Virgil's Dido, whose quiver was of gold, her golden hair knotted in gold and her purple robe girdled with gold, the horse's reins and everything of gold, I would not wish to use gold at all for it is in colours imitating the rays of gold that there is most admiration and praise for the artist.' Alberti does not appear to be adducing parallels even from classical works of art which he had seen. The predominance of classical references has a literary basis like the examples of domestic economy in *Della Famiglia*.

Moreover in two important respects the substance of Alberti's attitude was clearly influenced by his classical sources. First, the selection of naturalistic realism as an ideal if not inspired, must at least have been strongly encouraged, by classical writers who praised it in the works which they prized. Alberti's main source of examples of classical works of art was the comprehensive history of ancient painting in Book 35 of Pliny's *Natural History*. Pliny consistently praised artists for their realism and this attitude was taken over by Alberti. Secondly the notion of the visual artist as an individual genius who moved in the highest circles, must, apart from its reflection of the Ciceronian oratorical ideal,[1] be derived from reading Pliny and Vitruvius who portrayed artists of antiquity in this way. Pliny had said that Painting was a liberal art in which no slave had ever executed any important work[2] and Vitruvius had given an account of the liberal accomplishments necessary for an architect. It was from Pliny that Alberti took the story of Zeuxis giving his paintings away because their value was too great for any price to be set upon them. There is a long historical movement in which art escapes from its subservience to religion and becomes itself the object of religious awe and the source of religious inspiration. *Della Pittura* is an important early stage in this and it did much to encourage a new view of art. But since Pliny and Vitruvius were not unknown before Alberti we must reckon with the possibility that it was not entirely a new influence, that perhaps the classical reading of earlier humanists had led them to spread such ideas before they were crystallised in this book.

If we try to move backwards behind the period of Alberti's impact we find first of all that by the late 1420s there is clear evidence of contacts between humanists and artists and of an interest by humanists, in art, of a kind which could well have affected the practitioners. In September 1428 Nanni di Miniato, a former assistant of Donatello and Michelozzo, wrote from Naples to Matteo Strozzi, a friend of Bruni and Marsuppini and an amateur collector of manuscripts and student of Greek. He had evidently been on the lookout for pieces of classical art on Strozzi's behalf and he reported two sarcophagi that he had seen between Lucca and Pisa, adding the recommendation that Donatello had pronounced them good.[3] In 1430 Poggio wrote from Rome to

[1] J.R.Spencer, 'Ut Rhetorica Pictura', *Journal of the Warburg and Courtauld Institutes*, xx, 1957.

[2] *Natural History*, xxxv, xxxvi, 77.

[3] C. von Fabriczy, 'Nanni di Miniato, detto Fora', *Jahrbuch der königlicher Preussischen Kunstsammlungen*, xxvii, 1906, pp. 74-6. On Strozzi as a humanist, A.Della Torre, *Storia dell'Accademia Platonica di Firenze* (Florence, 1902), pp. 287-91.

Niccoli in Florence about three marble heads, alleged to be by Polycletus and Praxiteles, which an agent had found for him in Chios and which he hoped to put in his study. He added, 'I have here also something I shall send home. Donatello has seen it and praised it greatly.'[1] In both cases the practising artist is accepted in humanist circles as the judge of classical art. That Poggio at this time admired classical sculpture not merely because it was ancient but also because of its realism can be seen from a letter which he wrote in 1431 to a correspondent at Rhodes, whom he hoped might supply him with specimens, in which he says that he admires the art of the ancient sculptors because, 'they transform the mute and senseless substance so that it seems to breathe and speak and they sometimes represent the passions of the soul so that matter which can feel neither joy nor grief seems to be smiling or grieving'.[2] This is a particularly interesting comment because the humanist is adopting from classical art a critical standard which is clearly related to the novelties of Donatello and Masaccio. Much earlier, in 1417, Poggio had demanded the erection of a monument to one of his heroes, Zabarella, in what he considered to be the classical manner:

A magnificent monument should be raised to him at public expense on which an account should be inscribed of his deeds as used to be done for those who laid down their lives for the fatherland. Above it should be placed a golden statue in the ancient manner on whose base should be written *Parenti Patriae*. But since this custom has gone into disuse among us it will be enough to set up a monument and decorate it in the manner of our ancestors with an inscription to his honour and for the imitation of posterity.[3]

No doubt similar ideas were behind the new fashion started by the classicising tomb erected for Baldassare Cossa. A contemporary description of a visit to Florence by Ciriaco d'Ancona about 1431-2, which seems to be preserved in an account of his life put together much later, includes artists together with humanists and their patrons among the notables of the city whom he visited. He

[1] Poggio, *Epistolae*, I, p. 322.

[2] Poggio, *Epistolae*, IV, 2.

[3] Poggio, *Opera*, pp. 260-61.

said that he had met Cosimo, Niccolò da Uzzano (one of the leading city politicians), Palla Strozzi, Bruni, Marsuppini, Filelfo (it was during Filelfo's stay at Florence), and Niccoli, 'the great *biblicultor*'. Together with Marsuppini he visited Niccoli's library and told him of the antiquities he had seen in the Levant and saw his collection of antique works of art. He also apparently saw both ancient works and their own creations of bronze and marble at the workshops of Donatello and Ghiberti.[1]

By 1434 the renaissance of the visual arts seemed sufficiently striking in those circles for an austere humanist, Marsuppini, to use it with a rather surprising reversal of priorities as a model for the revival of ancient philosophy. If the painters, sculptors and architects of our time can in some part emulate the temples, the gates, the columns, the paintings, the marble figures and bronze statues of the ancients ... shall we not imitate those ancients whom as Statius says we follow long after and whose traces we adore.'[2] About 1440 Poggio could open his dialogue *De Nobilitate* with a joke about the humanists' established veneration for classical art. Poggio imagined himself in his country house near Florence visited by Niccoli and Lorenzo de' Medici, Cosimo's brother, to whom he wished to show some pieces of sculpture which he had brought from Rome. Lorenzo, smiling, says that Poggio has been reading how the ancients decorated their houses with paintings and sculpture and statues of their ancestors and, since he has no portraits of his own forbears, 'wants to make this place and himself noble with these trifling and broken relics of marbles'.[3]

Direct evidence of contacts between artists and humanists and of humanist interest in contemporary and classical art is common enough then after 1425. But by that date the essential artistic advances had already been made by Donatello and Masaccio. Direct evidence from the crucial first quarter of the fifteenth century is rare. There are traditions which stress the early connection between humanists and artists but they were mostly

---

[1] 'Et apud donatellum Nenciumque statuarios nobiles plera vetusta novaque ab eis aedita ex aere marmoreve simulachra' (*Antichità Picene*, xv, p. xcii).

[2] P.G.Ricci, 'Una consolatoria inedita del Marsuppini', p. 397.

[3] Poggio, *Opera*, p. 65.

written down by biographers much later and must be discounted as evidence for its origins. We can only make a hypothetical reconstruction out of the fragments of evidence of classical influence in art, of patronage and of the occasional humanist remarks. Examples of the affinities of classical models with the art of this period are not difficult to find. The most obvious of the generic types is the Roman statue of the toga-clad emperor or senator which lies behind the prophets and saints of Nanni, Donatello and Ghiberti and from which they borrowed both the general realism and the particular stances. It is possible that the new technique of low relief was partly inspired by ancient gems. Donatello, who many years later reproduced such a gem on the helmet of Goliath in the bronze David, may well have used such a model for the horse in the St George relief.[1] One of the best things in Ghiberti's *Commentarii* is his enthusiastic description of the effect of light in a chalcedony engraved with Diomedes' theft of the Palladium which he had seen in the collection of Niccoli.[2] The other figure in the St George relief, the princess in swirling robes, seems to have been inspired by the Maenad type in ancient relief sculpture which reappears as the Salome in both the Siena and the Lille panels. Another possible generic influence which may have been of wide significance is the use of light in ancient wall paintings as an inspiration for Masaccio's use of light in his frescoes. There are also cases where modern works appear to reflect identifiable ancient remains. A striking example which has recently come to light is the resemblance of the Child in Masaccio's Uffizi Madonna to a surviving Etruscan bronze.[3] The head of Donatello's beardless prophet bears a strong resemblance to an ancient bust and some features of the head of his Jeremiah recall portraits of the third-century Emperor Gallienus.[4] To link bor-

---

[1] G.Castelfranco, *Donatello* (London, 1963), pp. 20-21.

[2] *Lorenzo Ghibertis Denkwürdigkeiten (I Commentarii)*, ed. J. von Schlosser (Berlin, 1912), I, p. 64. The gem is known; see E.Kris, *Meister und Meisterwerke der Steinschneidekunst in der italienischen Renaissance* (Vienna, 1929), I, pp. 18-19.

[3] R.Offner, 'Light on Masaccio's Classicism', *Studies in the History of Art presented to William E.Suida* (London, 1959).

[4] A.Nicholson, 'Six Portrait Statues', *Art in America*, xxx, 1942; cf. G.de Francovich, 'Appunti su Donatello e Jacopo della Quercia', *Bollettino d'Arte*, ix, 1929.

rowings with the teachings of humanists is a more difficult matter. Does the Hercules motif on the Porta della Mandorla reflect Salutati's interest in the allegorical interpretation of the Hercules story?[1] This is a possibility that can hardly become a certainty. A humanist influence that comes near to being a certainty, however, is revealed by the use of classical lettering for inscriptions on works of art. It appears first in Ghiberti's St John the Baptist about 1412-16, on Nanni's St Philip (c. 1415), on Masaccio's early Madonna at S.Giovenale di Cascia (1422) and on Donatello's *Zuccone* (c. 1425)[2] (Plate 44). The form of lettering in these inscriptions often seems to be more closely related to ancient inscriptions than to contemporary humanist scripts but it seems likely that the interest of the artists was first inspired by the passion of Niccoli and Poggio for reviving classical forms of lettering. The natural link between imitation of the classics and a certain kind of aesthetic austerity comes out in a remark made by Bruni to Niccoli in a letter about the new script in 1407. He is asking Niccoli to do some capital letters in a volume of Cicero's orations for Bartolomeo Capra. The point of entrusting the job to Niccoli was that he would do it, 'not in gold or in pointed script but in the ancient manner. . . . He (Capra) could have gilding done here if he wanted such a thing. But he scorns that and is devoted to antiquity.'[3] There is something in common between this and Alberti's prohibition on gold in painting.

The evidence of the humanists' interest in art at this period is really confined to the two figures of Niccoli and Chrysoloras. We have seen that in 1413, when Guarino was writing his denunciaciation of Niccoli, one of the despicable traits which he mentioned was the habit of adducing evidence from coins and marble sculptures in support of his theories about orthography. Probably in 1407, Bruni wrote to Niccoli from Rome saying that, 'a certain Roman promised me a little stone with Narcissus seeing himself in the water which he had found at Ostia when he was digging. I

---

[1] Krautheimer, *Ghiberti*, p. 280.

[2] M.Meiss, 'Toward a More Comprehensive Renaissance Palaeography', *Art Bulletin*, XLII, 1960; L.Berti, 'Masaccio a S.Giovenale di Cascia', *Acropoli*, II, 1962.

[3] Bruni, *Epistolae*, II, x.

was waiting for it joyfully to please you who are a keen student of these things.' The Roman broke his promise.[1] In his *Dialogi* Bruni makes Niccoli use an artistic simile: 'What would you say of a painter who would claim to have such knowledge of his art that when he started to paint a scene people would believe that another Apelles or Zeuxis was born in their age, but when his paintings were revealed it would prove to be laughably painted with distorted outlines? Would he not deserve universal mockery?'[2] This is perhaps an indication that Niccoli was already at the very beginning of the century urging artists to be true to ancient realism just as he was certainly urging humanists to copy ancient orthography and script. There is plenty of evidence later on in the twenties and thirties that Niccoli was a keen collector of antiques.[3] In the earliest recollections of him, written soon after his death in 1437, Giannozzo Manetti said that, 'he delighted in ancient paintings and sculptures. There was nothing found in the whole of Italy from the hands of those ancient painters and sculptors that he did not try to collect, sparing no expense, in his own house.'[4] Many years later Vespasiano wrote in his life of Niccoli that, 'he not only favoured men of letters but, being greatly interested in painting, sculpture and architecture and well versed in them, he showed great favour to Brunelleschi, Donatello, Luca della Robbia and Ghiberti and he was on intimate terms with them.'[5] Taken together, the evidence strongly suggests that Niccoli already had a keen interest in classical art before 1410 and makes it possible that he had a decisive influence on the earliest stages of the movement in art.

Behind Niccoli it is possible that Chrysoloras was the original inspirer. He certainly had an uncommonly strong interest in art. Among the letters which he wrote from John XXIII's court (*c.* 1411-13) there is one in which his delight in exploring the works

[1] Bruni, *Schriften*, p. 106.

[2] *Prosatori Latini del Quattrocento*, p. 72, quoted by Gombrich, 'From the revival of letters to the reform of the arts', p. 80.

[3] Krautheimer, *Ghiberti*, pp. 301-4.

[4] *Traversari/Mehus*, I, p. lxxvii.

[5] Vespasiano da Bisticci, *Vite di Uomini Illustri del Secolo XV*, ed. L.Frati (Bologna, 1892-3), III, p. 90.

of art surviving in Rome led him to state a rudimentary aesthetic theory which laid stress on realism and the graphic expression of the passions.[1] His long letter of the same period about the cities of Rome and Constantinople contains passages which are curiously evocative of various future aspects of the Florentine Renaissance: delight in Roman relief sculpture done so that in the battle scenes the art of the sculptor rivals nature and you can see the individuals fleeing, laughing, weeping, aroused, angry; regret about the neglect of classical works of art inspired by religious distaste; admiration for the great dome of S.Sophia and for the engineering skill which enabled the architect to plan it, which Chrysoloras expresses in terms reminiscent of the later Florentine attitude to Brunelleschi.[2] Chrysoloras's appreciation of the material remains of antiquity was so strong that he may well have fired the imagination of his pupils in Florence with the idea of making a third Rome and directed their taste towards artistic realism. At any rate, if the letter to John Paleologus is any indication of his state of mind a decade earlier, he must have strengthened the Florentine sense of the connection between the literary, artistic and architectural aspects of classical civilisation. The traditional reputation of Chrysoloras is concerned mainly with his services as a teacher of the Greek language but this view of him is derived mainly from Bruni who was not much interested in art. There was probably a powerful aesthetic influence which was forgotten because it was transmitted through Niccoli and Poggio who had no occasion to write about it.

The evidence of patronage does not give a great deal of help in identifying direct relationships. Of Masaccio's major works, the commissioning of the Trinity fresco is obscure;[3] the Brancacci frescoes were commissioned by Felice Brancacci, a very prominent merchant famous as the commander of the first galley fleet

---

[1] Migne, *Patrologia Graeca*, CLVI, cols. 57-60; translation and comment in M. Baxandall, 'Guarino, Pisanello and Manuel Chrysoloras', *Journal of the Warburg and Courtauld Institutes*, XXVIII, 1965, pp. 197-8.

[2] *Patrologia Graeca*, CLVI, cols. 28, 48, 49; cf. above, p. 10.

[3] Borsook, *Mural Painters of Tuscany*, p. 143; von Simson, 'Über die Bedeutung von Masaccio's Trinitätsfresko', pp. 122-4.

sent to Alexandria in 1422 but without any known intellectual distinction;[1] the Pisa polyptych by a Pisan notary. Donatello's earlier works were mostly done for the big enterprises of the major gilds; his patrons therefore included a number of members of the richest layer in Florentine society who may or may not have been responsive to the latest intellectual fashions. After 1420 he worked more for other clients, mostly on ecclesiastical commissions outside Florence. The only clearly significant suggestion is that Cosimo may have spread his fame. The Cossa tomb was done in 1425-7 for the executors, of whom the chief was Giovanni di Bicci de' Medici so that the choice of the artist may have been influenced by his son.[2] The tradition that the work for the tomb of Cardinal Rainaldo Brancacci, an old supporter of Cossa, was ordered by Cosimo is supported by the fact that the money for it passed through Cosimo's bank in 1426-7.[3] Cosimo's links with Ghiberti, however, are better attested. He appears to have taken the lead in the supervision of the St Matthew Statue; Ghiberti made a shrine for the relics of Saints Protus, Hyacinth and Nemesius for Traversari's monastery at Cosimo's expense about 1425-7 and he mounted an ancient gem for Cosimo about 1430.[4]

The most interesting pieces of documentary evidence about the planning of works of art which have been unearthed from the records of the early fifteenth century both relate, as it happens, to Lorenzo Ghiberti. One of them is about the commissioning of the statue of St Matthew by the *Cambio*, the bankers' gild, to be placed in their niche on Or San Michele. From the very full records which survive we know that the consuls of the gild decided to proceed with the statue on 19 June 1419 and that they entrusted the control of the work, which was to be 'of bronze or brass, as beautiful as it can be made,' to a committee of four, one of whom was Cosimo de' Medici. In July it was decided to commission Ghiberti and his contract laid down that the statue was to be at least as big as the St John the Baptist, which he had done for

[1] C. Carnesecchi, 'Messer Felice Brancacci', *Rivista d'Arte*, I, 1903.

[2] Janson, *Donatello*, II, pp. 59-61.

[3] Janson, II, pp. 89-90.

[4] Krautheimer, *Ghiberti*, pp. 138-9, 300.

the *Calimala* gild, and was to be 'gilded entirely or in part as it shall seem to the consuls of the gild and the four *operai* or to two-thirds of them.' We learn that on 30 January 1422 Cosimo reported to the consuls on the progress of the work, saying that the casting of the statue was now finished and that 200 florins were needed for cleaning and chasing it, putting it in place and decorating the niche. Of the dozens of banking firms which contributed to the fund the most generous were Cosimo's and the company of Lorenzo, son of Palla Strozzi.[1] Though they are not so well documented the works at the Baptistry and the cathedral were presumably administered similarly by the *Lana* and *Calimala* gilds. The result was a competition between committees to commission the most splendid works and between artists to produce the most effective monuments. Amateurs with classical tastes like Cosimo must often have been able to influence the choice of artists and styles through this system of patronage.

The other piece of evidence sheds some light on humanist connections. In 1424 Leonardo Bruni supplied the *Calimala* gild with a programme of *Old Testament* scenes for the Baptistry door. He ended his letter: 'Whoever has them to design must be well instructed in each episode (*historia*) so that he can arrange the persons and events and must have gracefulness to ornament them well. But I would like to be close to the designer to make him grasp every point of significance that the episode carries.' This is interesting, but Bruni's design was not the one which Ghiberti implemented. Traversari and Niccoli are known to have corresponded about the matter and it has been conjectured that they may have been the consultants for the final list of scenes. It reflects an original view of the *Old Testament*, perhaps indebted to St Ambrose, and in the final panel the meeting of Solomon and the Queen of Sheba is probably used to represent the ideal of the reconciliation of the Latin and Orthodox churches of which Traversari was a prominent supporter.[2] In view of this it is all the more interesting to find Traversari at the end of 1429 writing to a

[1] A. Doren, 'Das Aktenbuch für Ghibertis Matthäusstatue an Or San Michele zu Florenz', *Italienische Forschungen*, 1, 1906, pp. 19-55.

[2] Krautheimer. *Ghiberti*, pp. 161-2, 169-87.

foreign humanist Giovanni Aurispa on behalf of Ghiberti to ask for a loan of a manuscript of Athenaeus's *Ta Organika*, an ancient work on military machines which Ghiberti later quoted in his *Commentarii*, and Aurispa replying that 'that sculptor' could have the book only if he got two others in exchange.[1] All this suggests that some humanists had more appreciation of artists than others and that Bruni was one of those who held more aloof. He wrote later in 1441 that,

an artist who has acquired a certain perfection and standing in his art, such as Apelles in painting or Praxiteles in sculpture, does not need to understand military science or the government of the state or to have a knowledge of the nature of things. Indeed as Socrates says in the Apology it is a common vice in artists that one who excels in his own art deceives himself into thinking that he has other faculties which he has not. An art therefore should be distinguished from other intellectual virtues.[2]

This is very likely a conscious riposte to the *Della Pittura*, made at a time when Bruni and Alberti were at odds over the *Certame Coronario*, and a reaction against the high valuation of artists which had been popularised by other humanists. The main significance of the case of the Gates of Paradise, however, is that it gives us some idea of the kind of close contact between artists and humanists that could have occurred frequently in the first quarter of the fifteenth century when the great sculptural enterprises were being planned by committees of gild members who would naturally turn for advice not to ecclesiastics but to humanists.

The career of Ghiberti, the artist involved in these commissions, provides good illustrations of both the extent and the limitations of the humanists' influence over artists in general. Ghiberti was a slightly older contemporary of Donatello, born about 1380. Unlike Donatello he was by training a goldsmith and painter rather than a sculptor in stone and most of his work was done in metal with a very high finish. This probably helped to attract him to the elegant styles emanating from the northern courts. He achieved an early striking success in winning the con-

[1] *Carteggio di Giovanni Aurispa*, ed. R.Sabbadini (Rome, 1931), pp. 67-9.
[2] Bruni, *Epistolae*, IX, 2.

tract for the North Doors of the Baptistry in 1403, which launched him on an extremely successful career lasting until his death in 1455. Considered in relation to the features which have been isolated here from the works of Nanni di Banco, Brunelleschi, Donatello and Masaccio, Ghiberti was a conservative, more interested in elegance than in realism. At various points in his career, however, he can be seen taking up hints from his advanced contemporaries. The St Matthew which he did for the *Cambio* about 1420, after the completion of some of Donatello's statues, shows their influence. (Plate 45.) It is still more stylised but Ghiberti has taken over some of the interest in body structure and the orator's pose. Between 1429 and 1437 Ghiberti was working on the series of *Old Testament* reliefs for the west door of the Baptistry, the Gates of Paradise. Most of the plaques rely on exquisite sculptural detail and sensuous outlines in the international style and show little interest in spatial realism; the famous Genesis relief is a good example. But among them are two in which the artist has decided suddenly – and in fact only temporarily, since later work does not conform to the same principles – to take space seriously. Both belong to about the same period as Alberti's *Della Pittura* and Donatello's Lille Feast of Herod. The Isaac panel is, from the temporal point of view, a composite affair including half a dozen episodes from the story with the same characters appearing several times (Plate 46). Spatially, however, it is grouped around a large open building made up of high rounded arches between corinthian pilasters. The space in and around the building is mostly, though not entirely, arranged according to strict perspective with the figures made in appropriate diminishing sizes and the *braccio*, one third of the height of a foreground figure, has been used as a module. To a lesser extent the same is true of the Joseph panel (Plate 47). Here the buildings in perspective are more ambitious but there is a scene in the background which is spatially quite separate from the rest of the picture.[1]

As Alberti was the humanist who dabbled in art, Ghiberti was the artist who dabbled in literature. In the last years of his life

[1] Krautheimer, *Ghiberti*, pp. 249-53.

Ghiberti set down his views on art, the only artist of this period to do so, in three books of memoirs with the humanist title *Commentarii*. The *Commentarii* are a curious mixture of laborious plagiarism and original insights. Book I, which discusses the culture necessary for a sculptor and the history of classical art, is almost entirely lifted from Vitruvius and Pliny. Book II is a largely independent account of modern art since Cimabue, followed by an artistic autobiography. Ghiberti used some of the same classical authors as Alberti had used in the *Della Pittura*, without his grace or originality, and presented his version of some of the same attitudes. Reflecting on his own life, he claimed to have followed the Vitruvian precept of devotion to study rather than money-making – taken over by Alberti also – and to have concerned himself especially with nature and perspective. 'I have sought to investigate how nature proceeds in herself and how I could approximate to her, how the *species* come to the eye and how much effect the visual virtue has and how visual things go and what should be the theory of statuary and of painting.' At several points he speaks of perspective as a matter of great importance. He adds it to a list of necessary accomplishments for artists taken from Vitruvius. In recounting the story of the competition between Protogenes and Apelles from Pliny he adds his own view that it must have been a competition in perspective. When he comes to describe his own achievement in the Gates of Paradise he does it in these terms:

I strove to observe with all the scale and proportion and to endeavour to imitate nature in them as much as I might be capable. . . . There were ten stories all in architectural settings in the relation with which the eye measures them, and real to such a degree that if one stands far from them they seem to stand out in high relief. They are actually in very low relief and on the standing planes one sees the figures which are near appear larger and those that are far off smaller as reality shows it.[1]

This is Ghiberti's expression in cruder language of Alberti's ideal of imitation of nature. It corresponds to the Isaac and Joseph

[1] *Lorenzo Ghibertis Denkwürdigkeiten*, I, pp. 45, 4, 24-5, 48-9; translation, Krautheimer, *Ghiberti*, p. 14.

panels but not, as he implies, to the whole series. In the third book of the *Commentarii*, in which he went at length into the question of light and optics, what he produced was a chain of quotations from medieval lore, the writings of Arabic and schol-astic philosophers without a presentation of the Albertian scheme. Ghiberti's grasp of the idea of pictorial space was fleeting and imperfect and rather superficially related to the aims which actually dominated his own artistic production. His desire to present himself as an understanding devotee of the new ways, although he was an artist who lacked neither success nor admira-tion, shows the prestige of Albertian ideas in the artists' world.

The extreme emphasis on physical realism and the direct por-trayal of human emotions which gives distinction to the work of Masaccio and Donatello was a passing phase, a moment of intense effort in one direction which is not paralleled in the work of their contemporaries and did not persist in the work of their successors. We have already seen the half-hearted acceptance of their ideals by Ghiberti. Analogous reflections of their influence, falling far short of complete sympathy, are to be found in the works of the artists who collaborated closely with them, Michelozzo and Masolino. Michelozzo's Aragazzi monument (Plate 48) is a piece of advanced classical imitation but it has little of Donatello's interest in human emotions. Masolino, who worked with Masac-cio on the Brancacci frescoes and elsewhere, presents complicated problems of influence because the extent of the collaboration is uncertain. Masolino was a pupil of Ghiberti and a painter of delightful works with an inventive picturesque imagination and a preference for smooth flowing lines. His instincts were very different from Masaccio's and the collaboration between them was slightly bizarre. In the Brancacci frescoes themselves Masolino predominates in the sweet and fairly shallow figures of Adam and Eve before the Fall. On the other hand the scene depicting St Peter preaching to the people, though it is generally attributed to Masolino, shows a great deal of Masacciesque influence in its substantial figures and interesting faces. The famous double scene of the Resurrection of Tabitha and the Healing of the Cripple has a pair of charming but superfluous figures in the centre which are characteristically Masolino (Plate 49). The main scenes to either side are included in a unified perspective setting and they include some figures which would hardly have been composed by Masolino working quite alone. Similar problems of attribution arise in the other two sets of paintings in which they may well have collaborated, a set of panels for S. Maria Maggiore in Rome, probably done for Martin v, and the frescoes in S. Clemente, done for Cardinal Branda Castiglione. At S. Clemente the fresco of the crucifixion with its complicated, crowded scene at the foot of the cross, including many figures in a variety of attitudes, has been seen by some as an obvious creation of Masaccio and even suggested as the inspiration for Alberti's preference for paintings crowded with figures. The fresco technique on the other hand, as shown by the designs recently revealed below the paint, seems to prove the execution to be Masolino's. These problems and in general the degree of Masaccio's direct or indirect contribution are probably insoluble. It is certain that in his main later work, the frescoes which he did also for Branda Castiglione at Castiglione d'Olona in Lombardy, Masolino returned with renewed enthusiasm to Gothic sweetness. Most of the influence of Masaccio, which may have been deeply absorbed for a time, vanished, though the roundness of the figures in this later work sometimes shows that it was not totally forgotten.[1]

The most distinctive innovations of Donatello and Masaccio were not adopted by their immediate successors. One of the most original and powerful painters of the mid-fifteenth century, for instance, was Paolo Uccello who was born in 1397 and worked at an early age in Ghiberti's workshop, then went to Venice. He returned to Florence in the early 1430s when Albertian influence was strongest. Uccello was an aesthetically adventurous man, fascinated by the possibilities of perspective drawing. Some of the frescoes which he painted in the Chiostro Verde at Santa Maria Novella in the 1430s and 1440s, notably the Drunkenness of Noah and the Flood (Plate 50), reveal a most elaborate use of perspective drawing and a great interest in realistic foreshortening and the

[1] Masolino's work is conveniently surveyed by E. Micheletti, *Masolino da Panicale* (Milan, 1959).

drawing of complicated rounded objects. The Flood fresco and the later panels of the Rout of San Romano also show an interest in the illusory effects of light. Uccello was certainly much influenced by perspective theory – whether this came to him from Alberti or from the medieval writers on optics is less certain.[1] In him, however, it was a one-sided development. He was a designer of advanced visual tours-de-force, not much interested in human character. Piero della Francesca, who worked in Florence at the end of the 1430s was again fascinated by perspective. His later Flagellation (probably *c.* 1455-60) is one of the most famous exercises in elaborate, mathematically exact perspective with a framework of classical architecture. But his great cycle of frescoes of the History of the Cross at Arezzo, although it abounds in splendid exercises in the portrayal of figures and scenes in depth, is dominated by an elaborate, complex and beautiful iconographical pattern and shows little interest in drama or emotion.[2] Similarly Andrea Castagno and Filippo Lippi owe to Masaccio their ability to paint the human body but their realism is a tool used superficially for striking visual effects not for the exploration of the human personality. Apart from the later works of Donatello himself, we have to wait until the very end of the century before this quest is resumed.

Masaccio and Donatello were not therefore the founders of a school. Their immediate successors accepted only the technical part of their innovation, the control of body and space but not the dramatic realism. This is not simply a matter of the difference between the great and the merely good artist. Piero was an artist with very great powers, but he was trying to do something different. The achievement of Masaccio and Donatello required genius of course, but the peculiar tendencies of their work are most easily explained as the product of an intellectual climate. That climate was also, as we shall see, a temporary phenomenon. The

[1] A.Parronchi, 'Le fonti di Paolo Uccello', *Paragone*, 1957, and in *Studi su la dolce prospettiva* (Milan, 1964).

[2] R.Wittkower and B.A.R.Carter, 'The Perspective of Piero della Francesca's "Flagellation"', *Journal of the Warburg and Courtauld Institutes*, XVI, 1953; C. de Tolnay, *Conceptions Religieuses dans la peinture de Piero della Francesca* (Florence, 1963).

Florentine enlightenment which has been described in earlier chapters was replaced in the later fifteenth century by intellectual tendencies of a very different kind. One important element in the intellectual climate was certainly the passion for the revival of antiquity shared by all humanists. The emphasis on pictorial space and dramatic realism owed much in the later stages to Alberti's influence. The earlier stages are more mysterious but it is a fair hypothesis that the people of Donatello and Masaccio would not have been so human if it had not been for the humanists. 'When eloquence flourished so did painting . . . and when one was reborn the other raised its head again,' said Aeneas Sylvius,[1] probably speaking more truly than he knew. The humanists' admiration for the realistic expression of emotion in ancient art, combined with their preference for common-sense moral philosophy must, where they were influential, have created an atmosphere hostile to the romantic and symbolical in art. Ghiberti, the exponent of the flowing outlines of international Gothic, a great artist but without much interest in human psychology, was not well suited to bring the new realism to birth. In the works of Donatello and Masaccio, however, there is a clear logic of development. The pursuit of realistic sculpture of the human figure under classical influence was joined by Brunelleschi's invention of perspective space. Imagine a painter of genius impressed by these novelties, a temperamental realist of deep psychological insight who knew the works of Giotto, and it is possible to see how Masaccio came to create the Brancacci frescoes. Genius apart, the difference between him and the humanist litterateurs was that, while they had imprisoned themselves within an inflexible literary convention, he was practising an art capable of reaching the heights and of expressing the humane values which they had developed out of their literary passion.

[1] In a letter of 1452, quoted by J.R.Spencer, 'Ut Rhetorica Pictura', p. 27.

8

The Return to Metaphysics

One of the best epitaphs for the Florentine enlightenment was written appropriately by a grandson of that Cino Rinuccini whose invective against Niccoli's circle gave such a vivid impression of its early days. In 1489 Alamanno Rinuccini, who had been a young intellectual in mid-century – he was born in 1426 – wrote a letter in which he reflected on the changes which had come over the intelligentsia of his city since his youth. The change which he wished to point out was the revival of interest in philosophy, which forty years earlier had been an unfashionable pursuit:

> Not long ago few people concerned themselves with philosophy – which includes the understanding both of nature and of supernatural things; they thought they had done more than enough of that if they knew Aristotle's *Moralia*. I am thinking of our own citizens. Only those who had joined one of the religious orders or who wanted to practise medicine studied philosophy. You can tell this from the writings of those who professed humane studies in the last generation; you will find that very few of them were expert in philosophy with the exception of Giannozzo Manetti. I do not think I shall be boasting if I say that Donato Acciaiuoli and I introduced our fellow citizens to the love of philosophy. When John Argyropoulos, a man most expert in philosophy and all good arts, came to the city and we had spoken with him and got to know about his profession and the reasons for his travels we were the first to discuss with Cosimo de' Medici the possibility of employing him.[1]

We shall return to Donato Acciaiuoli and John Argyropoulos later. Rinuccini's main point, and he was certainly right, was that

[1] Alamanno Rinuccini, *Lettere ed Orazioni*, ed. V.R.Giustiniani (Florence, 1953), p. 189.

there had been a radical change in outlook among the intelligent-sia. In the second half of the fifteenth century the sophisticated world of Florence was beguiled by forms of philosophy and art in which the tendencies of the first Florentine Renaissance were not only abandoned but in a sense reversed. Marsilio Ficino, the protégé of Cosimo in his last years and later of Lorenzo the Magnificent, constructed a philosophy of the soul, one of whose explicit purposes was to reunite those things which the earlier humanists had been inclined to separate, to show the impiety of a separation of philosophy from religion.[1] Ficino's philosophy was an adaptation of Platonism or Neo-Platonism for use as a Christian metaphysic. This made it radically different from the Aristotelian scholasticism which the earlier humanists so much disliked; and Ficino, who was an expert Greek scholar and translated many of Plato's dialogues, could not be accused of the literary barbarity with which his predecessors had taunted the schoolmen. His philosophical work however was an effort of synthesis of a similar kind to that of the thirteenth-century scholastics, an attempt to use the insights of the Greek philosophers to construct a hierarchical explanation of the universe which would also be consistent with Christian doctrine. As the translator not only of Plato but also of Plotinus, Dionysius the Areopagite, Iamblichus and Proclus, Ficino had an unrivalled knowledge of both Platonic and Neo-Platonic ideas. The metaphysic which he presented elaborately in his *Theologia Platonica*, written between 1469 and 1474, was inspired by the Neo-Platonic conception of a hierarchy of being ascending from matter to God. He placed the human soul at the middle point of an ascending scale, below it the categories of matter and quality, above it the angelic soul, corresponding to Plotinus's 'Mind', and God. The hierarchy was defined by the ascent from the irrationality and divisibility of matter to the total unity and rationality of God. God, the highest principle, was equated with unity, self-sufficiency, reason. The justification for a belief in the immortality of the soul, towards

---

[1] 'Quicumque philosophiae studium impie nimium a sancta religione seiungant, agnoscant aliquando ...' (Marsile Ficin, *Théologie Platonicienne de l'Immortalité des Ames*, ed. R. Marcel (Paris, 1964), I, p. 36).

which Ficino directed the argument of the later part of the book, was that the soul in part shared these divine qualities and was therefore independent of the body. Neo-Platonist reason therefore supplied a satisfactory explanation of the world, defensible by rational argument, which was also consistent with Christianity. The best known paintings of the late fifteenth century, Botticelli's *Primavera* and Birth of Venus can only be understood as pictorial representations of the magical and mythological ideas which Ficino found consistent with his philosophy.[1] Ficino and Botticelli were not of course the only figures of the late fifteenth century. They were, however, outstanding innovators in their two fields and the distinction between the character of their creations and those of the early fifteenth century gave the intellectual world of their time a new colour. The contrast is as striking as that separating, say, the sceptical world of Voltaire from the mystical religiosity of Chateaubriand. Why did Florentine thought develop in this way?

The end of the old humanism and the beginning of the new one are not entirely separable phenomena. The world of Bruni came to an end, of course, because Bruni and his friends died; but the supersession of the ways of thought which they had created by an opposing tradition is something which demands further explanation. The circumstances in which they had flourished came to an end also. The change in circumstances is the main subject of this chapter.

Two main factors transformed the climate of Italian intellectual life in the middle of the fifteenth century. The first was the sudden and rapid recovery of the papacy from the degradation of the conciliar period during the decade between 1440 and 1450. This had the immediate effect of releasing the Pope from his political dependence upon Florence and of breaking once and for all the social links which bound the papal curia to the Florentine intellectual world. Within a very short time Rome became what it had never been before, the undisputed capital of Italian humanism. Though this age of supremacy was temporary it decisively turned

[1] See e.g., E.H.Gombrich, 'Botticelli's Mysteries', *Journal of the Warburg and Courtauld Institutes*, VIII, 1945.

back the intellectual currents of the first period of Florentine humanism. The second factor was the influence of the Greek emigrés who came to Italy as a result of the Council of Ferrara-Florence in 1438-9 and of the fall of Constantinople in 1453. They were few in number but they found a receptive audience for the expertise which they brought from the schools of Byzantium. Coming into an environment different from the one which had greeted Chrysoloras half a century earlier, they made a different contribution to the education of their Italian audiences. While Chrysoloras had confirmed his pupils in their neo-Latin prejudices the new wave of Greeks delighted Italians by initiating them into the arcane mysteries of Platonic and Neo-Platonic philosophy. The lip-service which had been paid to Plato on account of his ravishing literary grace was turned into a real acquaintance with his works and submission to the fascination of his doctrines. It is not too much to say that the dominant position held by Cicero in the imagination of the early Florentine renaissance was lost to Plato in the next fifty years.

In January 1443 the papal court had been so long at Florence that the connection was assuming the proportions of another Babylonish Captivity and the departure of Eugenius IV for his proper see in that month was witnessed with much head-shaking and regret. The Signoria itself posted a sonnet warning Eugenius against trusting false allies like Alfonso V rather than trusted friends like themselves.[1] The departure from Florence was part of a diplomatic revolution which unexpectedly confirmed the political wisdom of Eugenius's rigid opposition to the Council of Basle but also transformed the map of Italian alliances in such a way that the intimate connection between Florence and the Curia was broken. The normal political pattern of the late 1430s had been an alliance between Alfonso of Aragon and Filippo Maria Visconti, cautiously supporting the Council of Basle and facing an alliance of Florence and the Pope. In the years 1442-3 this structure broke down very rapidly and was replaced by another.[2] It is

[1] F.Flamini, 'La Lirica Toscana del Rinascimento', *Annali della Reale Scuola Normale di Pisa*, 1891, p. 125.

[2] There is no modern account of these events but the pattern is clear enough for

usually difficult to isolate decisive factors in diplomatic history and in this case it is hard to say whether the lead was taken by the Pope, by Alfonso or by Filippo Maria. From Eugenius's point of view the crucial irritation which caused him to contemplate a change of friends was perhaps provided by Cosimo's support of Francesco Sforza, exceedingly distasteful to Eugenius because of Sforza's conquests in the papal states. In April 1442 Sforza entered the service of King René and Eugenius for another assault, on the old pattern, on Alfonso's position in Naples. In the course of the summer, however, Eugenius also made an engagement with Sforza's enemy Piccinino who agreed to oust Sforza from the March of Ancona. Piccinino was the servant of Milan, the enemy of Florence. On the second of June 1442 Alfonso entered the city of Naples and thus became more obviously unbeatable, which may also have helped to change the Pope's mind. Two months later Eugenius foiled a plan of Cosimo to reconcile Sforza and Piccinino by releasing the latter from his oath. By the end of 1442 it was becoming clear that there was a quite new alignment of powers, Eugenius on friendly terms with Milan and Naples, facing Sforza supported by Florence and Venice. The new engagements were not entirely in the open. Eugenius still outwardly supported the Angevin claim to Naples when King René visited Florence in the autumn of 1442. In January 1443 he left Florence for Siena where he lifted the mask and for the first time recognised Alfonso as King of Naples, formalising this approval in the Treaty of Terracino in June. On the twenty-eighth of September 1443 Eugenius re-entered Rome and his exile was over.

Eugenius's diplomacy in 1442-3 repeated with much more permanent effects the pattern which had appeared temporarily in the pontificate of Martin v. Papal independence required control of the papal states and reasonable relations with Naples. On this basis it was possible to resist the menace of conciliarism in the rest of Europe. But the political independence of the papacy involved

detailed references to be unnecessary. The best account remains that in Perrens, *Histoire de Florence Depuis la Domination des Médicis*, i (Paris, 1888), supplemented by N. Valois, *La Crise Réligieuse du XVe Siècle*, ii.

a degree of coolness in relations with Florence. This aspect of the later years of Eugenius's pontificate is very prominent in contrast with the situation during the years in Florence. The clash of interests between Cosimo and Eugenius in their relations with Sforza introduced a surprising bitterness where there had once been friendship. Cosimo lost his favoured position as the Pope's banker. In 1446 he was reputed to be urging Sforza to attack and liberate Rome which Sforza might have done if Florentine money had not been inadequate. In the same year Eugenius seized Medicean property in Rome and imprisoned Bernadetto de' Medici.[1]

Unlike the recovery under Martin v, Eugenius's restoration of papal independence was permanent. The Council of Basle did not entirely cease to be a menace until the submission of Felix v to Eugenius's successor Nicholas v in 1449; but after 1443 it had lost the chance of building an irresistible party of opposition to the papacy. The end of the conciliar period cannot of course be explained simply in terms of Italian politics. There was a more complicated European loss of interest in the council and to understand why conciliarism did not effectively raise its head in the second half of the fifteenth century one would have to look to European rather than Italian history. In the short run, however, the Italian diplomatic revolution of 1442-3 was decisive in that it dictated that the conciliarists could no longer build their position on the support of Milan and Naples. When Eugenius iv died in 1447 he had redeemed the blunders of his earlier years. He had recovered secular control of the papal states and spiritual recognition in Christendom. He had effectually ended the conciliar period with its sixty years of papal humiliation. He bequeathed a strong papacy to his successor.

The political security which Nicholas v enjoyed and preserved is important in intellectual history because he used it to an extraordinary extent for intellectual and aesthetic purposes. Nicholas was a humanist pope who actually believed, in the face of the

---

[1] De Roover, *Medici Bank*, p. 198; Capponi, *Commentari* (Muratori, xviii), col. 1201; Perrens, i, p. 106. Eugenius's bitterness towards Florence is emphasised by Vespasiano da Bisticci (*Vite di Uomini Illustri*, ed. Frati, ii, p. 105).

more obvious arguments of sense and tradition, that the resources of the papacy should be harnessed to humanist ideals for the sake of its glorification. He was not of course the only pope of the Renaissance to be influenced by this notion, which is extremely prominent in the careers of his successors Pius II, Julius II and Leo X. Although his achievements were rather small, however, the novelty, completeness and sheer magnificence of his plans make him, not only the initiator, but by far the most whole-hearted exponent of the idea of the Renaissance Papacy. What was once said by an art historian of his plans for the rebuilding of Rome applies equally to his literary ambitions:

> Others have left more lasting traces. The monuments which proclaim the glory of Julius II or Leo X are more numerous than those bearing the name of Nicholas V. But, apart from the fact that they only followed the path which he opened, their programmes are not comparable with his. They lack the epic grandeur of conception, the youthfulness, freshness of impression and naive enthusiasm. . . . They concerned themselves with one building or another; Nicholas V wanted to change the face of Rome.[1]

Nicholas's literary ambitions have the same grandeur. He wanted to create a library in which the whole literature of classical antiquity would be made available to the Latin world.

Nicholas was originally a scholar of fairly humble origins from Sarzana called Tommaso Parentucelli.[2] According to tradition his introduction to Florentine humanist circles came during his student career at Bologna when he took a temporary position as tutor to the children of Rinaldo degli Albizzi and Palla Strozzi. This must have been around 1420. Later he entered the service of Niccolò Albergati and was in attendance on the cardinal at the papal Curia during its stay at Florence from 1434. According to Vespasiano, Parentucelli was fascinated by the humanist group around Bruni and Poggio who used to assemble to dispute and

---

[1] Müntz, *Les Arts à la Cour des Papes*, I, p. 69.

[2] His biography before 1447 depends partly on the account by Vespasiano da Bisticci, *Vite di nomini illustri*, ed. Frati, I. Much record evidence was collected by G. Sforza, 'La Patria, la Famiglia e la Giovinezza di Papa Niccolò V', *Atti della Reale Accademia Lucchese di Scienze, Lettere ed Arti*, XXIII, 1884.

confer morning and evening in front of the Palazzo della Signoria and 'Master Thomas as soon as he had accompanied the cardinal to the (papal) palace went to join them on a mule with two servants on foot.' He was already in those days sufficiently respected as a scholar to be asked to produce a list of Christian and pagan authors for Cosimo's library at S.Marco.[1] Whether or not there is any truth in Vespasiano's report that he was already a fanatical book-collector, employing more scribes than he could afford, he was certainly thoroughly imbued, by long acquaintance, with some of the literary passions of the Florentine humanist circle. His devotion to Florence and to Cosimo produced a marked improvement in Florentine-papal relations on his accession. Cosimo's banker in Rome, Roberto Martelli, wrote to Francesco Sforza two days after the election in confident expectation of the new pope's reliance on Cosimo[2] and in fact the Medici bank was restored to its privileged position, which in view of the new strength of papal finance during this pontificate must have added a substantial increment to Cosimo's wealth. Vespasiano records a story that the bank at one time had 100,000 florins of papal money in its hands. Curiously enough the change of attitude to Florence, which was not accompanied by any serious change in papal foreign policy, probably sprang largely from Nicholas's sentimental regard for Florentine humanism and for Cosimo as its patron. There are several instances of friendly correspondence between the pope and the banker about literary matters after his election.[3]

While his more eminent cardinals were dispatched on legations to placate and inspire other parts of Christendom – Bessarion to Bologna, Nicholas of Cusa to Western Germany, Guillaume d'Estouteville to France and Giovanni Capistrano to central Europe – Nicholas v devoted his energies to the replanning of Rome and the creation of the Vatican Library. He was the realisa-

[1] 'Inventarium Nicolai pape v, quod ipse composuit ad instantem Cosimo de Medicis . . .' (*ASI*, ser. 3, xxi, 1875, pp. 103-6).

[2] L.Osio, *Documenti Diplomatici tratti dagli archivi Milanesi* (Milan, 1864-72), iii, p. 488.

[3] E.g. *Cosmi Medicei Vita Auctore Angelo Fabronio* (Pisa, 1788-9), ii, p. 222, Nicholas asking Cosimo to allow a book in S.Marco library to be copied for him.

tion of the bookworm's wildest dream: a scholar pope, nurtured in Florentine humanism and determined to make its ideals, or what he understood to be its ideals, in defiance of the more obvious concerns of his office, the first object of policy for his pontificate. Giannozzo Manetti's sympathetic *Life*, written soon after the pope's death, which is still by far the most interesting commentary on his pontificate, tells us that he planned the rebuilding of Rome to enlarge the 'honour of the Roman Church and the glory of the apostolic see' and 'the devotion of the Christian peoples', and that he planned his library for the assistance of present and future students. The third reason for his activity, Manetti candidly adds, was desire for the glory and perpetuation of his own name (*propriae gloriae cujus suapte natura avidissimus erat, adeptionem, ac sui nominis propagationem*).[1] Though Nicholas was no doubt exceptionally ambitious, this must be regarded not merely as a personal trait but as an acceptance of the humanist scholar-great man image. The whole-hearted assumption that the humanist programme was a proper object for the resources of the papal see, shows how thoroughly the Curia, in which Nicholas had formed his ambitions, had been saturated by the ideals of the Florentine school. The finances of Nicholas's pontificate are obscure but there can be no doubt that he was lavish. The humanist correspondence of the time abounds in expressions of delight and gratitude about the new fount of patronage. The large gifts of 500 florins to Valla for his translation of Thucydides[2] and the same to Filelfo, as a token of appreciation when he passed through Rome in 1453,[3] might seem to be special recognitions of the most outstanding Italian Graecists of the day. But Niccolò Perotti, who was not in that class, also got 500 florins for his translation of Polybius.[4] Decembrio seems to have found the Pope's plans, even for a humanist, slightly exaggerated; he speaks of his 'incomprehensible thirst for books' (*in-*

[1] *Vita Nicolai Summi Pontificis auctore Jannotio Manetto Florentino* (Muratori, III, ii), col. 925.

[2] Voigt, *Wiederbelebung*, II, p. 90.

[3] Rosmini, *Vita di Francesco Filelfo da Tolentino*, II, p. 83.

[4] G.Mercati, 'Per la Cronologia della vita e degli scritti di Niccolò Perotti Arcivescovo di Siponto', *Studi e Testi*, 44, 1925, pp. 36-7.

explicabilis quaedam librorum sitis).[1] According to Manetti the final encouragement to these plans was given by the large sums of money raised for the Apostolic Chamber in the very successful jubilee of 1450 when Rome was flooded with pilgrims.

Pope Nicholas's main literary purpose was evidently to make Greek literature available in Latin translation. In order to achieve this he aimed to attract the best humanists into his service as translators. In 1452 for instance he tried to persuade Carlo Marsuppini to leave his post as Chancellor of Florence, in which he had succeeded Leonardo Bruni, and move to Rome for the sole purpose of translating Homer. Cosimo was enlisted to help in persuading Marsuppini, who went so far as to do a trial piece. The pope professed himself delighted with the '*versus suavitas admixta gravitate*' and invited him to Rome with the promise that he would be provided for in such a way as to be entirely freed of other cares. At the same time the *Signoria* of Florence was approached with a request to release Marsuppini from his duties for this purpose.[2] The Pope's chief of staff in this literary campaign was his librarian Giovanni Tortelli, who had been in Florence in the thirties, had visited Byzantium and was himself a competent translator from the Greek. The learned world recognised him as the Pope's most influential advisor and the key to patronage; as Perotti put it, Mercury to the Pope's Jupiter.[3] Between them they attracted a good deal of talent. Valla's longing to return to Rome was at last satisfied. The prejudice felt against him, not unnaturally, as a distinguished anti-papal propagandist was overcome partly through his friendship with Tortelli, partly through the intervention of Cardinal Bessarion, partly no doubt through recognition of his exceptional merit. In November 1448 he was installed at the Curia as an apostolic writer.[4] Other eminent

[1] M.Borsa, 'Pier Candido Decembrio e l'umanesimo in Lombardia', *Archivio Storico Lombardo*, ser. 2, XX, 1893, p. 377.

[2] R. Sabbadini, 'Bricciole Umanistiche', *Giornale Storico della Letteratura Italiana*, XVII, 1891, pp. 214-17; *Spicilegium Romanum*, I, pp. 574-5.

[3] R.Cessi, 'Notizie Umanistiche, III, tra Niccolò Perotto e Poggio Bracciolini', *Giornale Storico della Letteratura Italiana*, LX, 1912, p. 79 (Perotti to Tortelli, December 1453); G.Mancini, 'Giovanni Tortelli', *ASI*, LXXVIII, 1920.

[4] Mancini, *Giovanni Tortelli*, pp. 171-2; Sabbadini, *Studi sul Panormita e sul Valla*, pp. 114-21; Mancini, *Valla*, p. 237.

scholars who were attracted at one time or another into the papal service included Giannozzo Manetti, Decembrio, and the Greeks George of Trebizond and Theodore Gaza.

The actual product of Nicholas's large plans and expenditure was not in fact very impressive. The translations which were actually accomplished fall mainly into three groups, books of Aristotle, Greek historians, and Greek Fathers.[1] The quality of some of the work, particularly that done by the most active translator, George of Trebizond, was poor. The most impressive achievement was Valla's *Thucydides*. Nicholas's pontificate was short and money did not ensure quality. The very direction of the enterprise, however, shows how much Nicholas was enslaved by the assumptions of the Florentine school. Little effort was made to tackle the unknown works of Plato, who was represented only by a bad translation of the *Laws* by George of Trebizond. Aristotle who was already far more accessible received the most lavish attention. Apart from the historical works, therefore, the Western mind was not greatly enriched by Nicholas, who really had the instincts of a bibliophile – he did create an enormous library at the Vatican – rather than those of a creative scholar.

The unintentional effect of Pope Nicholas's patronage, linked with the new influx of scholars from the Byzantine world, was immense. By his emphasis on translation from the Greek the Pope created a centre of learning which completely stole the old glory of Florence and in which the chief criterion was not excellence in Latin prose composition but competence in Greek. This was brought out by the discomfiture suffered by Poggio, now an old man of over seventy with a lifetime of service in the Curia behind him but still the most characteristic of Florentine humanists in his deep Latinism. Poggio had greeted the election of Nicholas with a florid *oratio* which was a characteristic humanist mixture of idealistic exhortation and barefaced begging. He told the Pope of his duty to devote himself to the promotion of the study of literature and at the same time reminded him rather unctiously of their old friendship. He took the occasion to men-

[1] They are surveyed by Voigt, *Wiederbelebung*, II, pp. 180-98. The list given by Manetti does not entirely tally but is on the same lines.

tion that he had served the Curia for forty years, 'certainly at a lower salary than befits one who is not entirely lacking in virtue and humane studies.'[1] But Poggio lacked the equipment to take a leading part in the enterprise which Nicholas promoted and was too old to change. His first study of Greek had been undertaken in his sixties after the return to Rome in 1443, when he translated Xenophon's *Cyropaedia* with the help of George of Trebizond.[2] He compromised with the atmosphere of Nicholas's court so far as to translate the first five books of Diodorus Siculus, some Lucian and the *Golden Ass*, but by paraphrase rather than translation. George of Trebizond was probably not exaggerating wildly in saying that Poggio was 'ignorant of Greek letters'. George, whose only claim to distinction was precisely the knowledge of Greek which Poggio lacked, was one of two people at the Curia with whom Poggio quarrelled violently during the pontificate of Nicholas. The other was Valla, an old enemy, the most brilliant of the new luminaries and also a considerable Greek scholar. In both cases Poggio was the aggressor. He publicly accused George of Trebizond of lying and attacked Valla, choosing his own ground, for the views about Latin grammar which Valla had expressed in his *Elegantiae*.[3] He also quarrelled less spectacularly with Tortelli.[4] These quarrels probably arose from the fact that Poggio found the court of Nicholas v an uncomfortable place and he was no doubt glad to leave its novelties in May 1453 to spend his last years in the office at Florence vacated by the death of Marsuppini. His correspondence with old friends at the Curia after his return to Florence contains bitter complaints of the new order at Rome which he could not share. He wrote to Piero da Noceto complaining about Valla's secretaryship and other appointments procured by Tortelli. 'What moves the Pope to

[1] Poggio, *Opera*, p. 292.

[2] Walser, *Poggius*, pp. 228-31.

[3] The quarrel with George of Trebizond is surveyed by R. Cessi, 'La Contesa fra Giorgio da Trebisonda, Poggio Bracciolini e Giovanni Aurispa durante il pontificato di Niccolò v', *Archivio Storico per la Sicilia Orientale*, ix, 1912. The quarrel with Valla produced the voluminous *Invective* by Poggio and *Antidoti* by Valla (published in their respective *Opera*).

[4] Mancini, 'Giovanni Tortelli', pp. 248-9.

bestow our office so freely? Was there a shortage of secretaries? Were those he had inadequate? . . . . Does the mountain of work require new labourers in the vineyard destitute of grapes and leaves? I know that our lord the Pope is a wise man but I think he is too credulous of the importunity of place-seekers.'[1] To another correspondent he wrote about the war which these 'half-Greeklings' (*semigraeculi*) had declared against him.[2] Finally he felt compelled to write in a more conciliatory tone to Tortelli, but still with an edge. 'I am delighted that there should be learned men in the Curia expert in the translation of Greek literature: they will enrich the Latin language and if you like them you are doing your duty and I praise you for it. Indeed if we love people whom we have never seen for their virtue we ought to treat with even more affection those whom we see and speak with to whom we are superior in learning and morals.'[3]

Apart from creating a new centre, Nicholas's patronage assisted the formation of a new school of native Greek scholars with a wholly different background and a different view of their functions from the Italian Graecists of the age of Bruni and Guarino. Intellectual contacts between Italy and Byzantium had not been very uncommon in the generation before the Council of Florence but they had been sporadic and isolated, confined to Italian enthusiasts like Guarino or Filelfo and to occasional Greek visitors who served the purposes of Italian humanism, like George of Trebizond. His *Rhetorica* and *Dialectica*, both composed in Italy in the 1430s before he came into the orbit of the Curia, are works in which he makes use of his knowledge of Greek in ways which harmonise with the interests of Italian humanists.[4] In the generation after the Council of Florence the effects of the council itself, of the patronage of Nicholas v and of the extinction of the Byzantine Empire, combined to create a school of Greek emigrés in Italy with the numbers and the prestige to carry on their own intellectual debate in their own terms and eventually to insinuate

[1] Poggio, *Epistolae*, xi, xv.

[2] Poggio, *Epistolae*, xi, xxii.

[3] Poggio, *Epistolae*, xi, xxv.

[4] C. Vasoli, 'La Dialectica di Giorgio Trapezunzio', *Atti dell Accademia Toscana di Scienze e Lettere La Colombaria*, xxiv, 1959-60.

their interests into the Italian world. These interests were of a very different kind from those, springing from Chrysoloras's impact upon the rhetoricians, which had been current in the Florentine humanist world before 1438.

The most important figure in Greek emigré circles was Cardinal Bessarion who came to the Council of Florence as a young man who had already acquired a reputation as a scholar. He did not immediately stay in Italy but he was given the cardinal's hat as part of Eugenius's plan to prop up the Union, and joined the Curia when it was still at Florence in 1442. He remained at the Curia, mostly at Rome, until Nicholas v sent him as Legate to Bologna in 1450 and then returned to Rome after Nicholas's death in 1455.[1] George of Trebizond had been in papal employment since 1438. The coming of Nicholas v gave him new opportunities; he lived well on Nicholas v's generous payments for worthless translations of Eusebius and Aristotle until the quarrels with Poggio and Valla drove him from Rome in 1452. He found a temporary refuge with Alfonso at Naples but returned to Rome in the days of Calixtus III and Pius to continue his philosophical quarrels with the other Greeks. Theodore Gaza, a later emigré came to Italy about 1435. He taught at Ferrara in 1447 and refused an invitation from Cosimo to migrate to Florence but in 1450 he was attracted to Rome where he translated Aristotle and Theophrastus for the pope. After Nicholas's death he remained in contact with Rome through Bessarion's patronage.[2] These three main figures, attracting other less prominent people such as the Italian Niccolò Perotti and the Greek Michael Apostolios, formed, under the leadership of Bessarion, whose membership of the College of Cardinals gave him wealth and influence, a self-sufficient nucleus of learning strong enough to establish a new intellectual tradition. This was related essentially to the preoccupations of the Byzantine world rather than to those of Italy. Bessarion's circle at Rome was later dignified by Platina with the

---

[1] L.Mohler, Kardinal Bessarion als Theologe, Humanist und Staatsmann, I (*Quellen und Forschungen aus dem Gebiete der Geschichte*, xx, Paderborn, 1923).

[2] Voigt, *Wiederbelebung*, II, pp. 137-46; Cessi, op. cit.; E.Legrand, *Bibliographie Hellenique* (Paris, 1885), I, pp. xxxi-xlix.

title of 'Academy'. Whether or not it had in fact the degree of regularity and organisation which that seems to imply, Bessarion was certainly after 1455, and possibly before 1450, at the centre of frequent meetings and philosophical debates at Rome, while in the intervening period of his legation at Bologna he exerted an influence by recommendation on the direction of Nicholas v's patronage.

Bessarion and the other Greek scholars were well acquainted with the writings of Plato and Aristotle and they were heirs to a tradition of studying their works in the original, for their philosophical and theological significance, which had no parallel in the West. It happened moreover, that the Greeks' own interest in their native philosophers had been given an extra stimulus at this time by the extraordinary career of George Gemistos Plethon. Plethon, who died the year before the fall of Constantinople, probably more than 90 years old, was responsible for a very strange intellectual innovation. He advocated the philosophy of Plato, or rather a philosophy of his own in which the inspiration of Plato was predominant, with an enthusiastic acceptance of some specifically non-Christian ideas. He appears to have believed in the Platonic theory of ideas, in personal immortality, in determinism and in the worship of the pagan Greek gods. He founded at Mistra in the Peloponnese a community devoted to the revival of Hellenism with these doctrines. The book in which his doctrines were most fully set out was written very late in his life and destroyed shortly after his death on the orders of the Patriarch of Constantinople, but, long before this time, he seems to have exerted a profound influence over some of the leading Greek intellectuals of the age. Bessarion had been a pupil at Mistra in the 1430s. After Plethon's death he wrote to his sons in these terms:

I have heard that our common father and master has laid down his earthly substance and has gone to heaven ... to dance the mystic Iacchos with the Olympian Gods. I rejoice to have been the pupil of such a man. Since the great men of early times, Greece has born no one more like Plato, both in knowledge and in other virtues. If one accepted the teaching of Pythagoras and Plato on the periodical ascent and descent of souls one would not refuse to add that it was the soul of Plato, obliged by the inescapable decrees of Adrasteia ... which was sent to earth to take the body of Gemistos and his life.[1]

Even allowing for reasonable literary licence this is strange language from a cardinal of the Catholic Church. Bessarion was no doubt perfectly orthodox in his public utterances but he had probably come so strongly under the influence of Plethon that he allowed a very special value, in some now undefinable relationship with Christianity, to Platonic doctrines. In his circle in Italy the preoccupation with Platonic and Aristotelian philosophy was a marked characteristic which gave rise to an influential polemical literature probably inspired originally by the challenge of Plethon.

In 1439, when he was attending the Council of Florence, Plethon composed a work *On the differences between the Platonic and Aristotelian Philosophies*, which was a defence of Plato against the criticisms of Aristotle, dealing with such matters as the theory of ideas, immortality, creation.[2] Strangely, it appears that this work arose in part from the inspiration of debates with Italian scholars in Florence. Plethon took part in conversations in Florence, amongst others, with Giuliano Cesarini, Traversari and Cosimo. Many years later, in the dedicatory letter to his translation of Plotinus, Ficino affirmed that these conversations had been the original cause of Cosimo's interest in Plato and of his ambition to recreate the Platonic Academy. 'At the time of the council between the Greeks and Latins at Florence under Pope Eugenius the Great Cosimo, *pater patriae* by decree of the senate, frequently heard a Greek philosopher Gemistus Pletho disputing about the Platonic mysteries. He was so inspired by his fervent utterance that he conceived the idea of an Academy ...'[3] A correction by Plethon to the manuscript of Bruni's Greek treatise on the Florentine constitution testifies to the reality of the contact between these two widely differing schools of Hellenism.[4] Whether or not Ficino was right about the impact of Plethon on

[1] F. Masai, *Pléthon et le Platonisme de Mistra* (Paris, 1956), p. 307. Cf. E. Wind, *Pagan Mysteries in the Rennaissance* (second edition, London, 1967), pp. 244-5, 256-7.

[2] Migne, *Patrologia Graeca*, CLX, cols. 889-932.

[3] Ficini, *Opera* (Basle, 1576), p. 1537.

[4] Garin, *Cultura Filosofica*, p. 19.

Cosimo he took very little positive action to revive Platonism for many years. That question can be set aside for the moment. What is clear is that Plethon and some of the Italians he met in Florence made an impression on each other. He was sufficiently interested in their humanism to produce a work in which their anti-scholastic prejudices were linked with his more positive Platonism. Since it was written in Greek, however, the impact of his book was on the Byzantine rather than the Italian world.[1] Plethon's enthusiasms entered into the stream of Italian thought indirectly, not from his own speech or writing but through the controversies which he caused within the circle of Greek emigrés. His unexpected attack on Aristotle produced replies from other Greeks and an enquiry from the Byzantine Emperor himself. The argument dragged on intermittently for the rest of his lifetime.[2] After his death it was revived among the Italian Greeks by the composition of George of Trebizond's *Comparisons of the Philosophers Plato and Aristotle*, in which he chose to give expression to his anger and resentment about his treatment at Rome after the death of Nicholas v by delivering a violently injudicious attack on the philosophy of Plato, beloved of those Greeks who were still enjoying papal favour. The *Comparisons* was an absurd farrago in which abuse was heaped senselessly on Plato and his devotees. George argued that Plato had a poor style and no capacity for logical argument, that the Aristotelian prime mover was nearer to the Christian God than Plato's polytheism, that there were even hints of the Trinity in Aristotle while all the heresies were derived ultimately from Plato, that Plato wished to institutionalise sexual immorality, and so on.[3] Rather surprisingly this despicable effort drew from Bessarion, by way of reply, a long book of high quality, *Against the calumniator of Plato*, which he probably wrote in Greek about 1458 and published in a printed Latin translation in 1469. Though in its Greek form it could of course have had little or no impact on most Italians, it was the first balanced

---

[1] Filelfo, however, knew of the Greek controversy which it aroused (Masai, p. 406).

[2] Masai, p. 337; list of polemics in R. Marcel, *Marsile Ficin* (Paris, 1958), pp. 326-5.

[3] Mohler, *Kardinal Bessarion*, I, pp. 352-8.

account of Plato composed in the Western World.[1] Bessarion on the whole expresses a sensible disapproval of vulgar attempts to prove that either Aristotle or Plato was more Christian. However, in the second book of his treatise, the most interesting part, he presented an extended account of Platonic views about God, the soul, eternity and providence, linking them with Neo-Platonic writings of Dionysius the Areopagite, Plotinus and Iamblichus to show that there were important features of Platonism which were not repulsive to Christianity.

This was an aspect of Platonism which might have been available to the humanists of the early fifteenth century through the conversation of Manuel Chrysoloras, and could certainly have been derived from the texts of Plato and Plotinus which Aurispa brought from Constantinople,[2] but it does not figure largely in their statements about Plato or translations of his works. The character of Plato's influence, like that of most classical authors, depended as much on the interests of his readers as on the contents of his works. The medieval world before 1400 had known in translation Plato's *Timaeus, Meno* and *Phaedo*. In the early fifteenth century Chrysoloras and Uberto Decembrio translated the *Republic* and Bruni the *Letters* and *Phaedo, Gorgias, Crito, Phaedrus* and *Apology*. In the Florentine school at least, Plato the philosopher and theologian made little impact in spite of the greater availability of his works. Bruni's delight in the 'political' Plato, whom he found in the *Letters*, comes out in the preface to his translation of them which he addressed to Cosimo about 1427.[3] An entirely new Plato was revealed or created by the new wave of emigrés, the theological Plato of the *Parmenides* and the *Laws*, the inspirer of Neo-Platonic tradition. Curiously enough, a positive as well as a negative part was played in this by George of Trebizond. In 1450-1 he had translated the *Laws* and the *Epinomis* at the behest of the German philosopher-cardinal Nicholas of Cusa.[4]

---

[1] *In Calumniatorem Platonis Libri IV*, ed. L.Mohler (*Kardinal Bessarion*, ii, *Quellen und Forschungen ans dem Gebiete der Geschichte*, xxii, 1927). For the date Mohler, *Bessarion*, i, pp. 360-64.

[2] R.Klibansky, *The Continuity of the Platonic Tradition* (London, 1939), p. 32.

[3] Bruni, *Schriften*, pp. 135-6.

[4] On the history of Plato translations, see E.Garin, *Studi sul Platonismo Medievale*

Bessarion's book was the first literary demonstration of the possibility of a Christian-Neo-Platonist philosophy, a possibility which was to be fully explored by Ficino, partly under the inspiration of Bessarion, who sent him a copy of the Latin translation in 1469. In a literary sense it initiated a new school of philosophy in Italy.

By mid-century the protagonists of the old Florentine school were dying off. Niccoli died in 1437, Traversari in 1439, Bruni in 1444. Carlo Marsuppini, now the most venerated humanist in Florence, taught in the *Studio* as well as being Chancellor, filling Bruni's double role. He gathered an enthusiastic group of pupils but in 1453 he died, unexpectedly young. Poggio was still active: two of his characteristic dialogues, *On Hypocrisy* and the *Historia Tripartita*, were composed during the pontificate of Nicholas v and in 1453 he returned to Florence to fill the chancellorship until his death in 1459. But he was already 73 when he took up this onerous position and he does not seem to have filled it competently[1] or to have exerted any serious intellectual influence in Florence. The only remaining Florentine humanist of the first rank was Giannozzo Manetti. Manetti was a well-to-do member of a Florentine mercantile family who devoted himself to books instead of business. As a young man in the 1420s he learnt Greek from Traversari and, a more unusual accomplishment, Hebrew from a Jew. He was an outstandingly pious and sincere man. He was also a distinguished orator, frequently chosen to represent Florence in embassies. His hour-long Latin oration, congratulating Nicholas v on his accession in full consistory – to which the pope was said to have replied point by point with faultless recollection and elegance – was a famous episode in the annals of rhetorical diplomacy. His opposition to Cosimo's policy of alliance with Sforza seems, however, to have given rise to a political persecution which led to his exile from Florence in 1453 to spend the rest of his life in the employment of Nicholas v and Alfonso v. Manetti's exile has commonly been regarded as a

(Florence, 1958), pp. 5-7, 180-3; 'Ricerche sulle traduzioni di Platone nella prima metà del sec. xv', *Medioevo e Rinascimento Studi in Onore di Bruno Nardi*, i.

[1] Walser, *Poggius Florentinus*, p. 285.

disaster for Florentine humanism.[1] This judgement depends largely on the little work *De Dignitate Hominis* which he dedicated to Alfonso v about 1452,[2] which has been seen as a glorification of humanity foreshadowing later Renaissance theories. The book certainly has an unusual theme. It sets out to demonstrate the uniqueness and superiority of man with respect first to the structure of his body, secondly to the achievement of his mind and thirdly to his position at the summit of creation. It then goes on to attack the pessimism of a work by Pope Innocent III, *De Miseria Humanis Vitae*, by showing reasons for optimism about human nature. But there is little indication of an original position being adopted. Manetti seems to have been an exceptionally learned and accomplished rhetorician but there is no evidence that he would have been an inspiring or influential teacher.

By the mid-fifties the poverty of Florentine intellectual life was as striking as its richness had been twenty years before. The main reasons for this were quite simply the departure of the papal court and the extinction of the older generation of humanists by natural causes. It has sometimes been argued that the hostility of St Antonino to humanism made his tenure of the see of Florence from 1446 to 1459 a particularly unpropitious period.[3] Antonino was a Dominican of the strict obedience, a worthy successor in the tradition of Giovanni Dominici, who had been prior of strict observant houses, first Fiesole and then S. Marco, since 1421 and had held Dominici's old position of Vicar General of the Italian houses of Observant Dominicans.[4] He thought that the vogue for classical studies had gone too far and criticised priests who made a pleasure of the study of Latin, enjoying Virgil and 'filling their heads with the names of gods and devils'. Save for the story, which may well be true,[5] that Antonino effectively cautioned the

---

[1] Della Torre, *Accademia Platonica*, pp. 372-5. Manetti's biography is very fully supplied by Vespasiano's 'Commentario della Vita di Messer Gianozo Manetti' in Vespasiano da Bisticci's *Vite di Uomini Illustri del Secolo XV*, ed. L.Frati, II.

[2] *Clarissimi viri Ianoci De Manectis ... de dignitate et excellentia Hominis libri IIII* (Basle, 1532) (Book 4 in *Prosatori Latini del Quattrocento*).

[3] The argument of Della Torre, *Accademia Platonica*, pp. 253-65.

[4] R.Morçay, *St Antonin Archeveque de Florence* (1389-1459) (Paris, 1914).

[5] It is accepted by Marcel (*Marsile Ficin*, pp. 204-12) and connected with events about 1457.

young Ficino against too great a devotion to Plato and therefore perhaps made an important difference to the future shape of Neo-Platonism, there is no evidence that he exerted much direct influence on lay intellectuals. More significant is the fact that he was, in a more general sense, the first effective bishop for a century, exercising a severe jurisdiction over the clergy of his diocese, defending them from secular taxation, criticising local morals and interfering in secular politics. His upholding of ecclesiastical authority was in marked contrast to the weakness or indifference which had been characteristic of the episcopates of his predecessors almost continuously since the early days of the Great Schism. That age was now over. Antonino's appointment came a year before the accession of Nicholas v; the restoration of a strong episcopacy and a strong papacy coincided. The age of ecclesiastical subservience to Florentine secular society had ended.

The vacuum left in Florence was filled not by a revival of the old style of humanism but by a new variety stemming from the dead Byzantine world, an offshoot of the school centred on Bessarion in Rome. In the years after Marsuppini's death the leaders of the Florentine intelligentsia, young enthusiasts from the best families among whom the most prominent names are those of Donato Acciaiuoli, Alamanno Rinuccini and Piero de' Medici himself, were anxious to replace him with a worthy successor to lift classical studies in Florence onto a high level again. Among the possible nominees was a refugee from Byzantium called John Argyropoulos. Marsuppini died in the year Constantinople fell. Argyropoulos, who had been earlier to Italy with the delegation to the Council of Florence and had been patronised by the exiled Palla Strozzi, came to the West in 1454 probably seeking a position. It appears that no public money could be found to support him in Florence at that moment. He came back in 1456 as an envoy of the Despot of the Peloponnese and this time was given a chair at the *Studio* which he filled until 1471.[1] The lectures of Argyropoulos which have survived are on various books of Aristotle. He could introduce his audience, as

[1] For Argyropoulos's biography, G.Cammelli, *I Dotti Bizantini e le origini dell' umanesimo*, II, *Giovanni Argiropulo* (Florence, 1941).

they fervently desired, to the Greek text. He showed some contempt for things which had been held sacred in the old days. According to Politian he told them that Cicero 'knew neither philosophy nor Greek' and he was advised by Filelfo in 1457 to stop criticising Bruni if he wished to be respected by an Italian audience.[1] Argyropoulos's teaching in fact was not a continuation of the old Florentine tradition but a sharp break from it. This had been foreseen by Poggio. In the summer of 1455 Alamanno Rinuccini wrote a letter to Andrea Alamanni pointing out the absence of any good teachers of the humanities in Florence to perform the office once gloriously filled by Bruni, Marsuppini, Manetti and George of Trebizond, and suggesting that someone must be summoned from outside.[2] Poggio read the letter and wrote to Alamanni about it. The old man was affronted by the idea. Much of his letter is taken up with recapitulation of the great Florentines from Salutati to Manetti. The present weakness, he said, was entirely the fault of the younger generation. If they wanted to learn they had only to read the books of Cicero and Quintilian in which the 'precepts of the art of rhetoric' were contained and the resources of Florence were quite adequate for this instruction. He could not see what Rinuccini wanted with 'outside teaching' (*externa doctrina*) unless he had a longing for something new and unprofitable.[3] The bitterness of Poggio's letter was not misplaced. The Florentine youth were not content with the old diet of Cicero and Quintilian. They did want something new and they got it.

It seems that Argyropoulos did not confine himself to Aristotle but, even more momentously for the future, filled his pupils with enthusiasm for Plato. The evidence for this is not abundant but it is decisive.[4] Argyropoulos was very likely a disciple of Plethon;

[1] Cammelli, pp. 176-81.

[2] Qui cum nulli apud nos habeantur omnino. . . . Eos (the governors of the Florentine studio) igitur ut dictum quendam uirum ex his, qui nostra aetate habentur illustres, aduocare uelint hortare . . . (31 May, 1455, Rinuccini, *Lettere ed Orazioni*, p. 13).

[3] Poggio, *Epistolae*, XIII, iii, dated 27 June without the year.

[4] It is collected by Della Torre, *Accademia Platonica*, pp. 387-99 and by E. Garin, 'Donato Acciaiuoli Cittadino Fiorentino' in *Medioevo e Rinascimento* (Bari, 1954) and *Cultura Filosofica*, pp. 102-8.

at any rate he was addressed by another disciple in terms suggesting that he shared a pious attachment to the ancient gods.[1] He
replied approvingly to a gift of a copy of Bessarion's book on
Plato. His lectures on Aristotle's *Ethics* and the *De Anima* included full and sympathetic accounts of the differing doctrines
taught by Plato. A letter from Pier Filippo Pandolfini to Acciaiuoli, written presumably some time in the 1460s, described his
informal exposition of Plato thus:

In the afternoon I and Vespasiano went to see Master John and
found him reading Plato. Some of our friends were with him. He put
his book down and we had such a discussion as you would certainly
have enjoyed. He told us some absolutely incredible and unheard of
things about Plato, whom he had first praised enthusiastically. 'I will
show you,' he said, 'his great prudence and the wisdom of his doctrine which the ignorant regard with astonishment.' He started right
away. 'I will explain to you the dialogue called *Meno*. You ought to be
satisfied with this one work of Plato and, if you want to, you shall see
what valuable instruction, what eloquence and what judgement and
wisdom it contains.' He then explained it so systematically and with
such eloquence and powers of exposition that we admired him no less
than Plato, of whom we were hearing many divine things. . . . Naturally Plato dealt much with morals, with the nature of the world, with
the art of clear discourse. Argyropoulos also told us some things
which seemed to have been decided not by Plato's human ingenuity
but rather by some Delphic oracle.[2]

With Argyropoulos introducing his hearers to the mysteries of
Plato we are not far from the world of Ficino's developed Neo-
Platonism. By 1463 Acciaiuoli, who had bewailed the poverty of
Florence after the death of Marsuppini, could say that the youth
of the city were so well instructed in Plato and Aristotle 'that they
seem educated in the Academy'. This was all due to the work of
Argyropoulos who had translated several books of Aristotle and
'has revealed the opinions of Plato, his secrets and his obscure
discipline (*Platonis opiniones atque arcana illa et reconditam dis-
ciplinam*) to the great admiration of his hearers.'[3] Whether

[1] Masai, *Pléthon*, p. 313.

[2] Garin, *Cultura Filosofica*, p. 119.

[3] Garin, *Medioevo e Rinascimento*, p. 237.

Argyropoulos's instruction was the decisive influence on the young Ficino is uncertain. As a young man in his early twenties he had already expressed his desire to be concerned with philosophy rather than language and composed a brief Aristotelian *Summa* and *Institutiones Platonicae* before Argyropoulos came to Florence.[1] It was in 1462-3 that he learnt Greek properly, translated most of the *Corpus Hermeticum* and began the translation of Plato's dialogues. Thus he was well launched on his historic enterprise of reviving Neo-Platonism.[2] A number of personal influences may have combined to determine the path taken by Ficino: the enthusiasm of Cosimo who patronised his studies in order to be inducted into the precious wisdom of Plato and the hermetic writings, perhaps the example of Argyropoulos, perhaps that of Bessarion. It is clear, however, that by 1463 when he was translating the *Pimander* and the Platonic dialogues for the dying Cosimo the ground was well prepared: the Florentine intelligentsia was already forgetting the old humanism and taking up a new one.

The differences between the schools of humanism in the early and late fifteenth century in Florence might be summarised by saying that they were respectively concerned with (i) Latin prose style, classical archeology and history, and personal and political morality; (ii) metaphysical philosophy of a Neo-Platonic kind and magic. One was devoted to Cicero, the other to Plato. The second style of thought had a very wide influence throughout Europe, a much more spectacular influence than the thought of Bruni, Poggio or Valla. This was partly because the thought of Ficino was more traditional and easier to assimilate than that of the followers of Petrarch. Its characteristic desire to establish a rational hierarchy linking the natural and human world with the divine had much in common with scholasticism. The pagan gods and the Platonism, which would no doubt have shocked St Thomas as they shocked some of Ficino's contemporaries, should

---

[1] Letter to Antonio da S.Miniato, 1454, in P.O.Kristeller, *Studies in Renaissance Thought and Letters* (Rome, 1956), p. 146; the *Summa*, thought by Kristeller to be about 1455, ibid., p. 56; on the lost *Institutiones*, Marcel, *Marsile Ficin*, p. 197.

[2] Following the chronology of Marcel, pp. 247-63.

not mislead us into thinking that this is a more secular outlook. It was more mysterious and magical. The passions of Dante and Ficino have some similarities; those of Dante and Bruni have little in common. These striking contrasts between the early and late fifteenth centuries have tempted some historians to suppose that the change was the result of a transformation of Florentine society, or a political change from republicanism to Medicean tyranny. There is no evidence that any such radical change in social or political organisation took place. But it remains true that the outlook propagated by the early fifteenth-century humanists in Florence was a transient one. In this book its resemblance to some of the attitudes commonly regarded as characteristic of the Enlightenment of the seventeenth and eighteenth centuries has been stressed: the preference for a common-sense approach in philosophy, indifference or hostility to traditional religion and metaphysics, artistic realism. In explaining the subsequent change one must allow some significance to the ordinary swing of the pendulum in the history of ideas. The impetus died with the first group of rhetoricians and amateurs and Ficino's generation was repelled by the dryness of the rhetorical school as Bruni's had been by the obscurantism of the scholastics. Apart from this, the situation which had been uniquely favourable for the peculiar collection of attitudes held by Bruni and his contemporaries was not repeated. In the world of Florence and the Curia which they had inhabited, Florence had been dominant for a period. The situation disappeared not because of any striking internal transformation within Florence but because of larger changes in the Italian world. The papacy recovered from its subservience to the Florentine intellect as, in another sphere, it recovered from the constitutional theories of the conciliarists. Italy in the late fifteenth century was no longer an environment favourable to a movement of extreme secularisation.

Index

267

Index

Index

Index

Montaigne, xviii
Montaperto, 26
Monte Cassino, 19, 190
Montepulciano, Bartolomeo da, 84, 87, 147, 189, 194–5
Montone, Braccio da, 75, 153, 157
Morelli, Giacopo, 75
Mucius, 50, 65
Mugello, 162–3

Nanni di Banco, 208–9, 229–30, 236
Nanni di Miniato, 226
Naples, 45, 50, 69, 204; see also Alfonso V, Charles of Durazzo, Joanna II, Louis of Anjou, Ladislas, René of Anjou
Nero, 51
Niccoli, Niccolò, 8, 9, 11–15, 21–2, 26–7, 29, 31, 34, 37, 43, 64, 68, 78, 82–3, 88–93, 96–9, 101, 107, 118, 119–24, 127, 129–30, 148–9, 175, 182, 189–90, 227–32, 234, 242, 260
Nicholas V, Pope, 92, 119, 170, 247–56, 258, 260, 262
Noceta, Piero da, 253

Ockham, William of, 3, 29
Oleari, Bartolomeo, bishop of Florence, 55
Orcagna, 172, 203
Origen, 97, 122
Orsini, Cardinal Giordano, 81–2, 84, 191
Orsini family, 76
Ostia, 98, 189, 230
Ovid, 108
Oxford University, 3–4

Padua, 204, 222
Padua, University of, 7, 15, 30, 62, 85
Palmieri, Matteo, 137–8, 150–2, 154, 166, 168, 170

Pandolfini, Agnolo di Filippo, 108–11, 139, 150
Pandolfini, Pier Filippo, 264
Panormita, 86, 127–30
Parentucelli, Tommaso, see Nicholas V
Paris, University of, 3, 4, 7
Parthenon, 191
Paul, St, 122, 132
Pavia, University of, 126–7
Pericles, 109
Perotti, Niccolò, 250–1, 255
Perugia, 46, 162
Pescia, Antonio da, 97
Petrarch, xvii, xviii, 2, 4, 5, 6, 7, 8, 15, 17, 21, 30, 31, 34, 35, 50, 97, 101, 155, 203, 265
Phidias, 21, 224
Piccinino, Niccolò, 71, 76, 161–3, 165, 246
Piero della Francesca, 240
Pisa, 42, 45, 46, 58–9, 70, 151–2, 160, 183, 204, 217–8, 220, 233
Pisa, Council of, 16, 55, 58–9, 62, 81
Pisano, Nicola and Giovanni, 202–3
Pistoia, 159, 177, 183
Pitti, Buonaccorso, 159, 162
Pius II, Pope, 6 n., 78, 84, 93, 241, 248, 255
Platina, 255
Plato and platonism, 2, 5, 10, 13, 18, 30, 31, 95, 106–7, 114, 117, 121, 154, 156, 243, 245, 252, 256–9, 262–5
Plautus, 81–2, 104
Plethon, George Gemistos, 256–8, 263
Pliny the elder, xix, 23, 34, 226, 237
Plotinus, 243, 257, 259
Plutarch, 13, 14, 18, 28, 97, 112
Poggio, see Bracciolini, Poggio
Politian, 263
Polybius, 95, 250
Polycletus, 227

Index